Communications in Computer and Information Science 1191

Commenced Publication in 2007
Founding and Former Series Editors:
Phoebe Chen, Alfredo Cuzzocrea, Xiaoyong Du, Orhun Kara, Ting Liu,
Krishna M. Sivalingam, Dominik Ślęzak, Takashi Washio, Xiaokang Yang,
and Junsong Yuan

More information about this series at http://www.springer.com/series/7899

Klinge Orlando Villalba-Condori ·
Agustín Aduríz-Bravo · Jari Lavonen ·
Lung-Hsiang Wong · Tzu-Hua Wang (Eds.)

Education and Technology in Sciences

First International Congress, CISETC 2019
Arequipa, Peru, December 10–12, 2019
Revised Selected Papers

 Springer

Editors
Klinge Orlando Villalba-Condori (iD)
Universidad Católica de Santa María
Arequipa, Peru

Agustín Aduríz-Bravo (iD)
University of Buenos Aires
Buenos Aires, Argentina

Jari Lavonen (iD)
University of Helsinki
Helsinki, Finland

Lung-Hsiang Wong (iD)
Nanyang Technological University
Singapore, Singapore

Tzu-Hua Wang (iD)
National Tsing Hua University
Hsinchu, Taiwan

ISSN 1865-0929   ISSN 1865-0937   (electronic)
Communications in Computer and Information Science
ISBN 978-3-030-45343-5   ISBN 978-3-030-45344-2   (eBook)
https://doi.org/10.1007/978-3-030-45344-2

This Springer imprint is published by the registered company Springer Nature Switzerland AG
The registered company address is: Gewerbestrasse 11, 6330 Cham, Switzerland

Preface

The International Congress on Education and Technology in Sciences (CISETC 2019), was held during December 10–12, 2019, at the Catholic University of Santa Maria, Peru. CISETC is a global initiative framed in STEAM for the development of science and technology in various contexts. CISETC 2019 was the first edition of this conference series and had a great reception nationally and internationally with regard to the presentation of manuscripts and attendance of participants.

CISETC 2019 aimed to provide a good forum for participants to discuss best practices of STEAM (Science, Technology, Engineering, Art and Mathematics) in the different educational systems that according to PISA had the best results, as was the case with Singapore, Taiwan, Finland, Spain, and the USA. For this reason, this event was sponsored by the National Council of Science, Technology and Technological Innovation of Peru. With regards to the manuscripts, CISETC 2019 had two main themes:

- Pedagogical practice in the sciences, focused specifically on science education
- Complementary aspects of science teaching, which considers all the elements that can contribute to science education

This preface has been generated with the participation of the keynote speakers, because to a greater extent the manuscripts were linked to the development of teachers' skills. The proceedings were sponsored by the Peruvian Educational Research Society (SIEP), the Research Group on Interaction and eLearning (GRIAL) of the University of Salamanca, Spain, the Mackensie University of São Paulo, Brazil, and the Research and Development Group on Software Engineering of the University of Cauca, Colombia, who helped to ensure that the process of selecting manuscripts was relevant and appropriate to the scope of CISETC. The call for papers was made through EasyChair and wikicfp, and there were of two types of papers accepted: full paper (up to 10 pages) and short paper (6 pages). In total 96 manuscripts were received, which were submitted to the Program Committee for a blind peer review. In some cases, according to the score reached, there was more than one review to define the acceptance (or rejection) of the manuscripts. Of the 96 manuscripts presented (84 full papers and 12 short papers), both distributed in the corresponding thematic areas, 36 full papers were accepted. These papers were presented in the proceedings during the event. Later, and considering the higher scores obtained and after the discussion among the Program Committee (who prepared the preface), the extended version of 13 papers was requested, which correspond to the two thematic axes presented below and focused on the central theme of CISETC 2019.

Considering the scope of this first edition of CISETC, we are satisfied with the impact generated within the national and international scientific community.

December 2019

K. O. Villalba-Condori
A. Aduríz-Bravo
J. Lavonen
L.-H. Wong
T.-H. Wang

Organization

Organizing Committee

Klinge Orlando Villalba-Condori	Universidad Católica de Santa María, Peru
Francisco José Garcia-Peñalvo	Universidad de Salamanca, Spain
Jari Lavonen	University of Helsinki, Finland
Agustín Aduríz-Bravo	Universidad de Buenos Aires, Argentina
Tzu-Hua Wang	National Tsing Hua University, Taiwan
Lung-Hsiang Wong	Nanyang Technological University, Singapore
Margarida Romero	LINE, Université Côte d'Azur, France
Ismar Frango	Universidad de Mackensie, Brazil
Antonio Silva-Sprock	Universidad Central de Venezuela, Venezuela
Ivan Montes Iturrizaga	Sociedad de Investigación Educativa Peruana, Peru
Gonzalo Dávila del Carpio	Universidad Católica de Santa María, Peru
Karina Rosas Paredes	Universidad Católica de Santa María, Peru
Julio Vera-Sancho	Universidad Católica de Santa María, Peru
Hermann Alcazar Rojas	Universidad Católica de Santa María, Peru
Sara Medina Gordillo	Universidad Católica de Santa María, Peru
Paulo Ramirez Lazo	Universidad Católica de Santa María, Peru
María del Pilar Ponce Aranibar	Universidad Católica de Santa María, Peru
Carlos Arbieto Batallanos	Universidad Católica de Santa María, Peru
Betsy Carol Cisneros Chávez	Universidad Católica de Santa María, Peru

Scientific Committee

Agustín Aduríz-Bravo	Universidad de Buenos Aires, Argentina
Agustín Caminero	Universidad Nacional de Educación a Distancia, Spain
Alicia García Holgado	Grupo Grial Universidad de Salamanca, Spain
Aman Yadav	Michigan State University, USA
Ana Morales	Universidad Central de Venezuela, Venezuela
Angel Fidalgo	Universidad Politécnica de Madrid, Spain
Angela Calabrese	Michigan State University, USA
Antonio Silva Sprock	Universidad Central de Venezuela, Venezuela
Ary Millyviita	University of Helsinki, Finland
Azeneth Patiño	Université Laval, Canada
Carina Gonzalez	Universidad de la Laguna, Spain
Carmen Batanero	Universidad de Granada, Spain
Carmen Díaz	Pontifica Universidad Católica del Perú, Peru

César Collazos	Universidad del Cauca, Colombia
Chan-Jong Kim	Seoul National University, South Korea
Claudia Deco	Universidad Católica de Argentina, Argentina
Cristian Cechinel	Universidade Federal Santa Catarina, Brazil
Cristina Bender	Universidad Nacional del Rosario, Argentina
Daniel Quineche	Universidad Peruana Cayetano Heredia, Peru
Deborah Fields	Utah State University, USA
Denis Arias Chávez	Universidad Continental, Peru
Diego Torres	Universidad Nacional de La Plata, Argentina
Esteban Gonzales Clua	Universidad de Fluminense, Brazil
Faraón Llorens-Largo	Universidad de Alicante, Spain
Fernando Bordignon	Universidad Pedagógica Nacional de Argentina, Argentina
Francisco José Garcia Peñalvo	Grupo Grial, Universidad de Salamanca, Spain
Francisco Javier Murillo Torrecilla	Universidad Autónoma de Madrid, Spain
Huizilopoztli Luna García	Universidad Autónoma de Zacatecas, Mexico
Ismar Frango	Universidad Presbiteriana de Mackensie, Brazil
Ivan Montes Iturrizaga	Sociedad de Investigación Educativa Peruana, Peru
Jaime Muñoz Arteaga	Universidad Autónoma de Aguas Calientes, Mexico
Jari Lavonen	University of Helsinki, Finland
Jhon Guerra	Universidad de los Andes, Colombia
João Vilhete Viegas d'Abreu	Universidad Estatal de Campinas, Brazil
Jorge Maldonado	Universidad de Cuenca, Ecuador
José Antonio Pow Sang Portillo	Pontificia Universidad Católica del Perú, Peru
José Antonio Ruipérez-Valiente	Universidad de Murcia, Spain
Juan Cabrera Ramos	Universidad Católica de Temuco, Chile
Juan Díaz Godino	Universidad de Granada, Spain
Julio Guerra	University of Pittsburgh, USA
Liina Malva	University of Tartu, Estonia
Lilliam Enriqueta Hidalgo Benites	Universidad Nacional de Piura, Peru
Luis Alberto Ponce Soto	Universidad Católica de Santa María, Peru
Lung-Hsiang Wong	Nanyang Technological University, Singapore
Mar Pérez-Sanagustín	Université Paul Sabatier Tolouse, France
Marcos Roman Gonzales	Universidad de Educación a Distancia, Spain
Margarida Romero	LINE, Université Nice Sophia Antipolis, France
María Popescu	National Defence University in Bucharest, Romania
Miguel Angel Conde	Universidad de León, Spain
Nguyen-Thinh Le	Humboldt Universität zu Berlin, Germany
Omar Antonio Vega	Universidad de Manizales, Colombia
Raidell Avello	Universidad de Cien Fuegos, Cuba

Contents

Importance of the Concept of "Competency" in Science Teacher Education: What Are the Professional Competencies for Science Teachers?

Klinge Orlando Villalba-Condori[1]([✉]) [iD], Agustín Adúriz-Bravo[2] [iD], Jari Lavonen[3] [iD], Lung-Hsiang Wong[4] [iD], and Tzu-Hua Wang[5] [iD]

[1] Universidad Católica de Santa María, Arequipa, Peru
kvillalba@ucsm.edu.pe
[2] Conicet/Universidad de Buenos Aires, Instituto CeFIEC, Buenos Aires, Argentina
aadurizbravo@cefiec.fcen.uba.ar
[3] University of Helsinki, Helsinki, Finland
jari.lavonen@helsinki.fi
[4] Nanyang Technological University National Institute of Education, Jurong West, Singapore
lunghsiang.wong@nie.edu.sg
[5] National Tsing Hua University, Hsinchu, Taiwan
tzuhuawang@gapp.nthu.edu.tw

Abstract. The idea of competency, which is widely disseminated through science curricula in various countries, has great potential for the professionalisation of science teachers. Moreover, teachers need competencies for introducing these competencies and for supporting students to develop them. In this chapter, we explore a characterisation of scientific competencies that can be productive for the pre-service teacher education. With such a definition, it would be possible to inspect some "paradigmatic" competencies in science teaching.

1 Introduction

In current educational research, the notion of "competency" is considered both problematic and promising [1, 2]. To a large extent, this problematic character arises from its exo-educational, economicist origins. The promising aspect of the concept, on the contrary, may be lying in its power to transform teachers' professional development in the 21st century.

In the context of the European Higher Education Area, one definition of competency that has already become classic characterises it as the general capacity based on knowledge, experiences, and values that a person has developed through their participation in educational practices [3]. Such a definition of competency could be considered, following [4], as "generic". It has the value of placing science as a noteworthy contribution to the integral education of people, but it entails a danger: separating the development of formal skills from the disciplinary ways of understanding the world. Therefore, it would also be necessary to have a "specific" definition of competency, set in context . In the

© Springer Nature Switzerland AG 2020
K. O. Villalba-Condori et al. (Eds.): CISETC 2019, CCIS 1191, pp. 1–5, 2020.
https://doi.org/10.1007/978-3-030-45344-2_1

case of professional competencies of science teachers, the specific context is the science classrooms, in which the specific activities of science teaching are developed.

One way to understand competencies for science teacher education is to think of them as abilities (cognitive, discursive, material, value-related) that operate on scientific content within a well-defined context, which is that of professional performance. However, this definition does not indicate any criteria for selecting the competencies that would be most relevant for teacher professionalisation. It is here that the need arises to make additional specifications in order to identify the most paradigmatic competencies in the professionalism of teachers.

2   Towards the Identification of Professional Competencies for Science Teachers

We start from the basis that the education of science teachers aims at preparing individuals that are competent in designing, implementing and evaluating a good quality science education in their classrooms. Thus, the competency *par excellence* for science teachers would be that they make their students scientifically competent. This competency is similar to what [5] recognised in her analysis of various national-level teacher competency frameworks, strategies and standards, which typically emphasise professional knowledge and practices in teacher profession. Specific teacher competencies, on the contrary, could be conceptualised as a set of knowledge-based strategies that enable teachers to successfully design a teaching of science directed to different audiences and to tackle with the conflicts and difficulties that arise in their professional practice.

Science teachers of course need scientific competencies aligned with those that they will foster in their students. But they also need competencies for the planning, execution and regulation of their teaching practices, which involve effective actions responding to complex demands. Science teaching, seen from the perspective of professional competencies, entails the integration of very different forms of knowledge–including, but not reduced to, disciplinary knowledge. When science teachers teach, they are expected to mobilise these different forms of knowledge adequately and efficiently.

A competency-based science teaching would include four dimensions [6]:

1. a body of scientific knowledge composed of theoretical models that should be taught;
2. the ability to effectively transform the world using those models according to various human aims;
3. a set of socially shared attitudes and values to meet the demands of citizenship; and
4. a critical understanding of the nature of the scientific activity.

These dimensions, therefore, should be central in pre-service science teacher education. In addition to competencies needed in a science classroom, science teachers need *professional engagement*, which includes teachers' own engagement in professional learning and engagement with colleagues, parents and the community [7].

Therefore, a central trait in the professionalisation of science teachers would be sound knowledge *of* science and *about* science; teachers' professional competencies, in relation to the discipline to be taught, would be both of scientific and meta-scientific nature (using here the Greek prefix "meta" to give an idea of a "second order reflection on") [8]. Among meta-scientific competencies, we could place the teaching, instructional or *didactical* competency.

School science could be understood as an intellectual and social activity in which students use scientific models to make sense of phenomena. The theoretical ideas carried by the models, together with the specialised language of science and the experimental activities to intervene on phenomena, would constitute "game rules" to explain the natural world and to understand the human aims and values that shape science. With this idea in mind, a key aspect of the professional responsibilities of the teachers is lying on teaching model-based competencies, that is, competencies that mirror the epistemic nature of scientific activities, requiring students to think, talk and act on scientific problems.

According to the "Future of Education and Skills 2030 (https://www.oecd.org/education/2030-project/)", proposed by the Organization for Economic Co-operation and Development (OECD), "competency" refers to flexible applications of knowledge and skills in daily life, which can be expressed in self-learning, problem-solving, and adapting to the future [9]. Interdisciplinary STEM/STEAM education seems to be an effective model for competency-based teaching and learning. According to these authors, STEM/STEAM education facilitates interdisciplinary applications of science, technology, engineering, art, design and mathematics so that students can achieve meaningful learning for their daily life. Some effective teaching models for STEM/STEAM education are recommended for science teachers to put into practice in their classroom. For example, the DDMT teaching model, which includes four steps: discover, define, model and modelling, and transfer, provides a scaffold for teachers to develop their competency-based and interdisciplinary STEM/STEAM teaching activities [9, 10]. The DDMT teaching model was adopted as the key teaching model for STEM/STEAM curriculum development in the "Tsing Hua STEAM School (https://tsinghuasteam.org)" alliance, which was initiated by the National Tsing Hua University (NTHU) in Taiwan. The "Tsing Hua STEAM School" emphasises K-12 students' gaining of interdisciplinary learning experiences by solving and understanding daily life phenomena and problems via maker practices.

What would then be some of the important competencies for teachers to teach, which they would therefore need to learn during their professional education? When we face this question, we are located on a continuum with two very recognisable ends: 1. competencies that belong to science, working as a sort of "Ockham's razor" to demarcate science from common sense and from other human activities, or 2. more general competencies directed to citizenship, for which science would be an instrument or a *context*.

Mid-way in between these two positions, we could talk about "paradigmatic" scientific competencies, modelled on central traits of science. Such competencies would satisfy, at the same time, two requirements: 1. they would show the most characteristic elements of the scientific activity (and this does not imply that we naively believe that such characteristics are exclusive of science); and 2. They would enable students to acquire ways of understanding the world with scientific concepts and, at the same time, to critically discuss the nature of science as a human endeavour.

Among the "good candidates" for paradigmatic competencies, we could identify those related to:

1. grasping the methodological dimension of science;

2. producing texts in the different scientific "genres" in order to elaborate, justify and communicate scientific ideas;
3. using models while understanding their nature as representations, and
4. producing and defending solid arguments in favour of established scientific understandings of phenomena. It is worth noting that these four competencies have a hybrid cognitive-linguistic nature.

The aforementioned competencies, and other instances that science teacher educators could collective define, are perhaps key constituents of the definition of a scientifically educated citizen: they help meet current social demands such as engaged social participation, informed decision-making, critical thinking, or the ability to critically manage information in mass media.

In the particular case of the competency of scientific argumentation, the careful selection of the (socio-) scientific problems and issues on which students are going to argue would help them to apply and evaluate the scientific models and, at the same time, to discuss and incorporate an educationally valuable "image of science" that presents it as a deeply human activity of enormous social relevance.

3   Concluding Remarks

Adopting an operational definition of competency for science teacher education requires the identification of content to be taught ("big" scientific ideas that are essential), but also of "modes of thinking" that give support to scientific activities and are valuable in order to educate our students of different educational levels. In this sense, it is interesting to cite Díaz Barriga [2] idea that "the best way to see a competency" is in the "amalgam" between abilities, data and information, situations, aims, etc.

Students could be characterised as scientifically competent when all those elements can be put into action not only in school situations, but also in a wide variety of new conditions, thus demonstrating a high level of "transversal" applicability to a diversity of contexts [11, 12]. In accordance with this, science teachers would be genuinely competent when they can guide their students in the application of what they have learnt to *meaningful and relevant* contexts. This would require for them the competency of carefully designing science classes that accompany the whole process.

References

1. Perrenoud, P.: Identifier des compétences clés universelles: Fantasme de technocrate ou extension des droits de l'homme? Documento de trabajo. Université de Genève, Ginebra (1999)
2. Díaz Barriga, Á.: El enfoque de competencias en la educación: ¿Una alternativa o un disfraz de cambio? Perfiles Educativos **XXVIII**(111), 7–36 (2006)
3. Eurydice (Red Europea de Información en Educación) Las competencias clave: Un concepto en expansión dentro de la educación general obligatoria. Madrid: Ministerio de Educación, Cultura y Deporte (2002)

4. Pavié, A.: Formación docente: Hacia una definición del concepto de competencia profesional docente. Revista Electrónica Interuniversitaria de Formación del Profesorado **14**(1), 67–80 (2011)
5. Caena, F.: Teacher competence frameworks in Europe: policy-as-discourse and policy-as-practice. Eur. J. Educ. **49**(3), 311–331 (2014). https://doi.org/10.1111/ejed.12088
6. Adúriz-Bravo, A.: Pensar la enseñanza de la física en términos de "competencias". Revista de Enseñanza de la Física **29**(2), 21–31 (2017)
7. APST Australian Professional Standards for Teachers. Melbourne: Australian Institute for Teaching and School Leadership (2014). http://www.aitsl.edu.au/australian-professional-standards-for-teachers/standards/list
8. Adúriz-Bravo, A.: Competencias metacientíficas escolares dentro de la formación del profesorado de ciencias. In: Badillo, E., García, L., Marbà, A., Briceño, M. (eds.) El desarrollo de competencias en la clase de ciencias y matemáticas, pp. 43–67. Universidad de Los Andes, Mérida (2012)
9. Wang, T.H., Lim, K.Y.T., Lavonen, J., Clark-Wilson, A.: Maker-centred science and mathematics education: lenses, scales and contexts. Int. J. Sci. Math. Educ. **17**(suppl 1), 1–11 (2019)
10. Wang, T.H.: Effective Interdisciplinary STEM/STEAM Education: DDMT Teaching Model and WACEL system for e-Assessment (2019). http://trh.gase.most.ntnu.edu.tw/en/article/content/74
11. Villalba-Condori, K.O., García-Peñalvo, F.J., Lavonen, J., Zapata-Ros, M.: What kinds of innovations do we need in education? In: Villalba-Condori, K.O., García-Peñalvo, F.J., Lavonen, J., Zapata-Ros, M. (eds.) Proceedings of the II Congreso Internacional de Tendencias e Innovación Educativa – CITIE 2018, Arequipa, Perú, 26–30 November 2018, pp. 9–15. CEUR-WS.org, Aachen (2018)
12. Villalba-Condori, K.O., Adúriz-Bravo, A., García-Peñalvo, F.J., Lavonen, J.: What is new in teaching science structured around the notion of 'scientific competence'? In: Villalba-Condori, K.O., Adúriz-Bravo, A., García-Peñalvo, F.J., Lavonen, J. (eds.) Proceedings of the International Congress on Educational and Technology in Sciences – CISETC 2019, Arequipa, Perú, 10–12 December 2019, pp. 12–15. CEUR-WS.org, Aachen (2019)

Interweaving Transmission and Inquiry in Mathematics and Sciences Instruction

Juan D. Godino[✉] and María Burgos

Universidad de Granada, Granada, Spain
{jgodino,mariaburgos}@ugr.es

Abstract. Despite the huge research efforts that have been made, the problem of how to teach mathematics and sciences remains open. Deciding between teacher-focused teaching models (transmissive teaching) or student-focused (inquiring learning) poses a dilemma for educational practice. In this paper we address this problem and propose a solution applying the Onto-semiotic Approach assumptions and theoretical tools. We argue that the learning optimization and achievement of an appropriate didactic intervention require interweaving in a dialectical and complex way, the teacher's moments of knowledge transmission with the student's inquiry moments. The implementation of efficient didactic trajectories implies the articulation of diverse types of didactic configurations managed through didactical suitability criteria on the teacher's part. These should take into account the epistemic, cognitive, affective, interactional, mediational and ecological dimensions involved in instructional processes.

Keywords: Didactical models · Constructivism · Objectivism · Onto-semiotic approach · Didactical suitability

1 Introduction

Research in mathematics and experimental sciences education is usually interested in describing and understanding teaching and learning processes, avoiding proposing norms on how these processes should be implemented. In research activities the descriptive-explanatory scientific component predominates against the technological component of effective action on educational practice. However, intervention in the real problems of teaching requires developing specific instructional theories that help the teacher to take decisions in the design, implementation and evaluation phases. It is necessary to develop educational theories that articulate the epistemic and ecological facets (curricular theories), together with the cognitive and affective facets (learning theories), oriented to the practice of teaching (instructional design theories). In particular, the optimization of the interactional facet, that is, the types of interactions between teacher and students, between the transmission and inquiry of knowledge, constitutes a problem: The dilemma between directly transmitting knowledge or facilitating the students' inquiry so that they discover and build that knowledge themselves, remains unclear [1].

In this paper, we address the problem of instructional design in mathematics and experimental sciences education from the point of view of the Onto-semiotic Approach

© Springer Nature Switzerland AG 2020
K. O. Villalba-Condori et al. (Eds.): CISETC 2019, CCIS 1191, pp. 6–21, 2020.
https://doi.org/10.1007/978-3-030-45344-2_2

to Mathematical Knowledge and Instruction (OSA) [2, 3]. We will use the onto-semiotic configuration notion to show the complexity of knowledge, since it allows us to recognize the system of objects and processes put at stake in a problem-solving activity, which constitutes the rationale for such knowledge. Likewise, the notion of didactic configuration helps to recognize the variety and dynamics of teachers and students roles involved in the instructional process of any learning content. The different types of didactic configurations [4] should be articulated forming didactic trajectories whose management by the teacher, have to be guided by suitability criteria [5] in order to achieve the efficiency of the teaching activity. In summary, with the application of the OSA analysis and didactic intervention tools, a theory of instruction has been built for the progressive improvement of mathematics and sciences teaching practice.

In this article we expand and review the invited conference presented at the CISECT [6], incorporating in the thematic thread of the same ideas from previous papers focused on the problem of articulating pedagogical models focused on the teacher or students [7, 8], and justifying the relevance of applying a mixed type instructional model. In this sense, an example is described that shows the onto-semiotic complexity of mathematical practices in the case of solving a task on geometric proportionality [9] and another example of an experience with elementary students, following the dialogic-collaborative model described in this article, who have a first encounter with the concept of proportionality [10]. In this article we introduce significant clarifications regarding the type of dialogic-collaborative didactic configuration that we consider suitable in the situations of the student's first encounter with a new content, as well as the relevance of applying this didactic model in the field of education in experimental sciences.

In Sect. 2 we describe in more detail the dilemma between two extreme positions on the types of didactic interactions that should be implemented in instructional processes: constructivism, with an emphasis on student inquiry and autonomy, and objectivism with an emphasis on knowledge transmission. In Sect. 3 we introduce a key factor to consider when deciding between the two extreme positions: recognizing the onto-semiotic complexity of mathematical and scientific knowledge, which must be taken into account, along with other cognitive reasons, in order to ponder constructivism. In Sect. 4 we describe some OSA tools for the analysis and instructional design, which are used in Sect. 5 to present the mixed type instructional model that we propose to optimize the efficiency of didactic activity. This model is explained with an application example in Sect. 6.

2 Constructivism Versus Objectivism

The family of instructional theories called "Inquiry-Based Education" (IBE), "Inquiry-Based Learning" (IBL), and "Problem-Based Learning" (PBL), postulates inquiry-based learning with little guidance from the teacher [11]. The different varieties of constructivism share, among others, the assumptions that learning is an active process, that knowledge is built instead of innate or passively absorbed and that in order to achieve effective learning it is necessary to approach students with significant, open and challenging problems [12, 13].

"The arguments that human beings are active agents constructing knowledge by themselves have made people believe that instructional activities should encourage learners to construct knowledge through their own participations. This constructivist view plays an important role in science teaching and learning and has become a dominant teaching paradigm" [1, p. 897].

The recommendations for implementing a teaching and learning of mathematics and sciences based on inquiry have been playing a significant role in the curricular orientations of various countries, in projects, research centres and reform initiatives. Linn, Clark and Slotta [14] define inquiry-based science learning as follows:

"We define inquiry as engaging students in the intentional process of diagnosing problems, criticizing experiments, distinguishing alternatives, planning investigations, revising views, researching conjectures, searching for information, constructing models, debating with peers, communicating to diverse audiences, and forming coherent arguments" [14, p. 518].

In the pedagogical models assuming constructivist principles, the teacher's role is developing a learning environment with which the student interacts autonomously. This means that the teacher has to select some learning tasks and ensure that the student has the cognitive and material resources needed to get involved in solving the problems. In addition, the teacher has to create a cognitive scaffolding, a "choice architecture" that supports and promotes the construction of knowledge by the students themselves. In some way, the aim is implementing a "paternalistic libertarian" pedagogy in the sense of the Thaler and Sunstein [15] "nudge theory", based on the design of interventions of the "nudge" type. "A nudge, as we will use this term, is any aspect of the architecture of choice that modifies the people's behaviour in a predictable manner without prohibiting any option or significantly changing their economic incentives" [15, p. 6].

In mathematical learning, the use of situations - problems (applications to daily life, other fields of knowledge, or problems internal to the discipline itself) is considered essential, so that students make sense of the conceptual structures that make up Mathematics as a cultural reality. These problems constitute the starting point of mathematical practice, since the problem solving activity, its formulation, communication and justification are considered key in developing the ability to face the solution of non-routine problems. This is the main objective of the "problem solving" tradition [16], whose emphasis is the identification of heuristics and metacognitive strategies. It is also the main aim of other theoretical models such as the Theory of Didactical Situations (TDS) [17], and the Realistic Mathematical Education (RME) [18, 19].

There are also positions contrary to constructivism, as is the case of Mayer [20] or Kirschner, Sweller and Clark [21], which justify, through a wide range of investigations, the greater effectiveness of instructional models in which the teacher, and the transmission of knowledge, have a predominant role. These postures are also related to objectivist philosophical positions [22], and to direct instruction or lesson-based pedagogy [23].

Sweller, Kirschner and Clark [24] state that the last half century empirical research on this problem provides overwhelming and clear evidence that a minimum guide during instruction is significantly less effective and efficient than a guide specifically designed to support the cognitive processes necessary for learning. Similar results are reflected in the meta-analysis performed by Alfieri, Brooks, Aldrich and Tenenbaum [25].

For objectivism, particularly in its behavioural version, knowledge is publicly observable and learning consists of the acquisition of that knowledge through the interaction between stimuli and responses. Frequently, the conditioning form used to achieve desirable verbal behaviours is direct instruction. Cognitive reasons can be provided in favour of applying a didactic model based on the transmission of knowledge (objectivism) versus models based on autonomous construction (constructivism). Kirschner et al. [21] point out that constructivist positions, with minimally guided instruction, contradict the architecture of human cognition and impose a heavy cognitive burden that prevents learning:

> "We are skilful in an area because our long-term memory contains huge amounts of information concerning the area. That information permits us to quickly recognize the characteristics of a situation and indicates to us, often unconsciously, what to do and when to do it" [21, p. 76].

Other reasons contradicting constructivist positions come from cultural psychology. According to Harris [26]:

> "Accounts of cognitive development have often portrayed children as independent scientists who gather first-hand data and form theories about the natural world. I argue that this metaphor is inappropriate for children's cultural learning. In that domain, children are better seen as anthropologists who attend to, engage with, and learn from members of their culture" [26, p. 259].

The metaphor of the child as a natural scientist, so durable and powerful, is useful when used to describe how children make sense of the universal regularities of the natural world, regularities that they can observe themselves, regardless of their cultural environment. However, the metaphor is misleading when used to explain cognitive development. Children are born in a cultural world that mediates their encounters with the physical and biological world. To access this cultural world, children need a socially oriented learning mode (learning through participant observation). "The mastery of normative regularities calls for cultural learning" [26, p. 261].

The debate between direct teaching, linked to objectivist positions on mathematical and scientific knowledge, which defends a central role of the teacher in guiding learning, and a minimally guided teaching, usually referring to the constructivist-type teaching model, is not clearly solved in the research literature. Hmelo-Silver et al. [27] argue that PBL and IBL "are not minimally guided instructional approaches, but provide extensive support and guidance to facilitate student learning" (p. 91). Supporters of problem-based learning and inquiry focus their arguments on the amount of guidance and the situation in which such guidance is provided. They consider that the guide given contains an extensive body of support and being immersed in real-life situations helps students make sense of the scientific content.

For Zhang [1], the tension between these two instructional models does not consist of whether one or another would participate in presenting more or less guidance or support to the students, but between explicitly presenting the solutions to the learners or letting them discover these solutions. "For the advocates of direct instruction, explicitly presenting solutions and demonstrating the process to achieve solutions are essential guidance" [1, p. 908]. Having the intention that students discover, explore and find solutions, as structured in IBE, eliminates the need to present such solutions. In constructivist positions, although a certain dose of transmission of information from the teacher to the student is admitted, it is still essential to hide a part of the content. On the contrary for supporters of direct instruction, who assume the theory of cognitive load with emphasis on the worked-examples, providing solutions, is considered essential. In the next section we introduce a new key in the discussion of didactic models based on constructivism (inquiry) and objectivism (transmission). It consists of recognizing the onto-semiotic complexity of mathematical and scientific knowledge [2–28], which must be taken into account in instructional processes intending to achieve the objective of optimizing student learning. By accepting anthropological, semiotic and pragmatic assumptions about mathematical knowledge, it is concluded that an essential part of the knowledge that students have to learn are the conceptual, propositional and procedural rules, agreed within the mathematical or scientific community of practices. To solve the problems that constitute the educational objective, students use their previous knowledge, a central part of which are rules, which must be available to understand and address the task. Intending students to discover those rules is nonsense, but also the objective is to find the solutions, which in turn are rules, and which must be part of their cognitive heritage to solve new problems. The assumptions of an educational-instructional model that would solve the dilemma between inquiry and transmission are obtained by taking into account the onto-semiotic complexity of mathematical and scientific knowledge, while recognizing the central role of problem solving as a rationale for the contents.

3   Onto-Semiotic Complexity of Mathematical Knowledge

The onto-semiotic, epistemological and cognitive assumptions of the OSA [2] serve as the basis for an educational-instructional proposal. Although this modelling of knowledge has been developed and applied for the case of mathematics, it is also relevant for the central core (concepts and principles) of scientific knowledge.

The OSA recognizes a key role in the transmission of knowledge (contextualized and meaningful for the student) in the mathematics teaching and learning processes although problem solving and inquiring also have an important part in the learning process. Instruction has to take into account the cultural/regulatory nature of the mathematical objects involved in the mathematical practices, whose competent realization by the students is intended. This competence cannot be considered as acquired if it is meaningless to the students and, therefore, it should be intelligible and relevant to them. Thus, students should be able to use mathematical objects in their own contexts with autonomy. But, according to OSA, due to the onto-semiotic complexity of mathematical knowledge, this autonomy should not necessarily be acquired in the first encounter with the object or in the determination of some of the senses attributed to it; for example, it can be achieved in a mathematical application practice.

How to learn something depends on what you have to learn. According to the OSA the student must make the institutional mathematical practices and the objects and processes involved in the resolution of situations-problems whose learning is intended, appropriate (Fig. 1).

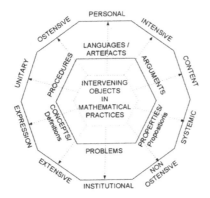

Fig. 1. Onto-semiotic configuration [18, p. 117]

An essential component of these practices are conceptual, propositional, procedural and argumentative objects whose nature is normative [28], and which have emerged in a historical and cultural process oriented towards generalization, formalization and maximizing the efficiency of mathematical work. It does not seem necessary or possible that students discover autonomously the cultural conventions that ultimately determine these objects.

In an instructional process, the student's realization of mathematical practices linked to the solution of some problematic tasks puts into play a conglomerate of objects and processes whose nature, from an institutional point of view, is essentially normative [28]. In the OSA mathematical ontology, according to Wittgenstein's philosophy of mathematics [29–32], the concepts, propositions and procedures are conceived as grammatical rules of the languages used to describe our worlds. They neither describe properties of objects that have some kind of existence independent of the people who build or invent them, nor of the languages by which they are expressed. From this perspective, mathematical truth is nothing more than an agreement with the result of following a rule that is part of a language game that is put into operation in certain social practices. It is not an agreement of arbitrary opinions, it is an accord of practices subject to rules.

The realization of the mathematical practices involves the intervention of previous objects to understand the demands of the situation - problem and to be able to implement a starting strategy. Such objects, their rules and conditions of application, must be available in the subject's working memory. Although it is possible to individually seek such knowledge in the workspace, there is not always enough time or the student does not succeed in finding that knowledge. Therefore, the teacher and classmates provide invaluable support to avoid frustration and abandonment.

Next, we exemplify the use of the onto-semiotic configuration tool for the case of the proportionality concept, contextualized with the puzzle enlargement task (Fig. 2).

It is intended to reveal the learning complexity of this mathematical object, discussing the pertinence of addressing such learning globally through a constructivist didactic model, or with a model based on the transmission of decontextualized and meaningless information for the student.

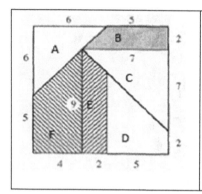

	- *You must cut a puzzle similar to this one (the model) on a card. But you have to make it bigger for kindergarten children. This side measuring 4 cm in the model should measure 7 cm in the enlarged puzzle.*
	- *You have to be able to make the same figures with the big puzzle as with the model.*
	- *To make the big puzzle you will divide into groups. Each group will make a single piece and we will put them all together at the end to fit.*

Fig. 2. Puzzle enlargement situation [17, p. 177]

In the puzzle enlargement situation (Fig. 2) the teacher tries to help the children reach a solution that involves the recognition and calculation of the proportionality constant (scale factor or unit value) through essays and discussions. However, the learning of proportionality requires that students progressively understand the algebraic-functional meaning, as indicated in the following sequence of practices:

- We intend to build a puzzle equal to that of the figure but bigger. That is, if a segment in the model is the union of two others, the associated segment will also be the union of the corresponding ones in the new figure. In addition, if the length of a segment s in the model is multiplied by a number, the length of segment S corresponding to s will be multiplied by the same number.
- Therefore, the correspondence established between the distances of the segments in the model (M) and the distances of the segments in the real puzzle (P), $f: M \rightarrow P$, is linear, $f(x) = kx$.
- The coefficient k of the linear function is the proportionality constant in the case of direct proportionality relations between magnitudes.
- Applying the properties of the linear function: $k = k \cdot 1 = f(1)$, and in our case: $f(4) = 7; 4f(1) = 7; f(1) = 7/4 = 1.75$.
- The length of a segment of length x in the model will therefore be $f(x) = 1.75x$ cm in the bigger puzzle.

This sequence of operative and discursive practices put at stake in an algebraic - functional solution involves a system of mathematical objects (Table 1) whose nature is essentially normative and that are the result of a long process of elaboration within the community of mathematical practices.

Table 1. Mathematical objects involved in the algebraic-functional solution of the puzzle situation

Object types	Objects
Languages	– *Symbolic*: function as correspondence between two numerical sets (f: M → P); value of a function f at a point x ($f(x)$); linear function of proportionality constant k ($f(x) = kx$) – *Numeric*: fractions, decimals – *Natural-mathematical*: correspondence, linear function, coefficient, segment, distance, multiplication, union, direct proportionality, magnitude
Concepts	– Magnitude; quantity; measure; numerical value of the measurements; sum of quantities, product by a scalar – Unlimited sequence of quantities and numbers; functional correspondence; direct proportionality; proportionality coefficient
Procedures	– Translation of expressions from natural to symbolic language – Calculation of the proportionality coefficient based on the definition conditions of the linear function – Calculation of the missing value based on the definition conditions of the linear function
Propositions	– The correspondence f: M → P is a linear function
Arguments	– Pragmatic conventions – The correspondence between the measurements of the two puzzles is additive and homogeneous

It does not seem pertinent to claim that the student autonomously reconstructs this network of knowledge that the mathematical culture has selected as adequate to respond to proportionality situations. Based on this onto-semiotic complexity, an instructional model based on the presentation of concepts, propositions, procedures and arguments cannot be considered pertinent if this information does not make sense to students.

4   OSA Tools for Didactical Analysis Instructional Design

In Godino et al. [4] some theoretical tools for the analysis of mathematical instruction processes are developed, by taking into account the previously developed onto-semiotic model for mathematical knowledge. In particular, the notions of didactic configuration and didactic suitability, serve as a basis to define a mixed didactic model that articulates the processes of inquiry and transmission of knowledge, related in a dialectical way in different types of didactic configurations.

4.1   Didactic Configuration

A *didactic configuration* (Fig. 3) is any segment of didactic activity put into play when approaching the study of a problem, concept, procedure or proposition, as a part of the instruction process of a topic, which requires the implementation of a didactical trajectory (articulated sequence of didactic configurations). It implies, therefore, taking into account the teacher's and student's roles, the resources used and the interactions with the context. In fact, there are different types of didactic configurations, depending on the interaction patterns, and the management of the institutionalization and personalization of knowledge.

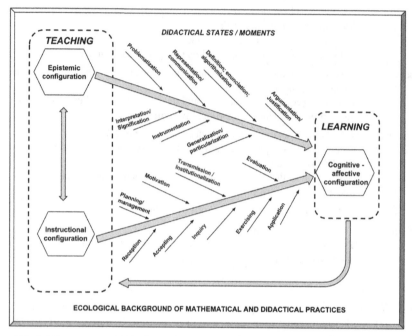

Fig. 3. Components and internal dynamic of a didactic configuration [33, p. 2646]

The task, which defines a didactic configuration, can be formed by different subtasks each of which can be considered as a sub-configuration. In any didactic configuration there is: (a) an *epistemic configuration* (system of institutional mathematical practices, objects and processes, required in the task), (b) an *instructional configuration* (system of teacher/learner functions and instructional means which are used in addition to the interaction between the different components) and (c) a *cognitive-affective configuration* (system of personal mathematical practices, objects and processes that describe the learning and the affective components which accompany it).

Figure 3 summarizes the components and internal dynamic of the didactic configuration, the relations between teaching and learning and the main mathematics processes lined to the onto-semiotic modelling of mathematics knowledge. This modelling takes into account the complexity of the relations that are established in the centre of any didactic configuration, not reducible to moments of inquiry or transmission of knowledge. In Fig. 3, with the bottom arrow, from learning to teaching, we want to point out that the relations are not linear but cyclical. In one particular moment of investigation, for example, the learner interacts with the epistemic configuration without the intervention of the teacher (or with less influence). This interaction conditions the teachers' interventions and so, should be taken into account in the instructional configuration, perhaps not totally in its content, but yes however in its nature, need and use. This is obviously not prerogative of the inquiry moments. The cognitive trajectory produces examples, meanings, arguments, etc., which condition the study process and as a result, the epistemic and instructional configurations, thus making possible and committing – in all cases, conditioning-, the conclusion of the instructional project planned.

4.2 Didactical Suitability

The detailed analysis of a process of mathematics study, which allows us to reveal the dialectic and synergy between the different components of the didactic system, requires to be divided into units where the notion of configuration and sub-configuration is useful. A *didactic fact* is significant if the actions or didactical practices that make it up carry out a function, or admit an interpretation, in terms of the instructional objective intended. The meaningfulness can be understood from the point of view of the teacher, of the student, or else from an institutional point of view which is external to the didactic system. The notion of didactic suitability [2–5], their facets and components, provide criteria to delimit the relevance of the didactic facts that occur in the processes of mathematics studies.

Didactic suitability of a process of instruction is defined as the degree to which the said process (or part of the same) meets certain characteristics that enable us to say it is optimum or adequate to be adapted among the personal meanings achieved by the students (learning) and the institutional meanings intended or implemented (teaching), taking into account the circumstances and the resources available (context). This supposes the coherent articulation of six facets or dimensions: epistemic, ecological, cognitive, affective, interactional and mediational [2].

5 A Mixed Transmissive - Inquiry Instructional Model

According to the students' previous knowledge and whether it is a first encounter with the object, or an exercise, application, institutionalization and evaluation moment, the didactic configurations can be of dialogical, collaborative, personal, magisterial, or a combination of these types (Fig. 4). The optimization of the learning process through the didactic trajectories may involve a combination of different types of didactic configurations. This optimization, that is, the realization of a suitable didactic activity, has a strongly local character, so that the didactic models, either student-focused (constructivist), or teacher-focused and content (objectivist), are partial visions that drastically reduce the complexity of the educational-instructional process.

In the student's first encounter with a specific meaning of an object, a dialogic - collaborative configuration, where the teacher and students work together to solve problems that put knowledge O at stake in a critical way can optimize learning. The first encounter should therefore be supported by an expert intervention by the teacher, so that the teaching-learning process could thus achieve greater epistemic and ecological suitability [34]. When the rules and the circumstances of application that characterize the object of learning O are understood, it is possible to tend towards higher levels of cognitive and affective suitability, proposing to deepen the study of O (situations of exercising and application), through didactic configurations that progressively attribute greater autonomy to the student (Fig. 4).

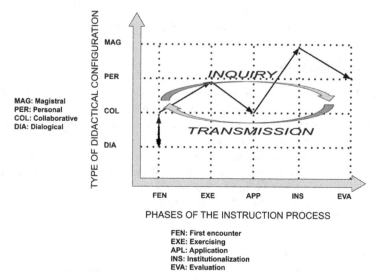

Fig. 4. A mixed inquiry – transmissive instructional model

In the moments or phases of the student's first encounter with a specific meaning of an object, it is considered that a dialogic - collaborative configuration can optimize learning. In these types of configurations, the teacher and students work together to solve problems that put knowledge O at stake in a critical way. The first encounter should therefore be supported by the teacher's expert intervention. The teaching-learning process could thus achieve greater epistemic, ecological and affective suitability [34]. In the phases of the first encounter, through a didactic model with minimal teaching guidance, students are exposed to the risk of not finding any solutions and fall into frustration and task rejection feelings.

"Even if the students find the solutions on their own, they do not know the most effective procedures as they have to wander around in the problem searching process, not to mention the cognitive loads they are imposed." [1 p. 909].

When the rules and the circumstances of application that characterize the learning object O are understood, it is possible to tend towards higher levels of cognitive and affective suitability, proposing to deepen the study of O (situations of exercising and application), through didactic configurations that progressively attribute greater autonomy to the student in a controlled manner (Fig. 4).

In summary, within the OSA framework, it is assumed that the types of didactic configurations that promote learning can vary depending on the types of knowledge sought, the students' initial state of knowledge, the context and circumstances of the instructional process. When it comes to learning new and complex content, the transmission of knowledge at specific times, already by the teacher, and by the leading student within the work teams, can be crucial in the learning process. That transmission can be meaningful when students are participating in the activity and working collaboratively. The didactic configuration tool helps to understand the dynamics and complexity of the interactions between the content, the teacher, students and the context. The optimization of learning can take place locally through a mixed model that articulates the transmission of knowledge, inquiry and collaboration, a model managed by criteria of didactic suitability [2–35] interpreted and adapted to the context by the teacher.

6 Working Together Introductory Situations of Proportional Reasoning in Primary School

Burgos and Godino [10] describe the implementation of the mixed type instructional model described in the previous section, with primary school students, whose aim was to create a first encounter with direct proportionality problems and initiate the development of proportional reasoning in the students. The sample under study consisted of a group of 23 students in fifth grade (10–11 years-old), who had a normal level of performance in mathematics and had difficulties in that course with the issue of fractions, as his tutor reported in an interview.

In a first didactic configuration, students were presented with different everyday situations in which the relationship between quantities of two magnitudes were of direct proportionality. The price paid for different quantities of an item, the distance travelled by a car at constant speed and time. In these situations, two series of numbers appeared, which were represented on the blackboard by means of tables, so that students could recognize the existence of a certain number (the proportionality ratio) that allowed them to write each value of the second series as product of the corresponding values of the first series by the said number. They were also presented with some situations of non-proportionality, in which the students had to decide whether they were or not and why; for example, the age and height of a child. Then the teacher - researcher provided the students with a worksheet with new introductory problem- situations. The students were organized in pairs, following the usual distribution to work in the classroom with their teacher.

In the second didactic configuration focused on the solution of the task "Laura visits her uncle" (Fig. 5), it was designed to stimulate inquiry and discussion by means of directed questions that serve as an approach to proportionality. The resolution of this task was carried out in a large group: the students intervene to complete the proportionality table, arguing at each moment the response and discussing with the classmates the strategy followed.

It is the end of the year party and the fifth classes want to order cakes to celebrate it. Laura's uncle is a pastry chef, he makes delicious cakes! So Laura has gone to visit him. That morning he used 3 liters of milk to make 18 equal pies. Laura wants to know how many pies she can make with 6, 2 and 5 liters of milk.

Laura, who is a very smart girl, reasons as follows to form a table like the one shown below.

−   First, 6 is double 3 (the number of liters of milk needed for 18 cakes). Put the number of cakes you can make with 6 liters of milk on the table.

−   Then she thinks that 2 liters is the third part of 6 liters. Put the following number of cakes on the table.

−   Finally 5 liters of milk are 2 liters plus the initial 3 liters.

Finish filling the table following these three ideas.

Liters of milk	3	6	2	5
Cakes	18			

Can you think of any other way that Laura could complete the table?

Fig. 5. Introductory task: "Laura visits her uncle"

At the end of each activity the ideas were discussed collectively, focusing the attention on the concept of proportionality and the properties whose knowledge and understanding are pursued to develop with the tasks. The students work on the worksheet in a collaborative way and the teacher-researcher could intervene to guide them, remember the necessary information and lead the discussion in the classroom.

One of the tasks that were used to evaluate the learning achieved was Brousseau's puzzle task (Fig. 2). 70% of the students correctly solved this task. Miyakawa and Winslow [36, p. 213] affirm, "It appears from experiments done by Brousseau and his colleagues that despite careful preparation in previous lessons, students spontaneously tend to construct the larger pieces by adding 3 cm to all known sides (since 7 cm is 3 cm more than 4 cm)". However, in our study, we found no evidence of this type of strategy, possibly because this task was preceded by other introductory tasks on arithmetic proportionality. The predominant resolution strategy was the reduction to unity, and some students used a resolution procedure that we describe as mixed, since they combine additive strategies with reduction to unity.

In the light of the results achieved, we believe that this model of collaboration between the teacher and the students, regarding the problem-situation that is intended to be solved and the mathematical content put at stake, achieves high levels of suitability in the interactional, cognitive and affective facets. An appropriate degree of dialogue, interaction and communication allowed:

− Detect intuitive, natural strategies and those that students develop with little guidance from the teacher (recurrent use of the tabular register, unit reduction strategy).
− Increase the degree of students' involvement and interest.
− Identify semiotic conflicts (greater difficulty when the proportionality constant is not integer) and resolve them.

7   Final Reflections

In this work of research we have complemented the cognitive arguments of Kirschner et al. [21] in favour of models based on the transmission of knowledge with reasons of onto-semiotic nature for the case of mathematical learning and science, especially in the moments of students' "first encounter" with the intended content: what they have to learn are, in a large dose, epistemic/cultural rules, the circumstances of their application and the conditions required for its relevant application. The learners start from known rules (concepts, propositions and procedures) and produce others, which must be shared and compatible with those already established in the mathematical culture. Such rules have to be stored in the subject's long-term memory and put into operation in a timely manner in the short-term memory.

The postulate of constructivist learning with little guidance from the teacher can lead to instructional processes with low cognitive and affective suitability for real subjects, and with low ecological suitability (context adaptation) by not taking into account the onto-semiotic complexity of mathematical knowledge or the potential development zone [37] of the subjects involved.

> "Children cannot discover the properties and regularities of the cultural world via their own independent exploration. They can only do that through interaction and dialogue with others. Children's trust in testimony, their ability to ask questions, their deference toward the use of opaque tools and symbols, and their selection among informants all attest to the fact that nature has prepared them for such cultural learning" [26, p. 267].

We believe that learning optimization implies a dialectical and complex combination between the teacher's roles as an instructor (transmitter) and facilitator (manager) and the student's roles as a knowledge builder and active receiver of meaningful information. The need for this mixed model is reinforced by the need to adapt the educational project to temporary restrictions and the diversity of learning modes and rhythms in large groups of students.

The teaching of mathematics and experimental sciences, should start and focus on the use of situations-problems, as a strategy to make sense of the techniques and theories studied, to propitiate exploratory moments of mathematical activity and develop research skills. However, configurations of mathematical objects (concepts, propositions, procedures, arguments) intervene in mathematical and scientific practice [28], which must be recognized by the teacher to plan their study. Such objects must be progressively dominated by students if we wish they progress towards successive advanced levels of knowledge and competence.

Acknowledgments. This work was carried out as part of the research project PID2019-105601 GB-I00, and it was supported by the Research Group FQM-126 (Junta de Andalucía, Spain).

References

1. Zhang, L.: Is inquiry-based science teaching worth the effort? Some thoughts worth considering. Sci. Educ. **25**, 897–915 (2016)
2. Godino, J.D., Batanero, C., Font, V.: The onto-semiotic approach to research in mathematics education. ZDM. Int. J. Math. Educ. **39**(1–2), 127–135 (2007)
3. Godino, J.D., Batanero, C., Font, V.: The onto-semiotic approach: implications for the prescriptive character of didactics. Learn. Math. **39**(1), 37–42 (2019)
4. Godino, J.D., Contreras, A., Font, V.: Análisis de procesos de instrucción basado en el enfoque ontológico-semiótico de la cognición matemática. Rech. Didactiques Math. **26**(1), 39–88 (2006)
5. Godino, J.D.: Indicadores de la idoneidad didáctica de procesos de enseñanza y aprendizaje de las matemáticas. Cuadernos Invest. Form. Educ. Matemática **11**, 111–132 (2013)
6. Godino, J.D.: How to teach mathematics and experimental sciences? Solving the inquiring versus transmission dilemma. In: Villalba-Condori, K.O., Adúriz-Bravo, A., García-Peñalvo, F.J., Lavonen, J. (eds.) Proceeding of the Congreso Internacional Sobre Educación y Tecnología en Ciencias - CISETC 2019, Arequipa, Perú, 10–12 December 2019, pp. 71–81. CEUR-WS.org, Aachen (2019)
7. Godino, J.D., Batanero, C., Cañadas, G.R., Contreras, J.M.: Linking inquiry and transmission in teaching and learning mathematics and experimental sciences. Acta Sci. **18**(4), 29–47 (2016)
8. Godino, J.D., Rivas, H., Burgos, M., Wilhelmi, M.D.: Analysis of didactical trajectories in teaching and learning mathematics: overcoming extreme objectivist and constructivist positions. Int. Electron. J. Math. Educ. **14**(1), 147–161 (2018)
9. Godino, J.D., Burgos, M., Wilhelmi, M.R.: Papel de las situaciones adidácticas en el aprendizaje matemático. Una mirada crítica desde el enfoque ontosemiótico. Enseñanza de las Ciencias **38** (1), 147–164 (2019)
10. Burgos, M., Godino, J.D.: Trabajando juntos situaciones introductorias de razonamiento proporcional en primaria. Análisis de una experiencia de enseñanza centrada en el profesor, en el estudiante y en el contenido. Bolema **33**(63), 389–410 (2019)
11. Artigue, M., Blomhøj, M.: Conceptualizing inquiry-based education in mathematics. ZDM Math. Educ. **45**, 797–810 (2013)
12. Ernest, P.: Varieties of constructivism: Their metaphors, epistemologies, and pedagogical implications. Hiroshima J. Math. Educ. **2**, 1–14 (1994)
13. Fox, R.: Constructivism examined. Oxford Rev. Educ. **27**(1), 23–35 (2001)
14. Linn, M.C., Clark, D., Slotta, J.D.: WISE design for knowledge integration. Sci. Educ. **87**(4), 517–538 (2003)
15. Thaler, R.H., Sunstein, C.R.: Nudge Improving Decisions About Health, Wealth and Happiness. Yale University Press, New Haven (2008)
16. Schoenfeld, A.H.: Learning to think mathematically: problem solving, metacognition, and sense-making in mathematics. In: Grouws, D. (ed.) Handbook of Research on Mathematics Teaching and Learning, pp. 334–370. MacMillan, New York (1992)
17. Brousseau, B.: Theory of Didactical Situations in Mathematics. Kluwer A. P., Dordrecht (2002)
18. Freudenthal, H.: Mathematics as an Educational Task. Reidel, Dordrecht (1973)
19. Freudenthal, H.: Revisiting Mathematics Education: China Lectures. Kluwer, Dordrecht (1991)
20. Mayer, R.E.: Should there be a three-strikes rule against pure discovery learning? Am. Psychol. **59**(1), 14–19 (2004)

21. Kirschner, P.A., Sweller, J., Clark, R.E.: Why minimal guidance during instruction does not work: an analysis of the failure of constructivist, discovery, problem-based, experiential, and inquiry-based teaching. Educ. Psychol. **41**(2), 75–86 (2006)

22. Jonassen, D.H.: Objectivism vs. constructivism: do we need a new philosophical paradigm? Educ. Technol. Res. Dev. **39**(3), 5–14 (1991)

23. Boghossian, P.: Behaviorism, constructivism, and Socratic pedagogy. Educ. Philos. Theory **38**(6), 713–722 (2006)

24. Sweller, J., Kirschner, P.A., Clark, R.E.: Why minimally guided teaching techniques do not work: a reply to commentaries. Educ. Psychol. **42**(2), 115–121 (2007)

25. Alfieri, L., Brooks, P.J., Aldrich, N.J., Tenenbaum, H.R.: Does discovery-based instruction enhance learning? J. Educ. Psychol. **103**(1), 1–18 (2011)

26. Harris, P.L.: The child as anthropologist. Infancia Aprendizaje **35**(3), 259–277 (2012)

27. Hmelo-Silver, C.E., Duncan, R.G., Chinn, C.A.: Scaffolding and achievement in problem-based and inquiry learning: a response to Kirschner, Sweller, and Clark (2006). Educ. Psychol. **42**(2), 99–107 (2007)

28. Font, V., Godino, J.D., Gallardo, J.: The emergence of objects from mathematical practices. Educ. Stud. Math. **82**, 97–124 (2013)

29. Baker, G.P., Hacker, P.M.S.: Wittgenstein: Rules, Grammar and Necessity. An Analytical Commentary on the Philosophical Investigations. Basil Blackwell, Glasgow (1985)

30. Bloor, D.: Wittgenstein: A Social Theory of Knowledge. The Macmillan Press, London (1983)

31. Wittgenstein, L.: Philosophical Investigations. The MacMillan Company, New York (1953)

32. Wittgenstein, L.: Remarks on the Foundations of Mathematics, 3rd edn. Basil Blackwell, Oxford (1978)

33. Godino, J.D., Batanero, C., Cañadas, G.R., Contreras, J.M.: Linking inquiry and transmission in teaching and learning mathematics. In: Krainer, K., Vondrobá, N. (eds.) Proceedings of the Ninth Conference of the European Society for Research in Mathematics Education. CEME9, 4–8 February 2015, pp. 2642-2648. Faculty of Education and ERME, Charles University in Prague, Prague (2015)

34. Godino, J.D., Font, V., Wilhelmi, M.R., de Castro, C.: Aproximación a la dimensión normativa en Didáctica de la Matemática desde un enfoque ontosemiótico. Enseñanza de las Ciencias **27**(1), 59–76 (2009)

35. Breda, A., Font, V., Pino-Fan, L.R.: Criterios valorativos y normativos en la Didáctica de las Matemáticas: el caso del constructo idoneidad didáctica. Bolema **32**(60), 255–278 (2018)

36. Miyakawa, T., Winsløw, C.: Didactical designs for students' proportional reasoning: an "open approach" lesson and a "fundamental situation". Educ. Stud. Math. **72**, 199–218 (2009)

37. Vygotsky, L.S.: Thought and Language. M.I.T. Press, Cambridge (1962)

Making Sense of Correlation and Regression

Carmen Batanero$^{(\boxtimes)}$ (iD) and María M. Gea (iD)

University of Granada, Granada, Spain
{batanero,mmgea}@ugr.es

Abstract. Although statistics is widely taught in high school and universities in many countries, the current teaching does not help student develop a complete understanding of many concepts. In this paper, we focus on the ideas of correlation and regression, which expand functional dependence and are the base of many other statistical concepts. We describe the main difficulties in understanding these concepts identified in the literature, analyse the components of statistical sense for the case of correlation and regression and suggest some ideas to improve the teaching of this topic.

Keywords: Statistical sense · Statistical literacy · Statistical reasoning · Correlation and regression

1 Introduction

The abundance of statistical information in the media and on the Internet, promoted by technology and by the increasing use of statistics in the workplace and in all the disciplines, has led to what we know as the information society, where the citizen is frequently involved in making decisions in an uncertain environment about various issues. As discussed by Engel [1], misinformation and ignorance in statistics are threats to our way of life in a complex world and are a risk for democracy. It is for this reason that current curricular reforms emphasize statistical reasoning and its role in decision making and professional work in many countries [2–5].

The teaching of statistics to all citizens has been justified because statistical thinking is a component of critical reasoning, as well as for the instrumental role of statistics in different disciplines [6, 7]. Another reason suggested by Batanero [8] is that improving statistical reasoning, prepares students for life, since we are surrounding by randomness since we are born.

However, the last reason is often forgotten and statistics is taught in a too formal way using non-realistic examples and a consequence is that students develop displeasure for the topic. Due to the need to complete a wide program in a short time, many teachers present only definition of concepts and procedures for solving statistical problems. Consequently, students do not acquire a deep understanding of the underlying concepts. In a previous paper [9] we describe the components of statistical sense, that include statistical literacy and reasoning and adequate attitudes towards statistics. In this new paper, we apply these ideas to the case of correlation and regression.

K. O. Villalba-Condori et al. (Eds.): CISETC 2019, CCIS 1191, pp. 22–35, 2020.
https://doi.org/10.1007/978-3-030-45344-2_3

Correlation and regression are included in curricula for middle and high school in Spain [4] and other countries [2, 3, 5]. Correlation and regression are fundamental statistical ideas that expand the previous knowledge about univariate distributions and mathematical functions. These methods are relevant when researchers are interested in finding relationships between quantitative variables in a statistical study (correlation problem) and, if possible, in finding a mathematical model that adequately fits to the data and that can be used to predict the values of a response variable when some values of another explanatory variable are known. Galton's [10] work on inherited characteristics of sweet peas led to the initial conceptualisation of linear regression. Bravais [11] is recognised as the author of the initial mathematical formulas for correlation, while Pearson [12] published the first complete treatment of correlation and regression. Subsequent joint efforts by Galton and Pearson served to develop the general technique of multiple regression.

Batanero and Borovcnik [13] offer an example of the interest of correlation and regression when analysing the variables that influence the Life expectancy in different countries, while Engel [1] analyses another situation dealing with income inequality. Both topics frequently appear in the media, together with different recommendations to act or judge the evolution of the variables involved. Other similar studies concern migration, pollution, crime, human rights, education, gender inequality, production or public expenditures [14]. Science also uses correlation and regression to make predictions about the future of our planet or the need to change some of our consumption habits to safeguard this future. To critically evaluate these arguments, we need to understand the way in which the data are analysed, and how the conclusions in these reports are obtained.

Moreover, correlation and regression form the foundation for many statistical procedures, including simple and multiple regression (with one or several explanatory variables), analysis of variance, and most multivariate methods (like factor analysis).

2   Main Difficulties in Understanding Correlation and Regression

In spite of the relevance of the topic, previous research suggests biases and misconceptions in the understanding of correlation. Batanero et al. [15] studied the intuitive conceptions of association in contingency tables in a sample of 213 high school students and Estepa and Batanero [16] investigated the accuracy of intuitive conceptions of correlation in a subsample of 51 of these students. The authors defined the *causal conception* of according to which the subject only considers association or correlation between variables, when it can be explained by the presence of a cause - effect relationship. They also described the *unidirectional conception,* where the student does not accept an inverse correlation, considering the strength of the correlation, but not its sign and assuming independence where there is an inverse association. In the *determinist conception* students only accept functional relationship between the variables and expect a correspondence that assigns only a single value in the dependent variable for each value of the independent variable. Finally, the *local conception* appears when the correlation is judged using only part of the data. Castro-Sotos et al. [17] described the *transitive conception* of correlation that consist in considering correlation is a transitive operation, that is, whenever there exist correlation between A and B, and between B and C, there should exist correlation between A and C; however, this is not always the case.

Moreover, research suggests poor results in people's estimation of correlation in everyday settings or in experiments where a scatter plot is offered to perform the estimation. Thus, Erlick and Mills [18] found that negative correlation is estimated as close to zero and Chapman [19] analysed the influence of previous theories about the context of the problem on the accuracy in estimating correlation. Chapman [19] showed that the estimation of correlation is more precise when people have no theories about the type of correlation (direct, inverse) in the data. If the person's previous theories agree with the correlation in the empirical data, then people overestimate the value of the correlation coefficient. But in case people's expectations about the correlation do not coincide with the correlation in the data, the estimation is poor. Estepa and Batanero [16] identified some additional variables that affect this estimation of correlation such as the sign or strength of correlation. Estimations are relatively good in tasks that involve linear, strong, and direct correlation, and poorer if inverse, non-linear, or moderate correlation is involved.

Some students do not distinguish the explanatory from the response variable and use the same regression line for prediction, no matter which variable should be predicted [20]. Moreover, students also may find problems in understanding the criteria to find a best-fitting function in the study of regression, that is, to understand the least-squares criterion or regression to the median (Tukey line). It is important to assure that students understand the chosen criteria; this understanding is needed to interpret the final approximation provided by the regression method, as well as the goodness of fit of the model to the data [13]. An explanation of the difficulty is that working with regression requires an advanced level of algebraic reasoning; more specifically, levels 4 and 5 in the six levels hierarchy proposed by Godino et al. [21], which are characterised by parameters and operation with parameters. In fact, parameters appear in statistics not only in the study of inference, but also in the study of regression. We need to operate with the parameters of the fitting function; for example, the slope and intercept in the line of best fit. To make the situation more complex, these topics are studied also by social sciences students, who generally do not have a strong algebraic background.

There are many calls to change the situation and try to decrease the level of formalization, in order to help students making sense of statistics [22]. In Batanero and Borovcnik [13] we recommend to use contexts familiar to the students, build on students' previous knowledge and introduce the concepts making students understand how statistical concepts help solve the given task. We also present examples of meaningful contexts and problems that can be used to make sense of the different concepts and methods to the students. Other suggestions include working with real data, adequate use of technology and using assessment to improve the students' learning. All of these suggestions are directed to increase the students' statistical sense, which is analysed below for the particular case of correlation and regression.

3 Statistical Sense: The Case of Correlation and Regression

As analysed in Batanero [9], suggestions for making sense of mathematics appeared early in relation to ideas of numeracy, that described the ability to cope with every day mathematical demands and as a way of understanding, which was opposed to routine learning. Soon the idea of number sense appeared, as a main outcome of school mathematics.

Number sense refers to a person's general understanding of number and operations along with the ability and inclination to use this understanding in flexible ways to make mathematical judgements and to develop useful strategies for handling numbers and operations It reflects an inclination and an ability to use numbers and quantitative methods as a means of communicating, processing and interpreting information [23, p. 3].

We found no similar ideas about statistical sense, although in [22] we discovered recommendations about helping students making sense of statistics. When comparing with the above definition of number sense, Batanero [9] argues that statistical sense should refer to general understanding of statistical concepts and the ability to use this knowledge in a flexible way in solving problems, that is, in statistical reasoning and thinking. It also includes the ability to use statistics to communicate, process and interpret statistical information. This statistical sense would be needed for everyday decision-making (e.g., taking an insurance policy, voting, evaluating risks of accident, interpreting coincidences, etc.).

Ideas related to statistical sense can be found in the notions of statistical literacy, reasoning and thinking, which are viewed by some authors [24] as three different levels of statistical knowledge. We, instead, prefer to include these three ideas in what we call *statistical sense,* and distinguish, on the one hand, statistical literacy as a set of knowledge and dispositions, and statistical thinking and reasoning as the ability and processes needed to solve statistical problems. Below we describe these components of statistical sense.

3.1 Statistical Literacy

The need of statistical knowledge for every citizen in a democratic society based on information has been widely recognized [6, 7] and led to the introduction of the term *statistical literacy,* which was defined by Wallman [25] in the following terms:

The ability to understand and critically evaluate statistical results that permeate daily life, coupled with the ability to appreciate the contributions that statistical thinking can make in public and private, professional and personal decisions [25, p.1].

While literacy means the ability to find, read, interpret, analyse and evaluate written materials (and to detect possible errors or biases in this information), to be statistically literate, people need a basic understanding of statistics. This includes knowing what statistical terms and symbols mean; being able to read statistical graphs and data; understanding the basic logic of statistics; understanding and critically evaluating statistical results that appear in daily life and a positive attitude towards statistics [7].

Statistical literacy describes the set of statistical competences needed to manage in our society and include general reading and writing literacy, mathematical and statistical knowledge, and attitude [26]. The authors of the GAISE project [6] suggest that statistics literacy is the final goal of statistics education, and that an investment in statistical literacy by a country will be reflected in that country's economy and development.

More recently, a group of researchers involved in the ProCivicStat project (http:// iase-web.org/islp/pcs/) have proposed the idea of *civic statistics* that describes eleven knowledge bases and processes needed to understand, evaluate, and reason with statistics about social phenomena, and a fundamental part of which is statistical literacy [1].

3.2 Fundamental Ideas in the Study of Correlation and Regression

A statistical literate citizen should acquire a minimum level of understanding of the fundamental statistical ideas [27]. These ideas commonly appear in statistical situations, can be taught with different levels of formalization along the curricula and have played a main role in the development of statistics as a science. In particular, the following fundamental ideas are basic in the study of correlation and regression.

Data: While data are also used in mathematics, in statistics the context of data is fundamental to interpret the results of statistical analyses and, for this reason, the understanding of the context is central to statistical literacy; we then should bring realistic contexts, in addition to statistical ideas to the classroom [14]. Moreover, there is a wider type of data in the work with statistics when compared with mathematics, because of the use of categorical variables. This mean the possibility of mathematising a wider range of situations that cannot be worked with mathematical methods.

Distribution: A pure statistical idea that describes the behaviour of a variable in a collective is that of distribution, which is characterized by its central tendency and spread. Instead of working with each isolated value of the variable, we work with the whole distribution, and a goal of statistics is predicting the model for the distribution of the variables in the study. In correlation and regression, we deal with bivariate data, since for every case we consider the values of the two statistical variables and try to relate them. When we add the corresponding joint frequencies for each different pair of values, we obtain the bi-dimensional distribution. Linked to this distribution we also need to take into account the marginal distribution (considering only one of the variables) and conditional distributions (fixing a particular value for one variable).

Representation: The values of a bi-dimensional distribution can be condensed in a graph (usually a scatter plot or a bivariate table). Other more sophisticate representations include bubble charts or bi-dimensional bar graphs and histograms. These graphical or tabular representation of a distribution are used as tools that help discovering patterns hidden in the raw data through a process of transnumeration [28]. For example, in Batanero and Borovnick [13], scatter plots are used to represent the Life expectancy in a series of countries against different variables and help students discover direct or inverse linear or non-lineal, strong and weak correlation with Life expectancy for these variables (An example of direct linear strong relationship is presented in Fig. 1).

Covariation and Correlation: Although variation also appear in the study of functions, statistics deal with random variation. In particular, variability appear in the spread of

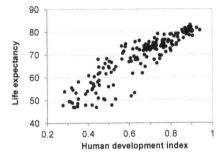

Fig. 1. Scatter plot of a strong and direct relationship between life expectancy and human development index

the scatter plot that represent the bivariate data. A main goal of statistics is identifying and measuring variability to predict, explain or control various phenomena. Contrary to mathematics that provides exact results, in statistics we often deal with approximation and randomness. In fact, we can think in terms of *signal* (the line fitting the bivariate data) and *noise* (the deviations or differences of the points to this line).

A statistic that considers these deviations is the covariance, which provides a measure of the direction (direct or inverse) and the strength of the correlation.

$$s_{xy} = \frac{1}{n} \sum_{i=1}^{n} (x_i - \bar{x})(y_i - \bar{y})$$

Since the covariance is not bounded, is difficult to compare the covariance for different scatter plots to decide which correlation is stronger. We then use the *Pearson correlation coefficient r*, which varies between -1 and $+1$ and takes the values $+1$ or -1 only if all the points have perfect linear dependence (i.e., they are all located on a straight line):

$$r = \frac{s_{xy}}{s_x s_y}.$$

The higher is the absolute value of the correlation coefficient the stronger is the linear correlation of the variables. If the variables are uncorrelated, then the value of the coefficient is zero.

Regression and Fitting Models. Once a strong correlation is found, the interest is to fit a model to the data that serves to predict the *response* variable from the known values of the *explanatory* variable. We use simple functions, such as linear, exponential, or power functions. When the tendency in the scatter plot suggests that a straight line with the equation $Y = a + bX$ is an adequate model, the parameters a and b should be estimated from the data. The common method to estimate these parameters is the *least-squares criterion* that consists in making the sum of squares of the errors of the predictions as small as possible. The solution is given by:

$$b = \frac{s_{xy}}{s_x^2}, \quad a = \bar{y} - b\bar{x}.$$

3.3 Correlational Thinking and Reasoning

In addition to knowledge of concepts, statistical sense requires the ability to apply this knowledge, as well as an adequate way of reasoning and thinking. Statistical thinking has been described by many authors, including a long discussion about how should we distinguish statistical thinking, reasoning and literacy [24].

We postulate that statistical thinking appears each time a person try to solve a statistical problem and that statistical reasoning is concerned with the arguments used by the person to justify his or her solutions to the problem or else to refute or agree with a statement based on statistical data. Consequently, the terms statistical thinking and reasoning will not be distinguished in the paper, and will be used with the broad meaning of solving problems in which variation and uncertainty are present.

A relevant model to explain statistical thinking and reasoning was proposed by Wild and Pfannkuch [28], who described the process of solving real statistical problems and considered the following components:

1. *The statistical investigation cycle* involves the phases of defining a statistical problem, planning for the solution, collecting the data, analysing the data and obtaining a conclusion about the problem. Many teachers use this PPDAC cycle as a framework for proposing activities or projects that help students to develop their statistical thinking and reasoning.
2. *Fundamental types of thinking.* There are five typical ways in which a statistician reasons: (a) Realizing what data are needed for a particular research or problem; (b) Trasnumeration, which consist in changing the way in which the data are represented to obtain new information not visible in the raw data; (c) Perceiving the variation and identifying the sources of variation, such as the sampling process, the variable being studied, or error in measurement; (d) Integrating statistical data and analysis with the context from which the problem has arisen; and (e) Selecting and using the appropriate statistical models.
3. *The interrogative cycle.* Along problem solving in statistics, there is a constant, recursive generic process of interrogation, which may start at any step of the process. In this interrogative cycle the solver tries to generate possibilities, searches for causes and explanations, and checks ideas and approaches for the solution to the problem. The ideas may come from the problem, the data or the statistical analysis. Another component of this process is the interpretation and criticism of data, representations or solutions.
4. In addition to the above components, statistical thinking requires *a series of dispositions,* such as engagement and perseverance, curiosity, imagination and scepticism. These dispositions take part of attitudes and beliefs that are discussed in Sect. 3.4.

All the components of statistical thinking can be applied in correlational thinking, which is a fundamental cognitive activity in diverse human activities [29, 30], since perceiving, interpreting and predicting many events that surround us depend on our ability to analyse covariations between these events.

Correlational thinking also includes the ability to interpret accurately the correlation presented between two variables. According to Barbancho [31], a correlation between two variables may be explained by the existence of a unilateral cause-effect relationship (one variable produces the other), but also to interdependence (each variable affects the other), indirect dependence (there is a third variable affecting both variables), concordance (matching in preference by two judges in the same data set) and spurious correlation. A good correlational thinking involve the discrimination of these types of relationships between variables; however, many students reduce correlation to unilateral cause-effect relationship.

3.4 Attitudes and Beliefs

The affective domain strongly influences the learning of mathematics, due to its impact on the cognitive processes related to mathematical thinking, such as, for example, creativity, visualization, intuition or argumentation [32, 33]. This domain includes, according to Phillip [33], emotions, attitudes and beliefs. According to this author, emotions are feelings or states of consciousness, distinguished from cognition, involve positive (e.g., satisfaction) and negative (e.g., panic) feelings, are transient and serve as a source for development of attitudes.

Di Martino and Zan [35] suggest that attitudes constitute a bridge between beliefs and emotions and their mutual relationships. They can influence the person's behaviour with respect to the topic and his/her willingness to continue studying or using what they learnt in the classroom and are difficult to change. Consequently, it is important that teachers are able to identify the affective aspects related to their teaching or the students' work in the classroom. Attitudes towards a topic (in this case correlation and regression) include different components, such as:

- *Affective*: feelings about the object in question, if the person is attracted or not by the study of the topic.
- *Cognitive*: the person's self-perception as regards the object, if the person believes he or she is capable to manage the topic.
- *Behavioural*: the person's inclination to act toward the attitude object in a particular way, for example, to use the topic to solve a problem or to study more deeply the topic.
- *Value*: appreciation of the usefulness, relevance and worth of the topic in personal or professional life.

Beliefs are psychologically held premises or propositions about the world that are thought to be true [34]. There are varied beliefs about a subject, which can refer to the topic itself. A well-known example in the case of correlation is that of illusory correlation described by Chapman [19, p. 151] as "the report by observers of a correlation between two classes of events which, in reality, (a) are not correlated, (b) are correlated to a lesser extent than reported, or (c) are correlated in the opposite direction from that which is reported". Another source of difficulty is the mixture of theoretical ideas and personal conceptions when people apply stochastic reasoning. Independence, for example, can be defined mathematically or reduced to the multiplicative rule. This definition, however, neither includes all the causality perceptions that students often relate to independence nor does it always serve to help decide if independence applies in a particular data set.

Among the beliefs that influence the motivation towards the topic, Goldin et al. [36] include interests and preferences, perception of the instrumental nature of the topic, as well as its relationship with the students' close or long-term objectives. All these beliefs are reinforced in a positive way, for the case of statistics, through project work [37].

4 Making Sense of Correlation and Regression

Taking into account the above components, making sense of statistics involve the work with statistical projects and real data that students can collect themselves of download from the many data servers available on the Internet. In Batanero and Borovcnik [13] and Batanero et al. [38], we describe a project based on data taken from the United Nations web server, where visualization and data analysis is based on simple tools, such as Excel. The aim of the project "Life expectancy in different countries" is investigate the relationship between the life expectancy in different countries and different international indicators of human development. To develop the project students are provided with an Excel file with the data set, containing data from 9 variables from about 175 countries:

- *Life expectancy at birth (years)*: Number of years a new-born could expect to live if prevailing patterns of age-specific, mortality rates at the time of birth stay the same throughout the infant's life.
- *Human Development Index (HDI) value*: A composite index measuring average achievement in three basic dimensions of human development-a long and healthy life, knowledge and a decent standard of living.
- *GDP per capita (2005)*: Sum of gross value added by all resident producers in the economy plus any product taxes and minus any subsidies not included in the value of the products, expressed in international dollars using purchasing power parity rates and divided by total population during the same period.
- *Adolescent fertility rate*: Number of births of women aged 15–19 per 1,000 women of these ages.
- *Under-five mortality*: Probability of child mortality between birth and exactly aged 5, expressed per 1,000 live births.
- *Expenditure on public health*: Current spending from government (central and local) budgets, external borrowings and grants (including donations from international agencies and nongovernmental organizations), and social (or compulsory) health insurance funds, expressed as a percentage of GDP.
- *HDI education index*: takes into account distribution of years of schooling.
- *Population, total* both sexes (in thousands).
- *Population, urban*: percentage of total population living in areas classified as urban according to the criteria used by each area or country.

The activities in the project include: (a) analysing the distribution and the statistical measures (centre and spread) of the Life expectancy in the set of countries; (b) producing scatter plots of the bivariate distribution of Life expectancy (response variable) with each explanatory variables described in the previous paragraphs (see an example in Fig. 1); (c) using these scatter plots to estimate the strength and sign of correlation for each bivariate distribution and ordering the explanatory variables by their power to predict Life expectancy; (d) Selecting a possible model to fit the data in each scatterplot and determining the line of best fit for the selected model.

In order to make students explore a variety of relationships with the Life expectancy, the following criteria were considered in selecting the explanatory variables:

- *Strength of correlation:* ranging from very strong correlation ($|r| = 1$) to independence ($r = 0$).
- *Sign of correlation:* including both positive and negative correlations, which are harder to be perceived by the students according to Sánchez-Cobo et al. [20].
- *Model fitting to the data:* including linear and nonlinear models.
- *Explanation of correlation:* we used relationships that may be explained by cause and effect, as well as interdependence and indirect dependence.

More details about the specific questions, graphs and calculations needed in the project are given in [13]. This project is useful to achieve the following learning goals:

- Becoming familiar with the concept of distribution, the difference between absolute, relative and cumulative frequencies and understanding the usefulness of each of these types of frequencies.
- Making sense of measure of location such as mean, median and mode and being able to select the most adequate measure for each type of variable and shape of the distribution.
- Understanding variability in the data and making sense to each different measures of spread.
- Interpreting covariation and correlation and discriminating different types of correlation (direct, inverse, lineal or no).
- Learning to identify a linear tendency in a scatter plot as well as identify other simple functions that fit the data when the tendency is not linear.
- Fitting models to bivariate data and understanding the usefulness of the line of best fit as a summary of a bivariate data.
- Understanding the asymmetric roles of the explanatory and response variables in the model. Hence, there are two different regression lines that coincide only in case of perfect linear regression.

The brief summary of this project suggests the many possibilities of expansion by just including other variables or research questions. A project is a simplified investigation that can be carried out by the students, help improving their attitudes towards the topic and understand and make sense of the different concepts and procedures we try to teach them. The computations need to complete the project can be facilitated by the widely available software. For example, we recently count with the platform CODAP, a user-friendly statistical software freely available online at https://codap.concord.org/. Moreover, there is also a simulator available, that help exploring probability problems and models, as well as many examples of data sets and projects that can be used in the classrooms.

5 Implications for the Teaching of Correlation and Regression

Statistics is today taught to almost all students in the different educational levels, but errors and misinterpretation of statistics published in the media and used in professional work is pervasive. In this paper we have suggested the need to change the approach in teaching, by focusing on conceptual understanding and making sense of statistics. The explanation for the poor learning of statistics is that teachers often forget the nature of statistics, which was described by Cabria [38] in the following way:

> Statistics studies the behaviour of the so-called collective phenomena. It is characterized by information about a collective or universe, which constitutes its material object; a specific type of reasoning, the statistical method, which is its formal object and predictions for future involving an uncertain atmosphere, which constitute its final object or cause [39, p.22].

The nature of statistics requires then to couple its study with that of probability, in considering settings where chance is present and at the same time should consider both statistical literacy and reasoning. We also discussed the relevance of context to statistical literacy; as suggested by Gal [14], most statistical methods emerged from the need to solve problems in disciplines different from mathematics. It is therefore necessary to find adequate contexts that serve to make sense of different statistical methods. This is very easy today given the abundance of real data available on Internet.

Working with statistical projects and investigation is a didactic method recommended by many statistical educators to better educate statistical literate citizens. There are many examples of such projects available, since different institutions organize statistical projects competitions for schools. Some examples are the Best cooperative project award (http://iase-web.org/islp/) promoted by the International Association for Statistical Education as a part of the International Statistical Literacy Project or the competition organized by the Canarias Statistical Office (http://www3.gobiernodecanarias.org/istac/webescolar/index.php), which also provides didactic materials in its web page.

This project work can be reinforced with other activities, in particular those based on simulations and microworlds that are easily available on the web. Many resources are today available to increase statistical literacy and reasoning, for example, those listed at the Civic-Stat project (http://iase-web.org/islp/pcs).

All of this involve a previous preparation of teachers, since the impact of curricular changes directly depends on teachers' willingness and interest in teaching the given topic. Because of a routine learning when they were students some teachers may not value statistics, feel scared with the idea or introducing statistical projects in the classroom or consider themselves not well prepared to teach statistics with this approach [40]. Souza et al. [41] indicate that teachers may not be aware of the possibilities that statistical projects offer or the way they can be used to make sense of reality. According to McGilliwray and Pereira-Mendoza [37], the use of data investigation projects is ideal to develop both statistical and didactic knowledge for teachers; therefore, it is important to immerse teachers in a reasoning and learning environment centred on this type of work.

We hope this paper help interesting these teachers to work with projects and encourage them to reinforce the teaching of statistics in the classrooms in order that all the students acquire an adequate sense of statistics.

Acknowledgments. Research supported by the project: EDU2016-74848-P (AEI, FEDER).

References

1. Engel, J.: Statistical literacy and society. In: Contreras, J.M., Gea, M.M., López-Martín, M.M., Molina-Portillo, E. (eds.) Actas del Tercer Congreso Internacional Virtual de Educación Estadística (2019). https://www.ugr.es/~fqm126/civeest/ponencias/engel.pdf
2. Australian Curriculum, Assessment and Reporting Authority (ACARA). The Australian curriculum: Mathematics, Sidney, NSW (2013)
3. Common Core State Standards Initiative, CCSSI. Common Core State Standards for Mathematics. National Governors Association Center for Best Practices and the Council of Chief State School Officers, Washington, DC (2010). www.corestandards.org/assets/CCSSI_Math%20Standards.pdf
4. MECD, Ministerio de Educación, Cultura y Deporte. Real Decreto 1105/2014, de 26 de diciembre, por el que se establece el currículo básico de la educación secundaria obligatoria y del bachillerato. (Royal Decree establishing the basic curriculum for secondary and high school), Madrid (2015)
5. Ministry of Education: The New Zealand curriculum, Wellington, NZ (2015)
6. Franklin, C., et al.: Guidelines for assessment and instruction in statistics education (GAISE report): a Pre-K-12 curriculum framework. American Statistical Association, Alexandria, VA (2007). www.amstat.org/Education/gaise/
7. Gal, I.: Adults' statistical literacy: meanings, components, responsibilities (with discussion). Int. Stat. Rev. **70**(1), 1–51 (2002). https://doi.org/10.1111/j.1751-5823.2002.tb00336.x
8. Batanero, C.: Understanding randomness: challenges for research and teaching. In: Krainer, K., Vondrová, N. (eds.) Proceedings of the Ninth Congress of the European Society for Research in Mathematics Education, pp. 34–49. European Society for Research in Mathematics Education, Prague (2016). hal.archives-ouvertes.fr/hal-01280506/document
9. Batanero, C.: Statistical sense in the information society. In: Villalba-Condori, K.O., Adúriz-Bravo, A., García-Peñalvo, F.J., Lavonen, J. (eds.) Proceeding of the Congreso Internacional Sobre Educación y Tecnología en Ciencias - CISETC 2019, Arequipa, Perú, 10–12 December 2019, pp. 28–38. CEUR-WS.org, Aachen (2019)
10. Galton, F.: Natural Inheritance. Macmillan, London (1889)
11. Bravais, A.: Analyse mathématique sur les probabilités des erreurs de situation d'un point (Mathematical Analysis of the Probabilities for Selecting a Point), vol. 9, pp. 255–332. Memoires presentés par divers savants à l'Académie Royale de l'Institut de France (1846)
12. Pearson, K.: Mathematical contributions to the theory of evolution. III. Regression, heredity and panmixia. Philos. Trans. R. Soc. Lond. (A) **187**, 253–318 (1896)
13. Batanero, C., Borovcnik, M.: Statistics and Probability in High School. Sense Publishers, Rotterdam (2016). https://doi.org/10.1163/9789463006248
14. Gal, I.: Understanding statistical literacy: about knowledge of contexts and models. In: Contreras, J.M., Gea, M.M., López-Martín, M.M., Molina-Portillo, E. (eds.) Actas del Tercer Congreso Internacional Virtual de Educación Estadística (2019). www.ugr.es/local/fqm126/civeest.html

15. Batanero, C., Estepa, A., Godino, J.D., Green, D.R.: Intuitive strategies and preconceptions about association in contingency tables. J. Res. Math. Educ. **27**(2), 151–169 (1996). https://doi.org/10.2307/749598

16. Estepa, A., Batanero, C.: Judgements of correlation in scatter plots: students' intuitive strategies and preconceptions. Hiroshima J. Math. Educ. **4**, 21–41 (1996)

17. Castro-Sotos, A.E., Vanhoof, S., Van Den Noortgate, W., Onghena, P.: The transitivity misconception of Pearson's correlation coefficient. Stat. Educ. Res. J. **8**(2), 33–55 (2009). http://www.stat.auckland.ac.nz/iase/serj/

18. Erlick, D.E., Mills, R.G.: Perceptual quantification of conditional dependency. J. Exp. Psychol. **73**(1), 9–14 (1967)

19. Chapman, L.J.: Illusory correlation in observational report. J. Verbal Learn. Verbal Behav. **6**(1), 151–155 (1967)

20. Sánchez-Cobo, F.T., Estepa, A., Batanero, C.: Un estudio experimental de la estimación de la correlación a partir de diferentes representaciones. Enseñanza de las Ciencias **18**(2), 297–310 (2000)

21. Godino, J.D., Neto, T., Wilhelmi, M., Aké, L., Etchegaray, S., Lasa, A.: Algebraic reasoning levels in primary and secondary education. In: Krainer, K., Vondrová, N. (eds.) Proceedings of CERME 9-Ninth Congress of the European Society for Research in Mathematics Education, pp. 426–432. ERME, Prague (2015)

22. Shaughnessy, J.M., Chance, B., Kranendonk, H.: Focus in High School Mathematics: Reasoning and Sense Making in Statistics and Probability. National Council of Teachers of Mathematics, Reston (2009)

23. McIntosh, A., Reys, B.J., Reys, R.E.: A proposed framework for examining basic number sense. Learn. Math. **12**(3), 2–44 (1992)

24. Garfield, J.B., Ben-Zvi, D.: Developing Students' Statistical Reasoning: Connecting Research and Teaching Practice, 1st edn., p. 408. Springer, Dordrecht (2008). https://doi.org/10.1007/978-1-4020-8383-9

25. Wallman, K.K.: Enhancing statistical literacy: Enriching our society. J. Am. Stat. Assoc. **88**(421), 1–8 (1993)

26. Watson, J.M.: Statistical Literacy at School: Growth and Goals. Lawrence Erlbaum, Mahwah (2006). https://doi.org/10.4324/9780203053898

27. Burrill, G., Biehler, R.: Fundamental statistical ideas in the school curriculum and in training teachers. In: Batanero, C., Burrill, G., Reading, C. (eds.) Teaching Statistics in School Mathematics-Challenges for Teaching and Teacher Education. New ICMI Study Series, vol. 14, pp. 57–69. Springer, Dordrecht (2011). https://doi.org/10.1007/978-94-007-1131-0_10

28. Wild, C.J., Pfannkuch, M.: Statistical thinking in empirical enquiry. Int. Stat. Rev. **67**(3), 223–265 (1999)

29. Moritz, J.: Reasoning about covariation. In: Ben-Zvi, D., Garfield, J. (eds.) The Challenge of Developing Statistical Literacy, Reasoning and Thinking, pp. 221–255. Kluwer, Dordrecht (2004)

30. Zieffler, A.S., Garfield, J.B.: Modeling the growth of students' covariational reasoning during an introductory statistics course. Stat. Educ. Res. J. **8**(1), 7–31 (2009). https://www.stat.auckland.ac.nz/~iase/serj/SERJ8(1)_Zieffler_Garfield.pdf

31. Barbancho, A.G.: Estadística elemental moderna (Modern Elementary Statistics). Ariel, Barcelona (1992)

32. Attard, C., Ingram, N., Forgasz, H., Leder, G., Grootenboer, P.: Mathematics education and the affective domain. In: Makar, K., Dole, S., Visnovska, J., Goos, M., Bennison, A., Fry, K. (eds.) Research in Mathematics Education in Australasia 2012-2015, pp. 73–96. Springer, Singapore (2016). https://doi.org/10.1007/978-981-10-1419-2_5

33. Gea, M.M., Batanero, C., Estrada, A.: Assessing prospective teachers' affective component related to working with statistical projects. Acta Sci. **21**(3), 112–130 (2019)

34. Philipp, R.A.: Mathematics teachers' beliefs and affects. In: Lester, F. (ed.) Second Handbook of Research on Mathematics Teaching and Learning, pp. 257–315. Information Age Publishing & National Council of Teachers of Mathematics, Charlotte (2007)

35. Di Martino, P., Zan, R.: The construct of attitude in mathematics education. In: Pepin, B., Roesken-Winter, B. (eds.) From beliefs to dynamic affect systems in mathematics education. AME, pp. 51–72. Springer, Cham (2015). https://doi.org/10.1007/978-3-319-06808-4_3

36. Goldin, G.A., et al.: Attitudes, Beliefs, Motivation and Identity in Mathematics Education. ITS. Springer, Cham (2016). https://doi.org/10.1007/978-3-319-32811-9

37. MacGillivray, H., Pereira-Mendoza, L.: Teaching statistical thinking through investigative projects. In: Batanero, C., Burrill, G., Reading, C. (eds.) Teaching statistics in school mathematics-challenges for teaching and teacher education, vol. 14, pp. 109–120. Springer, Dordrecht (2011). https://doi.org/10.1007/978-94-007-1131-0_14

38. Batanero, C., Gea, M.M., Díaz, C., Cañadas, G.R.: Building high school pre-service teachers' knowledge to teach correlation and regression. In: Makar, K., de Sousa, B., Gould, R. (eds.) Proceedings of the Ninth International Conference on Teaching Statistics. International Statistical Institute, Voorburg (2014)

39. Cabriá, S.: Filosofía de la estadística (Philosophy of Statistics). Servicio de Publicaciones de la Universidad, Valencia (1994)

40. Groth, R., Meletiou-Mavrotheris, M.: Research on statistics teachers' cognitive and affective characteristics. In: Ben-Zvi, D., Makar, K., Garfield, J. (eds.) International Handbook of Research in Statistics Education. SIHE, pp. 327–355. Springer, Cham (2018). https://doi.org/10.1007/978-3-319-66195-7_10

41. Souza, L.D., Lopes, C.E., Pfannkuch, M.: Collaborative professional development for statistics teaching: a case study of two middle-school mathematics teachers. Stat. Educ. Res. J. **14**(1), 112–134 (2015)

The UTAUT Model Applied to Examine the STEM in Hight School Robot Subject Instruction

Chi-Chieh Hsieh and Fu-Yuan Chiu[✉]

National Tsing Hua University, Hsinchu, Taiwan R.O.C.
magic2000566@gmail.com, chiu.fy@mx.nthu.edu.tw

Abstract. Since the rise of the waves toward artificial intelligence, more and more countries' robot education has changed from Robot-Assisted Instruction (RAI) to Robot-Subject Instruction (RSI). This study mainly compares the differences between the two teaching methods of RSI using traditional single subject teaching and STEM cross-disciplinary teaching. Through the data of Unified Theory of Acceptance and Use of Technology (UTAUT) and Course Satisfaction, this study finds out the advantages and disadvantages of STEM integration into RSI. The results of this study show that the Traditional RSI has a lower learning burden in the knowledge learning units, so the satisfaction is higher, but the Competition activities unit at the end of the period is prone to problems, causing a decline in satisfaction, while the STEM-based RSI students are the opposite, and the validation of students' positive attitude towards STEM model learning after participating in robotics activities.

Keywords: Robot Subject Instruction · STEM education · Unified Theory of Acceptance and Use of Technology

1 Introduction

In the new 12-years basic education curricula in Taiwan, a new field of technology has been added, and a course called "Robotics Project" has been developed in this field. It means that Taiwan's robot education has changed from Robot-Assisted Instruction (RAI) to Robot-Subject Instruction (RSI). The course focuses on developing student competencies including programming, data access and computing, electromechanical integration, computational thinking and design thinking. This study conducted a two-year lead study before the start of the new RSI. The first year of RSI used traditional teaching, meaning that the course taught only the hardware and software operations of the robot, and then began using the STEM-based RSI in the second year. The research tools section of this study used a unified theory of acceptance and use of technology (UTAUT) and course satisfaction to compare the differences between the two teaching methods. The results of the study can be used as a reference for future RSI schools. The overarching research question for this study is "To find out the advantages and disadvantages of STEM integration into RSI". To focus the study, this overarching question is divided into the following three sub-questions:

K. O. Villalba-Condori et al. (Eds.): CISETC 2019, CCIS 1191, pp. 36–46, 2020.
https://doi.org/10.1007/978-3-030-45344-2_4

RQ1. What is the difference in UTAUT Questionnaires between traditional RSI and STEM-based RSI?

RQ2. What is the difference between the pre-test and post-test of the UTAUT questionnaire for implementing STEM-based RSI?

RQ3. What is the difference in Course Satisfaction between traditional RSI and STEM-based RSI?

2 Literature Review

2.1 Robot Subject Instruction, RSI

With the advent of artificial intelligence, the application of robots in education has become more diverse. Qi, Dong, Chen, Qi, and Okawa proposed such as "Robot Subject Instruction (RSI)", "Robot-Assisted Instruction (RAI)" and "Robot-Managed Instruction (RMI)" [1]. Dr. Fridin suggests that robots are developmental and potential educational tools with broad appeal and learning relevance [2]. Chalmers proposed that the educational robot interface design has an intuitive visual effect, which helps students to learn programming at the teaching site [3], but the biggest bottleneck of the existing curriculum is the lack of specific teacher training [4]. The use of educational robots in both formal and informal learning can effectively build students' critical thinking and problem-solving skills and improve the study of mathematics and science. [5–7], Nag, Katz, and Saenz-Otero mentioned that robotics courses combined with competitions even helped students to cross-domain learning in STEM (science, technology, engineering, mathematics) Education [8], Kim and Kim used robotics in Korea for STEAM (STEM+ART) and Coding Education [9].

2.2 Unified Theory of Acceptance and Use of Technology, UTAUT

The UTAUT model was used to evaluate human-machine interaction evaluation using Humanoid robot (Nao Robot) in educational environment [10], UTAUT model comes from the Technology Acceptance Model (TAM) proposed by Davis [11]. The TAM has two major determinants are "Perceived Usefulness" and "Perceived Ease of Use". Perceived Usefulness means that the user's operation of a specific application or system will improve the performance or learning of the individual, while another Perceived Ease of Use refers to the user's learning to use the operating application or the ease of the system. The UTAUT model through the past research on "users accepting behaviors in technology", and this model found that predicting and interpreting users' access to information technology has more than 70% explanatory power [12]. Therefore, most of the follow-up studies will omit attitudes. The facets and Moderators of UTAUT as follows:

Performance Expectancy (PE), PE as the extent to which users believe that using the system will help improve or improve job performance. PE is affected by three moderators such as Gender, Age, and Experience, which affects male more obvious.

Effort Expectancy (EE), EE as the extent to which users can easily manipulate new technologies, systems, and applications. For example, the user interface of the IT device and the design of the operating system will affect the user's information technology acceptance. EE is affected by three moderators such as Gender, Age and Experience, which affects female more obvious, but EE will decrease with the growth of experience.

Social Influence (SI), SI as the extent to which the user feels that the existing organization believes that the user should use this new technology and system to what extent. SI is affected by four moderators such as Gender, Age, Experience and Voluntariness of Use, which affects female more obvious, but SI will decrease with the growth of experience. SI will directly affect the intent of the user to use the new technology, coupled with Ahmad and Love research indicates that lecture incentives can help them adapt to the new technology to learn [13]. In this study, SI was defined as the use of robots for students to be recommended by teachers. Students also believe that it is feasible to use robots to learn.

Facilitating Conditions (FC), FC as the extent to which users believe that existing organizations support users in using new technologies and systems. FC is affected by two moderators such as Age and Experience, which affects older workers more obvious and increasing as experience increases. Since the quality of RSI equipment provided by the school will affect the students' learning behavior and willingness, FC is defined in this study as the degree to which students assessed the school's support for the RSI by equipment quality.

Behavioral Intention (BI) was originally proposed by Fishbein and Ajen [14] and is defined as the degree of personal willingness of users to participate in certain behaviors. However, in this study, behavioral intentions were defined as students' willingness to continue to support RSI in the future or would like to further recommend RSI to others.

Since RSI is an open innovation course, users with a high degree of Personal Innovation are more likely to develop new technologies [13], and personal innovations in new information technologies will positively influence the adoption behavior [15], so this study adds the "Personal Innovation" proposed by Agarwal and Prasad to investigate the willingness of users to accept and use new technologies [16].

Based on the above, this UTAUT model will explore the changes of the six items including Performance Expectancy, Effort Expectancy, Social Influence, Facilitating Conditions, Behavioral Intention, and Personal Innovation.

3   Methodology

In the first year of the study, RSI carried out traditional teaching (only teaching software and hardware operations). In the second year, STEM was integrated into RSI. After completing the six-unit course, Course Satisfaction and Traditional UTAUT questionnaire were performed, only in the second. The experiment of the year was added to the "UTAUT-based Expectation situation questionnaire" for pre- and post-test analysis (Fig. 1).

As shown in Fig. 1, the RSI course has six units including Servo motor control, Infrared sensing module, Bluetooth communication module, Ultrasonic sensing module, Line following control, and Bluetooth control self-propelled obstacle avoidance control. The Course Satisfaction has four dimensions including Course Content, Teaching Activity, Learning Outcome, and Learning Attitude. The UTAUT questionnaire and the

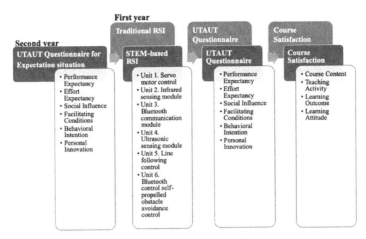

Fig. 1. Research architecture diagram

UTAUT-based Expectation situation questionnaire have six items including Performance Expectancy, Effort Expectancy, Social Influence, Facilitating Conditions, Behavioral Intention, and Personal Innovation.

3.1 Participants

In this study, two consecutives 12th grade students in a high school in northern Taiwan were Participants. The experiment lasted for two years. In the first year, 41 students participated in the study and 49 students participated in the second year. The two-year class hours (three hours a week for a total of 18 weeks) and the instructors are the same, the difference is that the second year of the course has introduced STEM cross-disciplinary teaching.

3.2 Research Tools

In this study, the robot uses Explore Board as the main controller, control software for the InnoBASIC ™ Workshop, this software platform provides students to write programs, functional testing, to download code to the robot.

3.3 Research Framework

The RSI contains the following six units, as explained below:

Unit 1. Servo motor control: After explaining through the teacher's instructions, the student programmatically controls the robot to move forward, backward, turn left, and turn right.

Unit 2. Infrared sensing module: After the teacher explained the working principle of the infrared sensor, the student programmed to control the robot to walk along the black line.

Unit 3. Bluetooth communication module: After the teacher explained the working principle of the Bluetooth communication module, the student programmed to control the robot by the mobile APP.

Unit 4. Ultrasonic sensing module: After the teacher explained the working principle of the ultrasonic sensor, the student programmed to control the robot to detect the distance of the obstacle and return the data to the computer.

Unit 5. Line following control (Competition activities I): In this unit, students must use the Bluetooth device of the mobile phone to control the robot to follow the line from the starting point to the end point.

Unit 6. Bluetooth control self-propelled obstacle avoidance control (Competition activities II): In this unit, students must use the Bluetooth device of the mobile phone to control the robot to automatically avoid obstacles and get out of the maze with the ultrasonic sensor.

3.4   STEM-Based RSI

The learning contents of STEM-based RSI are divided into four items according to science, technology, engineering, and mathematics in every unit.

In Unit 1 Science content includes Fleming's Left-Hand Rule, Amperes right-hand rule, and DC motor principle. Technology content includes Servo motor installation settings and fine-tuning. Engineering content includes Servo motor drive circuit production and application. Mathematics content includes Calculate the Pulse Width Modulation (PWM) parameter of the servo motor.

In Unit 2 Science content includes Infrared frequency range, Infrared sensor transmitting and receiving principle, and Optical principle. Technology content includes Infrared sensor installation settings and fine-tuning. Engineering content includes Infrared sensing circuit production and application. Mathematics content includes Infrared measurement signal operation.

In Unit 3 Science content includes Bluetooth communication principle. Technology content includes Bluetooth communication module installation and setting. Engineering content includes Bluetooth communication module circuit production and application. Mathematics content includes Bluetooth communication data transmission conversion, ASCII code conversion.

In Unit 4 Science content includes Ultrasonic frequency range, Ultrasonic transmitting and receiving sensing principle, and Doppler effect. Technology content includes Ultrasonic sensing installation settings and fine-tuning. Engineering content includes Ultrasonic sensing circuit production and application. Mathematics content includes Ultrasonic echo back signal calculation.

In Unit 5 Science content includes the Integration of Science application unit 1–4. Technology content includes the Integration of Technology application units 1–4. Engineering content includes the Integration of Engineering application units 1–4. Mathematics content includes the Integration of mathematical application units 1–4.

In Unit 6 Science content includes the Integration of Science application unit 1–4. Technology content includes the Integration of Technology application units 1–4. Engineering content includes the Integration of Engineering application units 1–4. Mathematics content includes the Integration of mathematical application units 1–4.

3.5 UTAUT Questionnaire

The questionnaire was revised to the original UTAUT and adopted a five-point Likert scale according to 5, 4, 3, 2, 1 score. The content of the questionnaire is divided into two parts. The first part is translated and modified [17] There are 4 questions for students to assess their current status, and the second part is a study modified from Milošević, Živković, Manasijević and Nikolić [18]. The questionnaire topics of pre-tests used "I expect" means expectation situation and the questionnaire topics of post-test used "I think", there are six facets such as:

"Performance Expectancy" includes PE1. I expect/think that using a robot teaching module would help me learn robots; PE2. I expect/think that using the robot teaching module will allow me to complete the homework that the teacher has explained; PE3. I expect/think that using the robot teaching module can speed up my learning; PE4. I expect/think that using the robot teaching module can improve the cooperation between me and my classmates.

The "Effort Expectancy" includes EE1. I expect/think that I will find a flexible and easy to use robot teaching module to learn; EE2. I expect/think that it is not difficult to learn to operate the robot teaching module; EE3. I expect/think that using the robot teaching module to learn interactively will be clearer and easier to understand.

"Social Influence" includes SI1. I expect/think that the teacher recommended me to use the robot teaching module, I will use the robot teaching module to learn; SI2. I expect/think that if the teacher assists me in using the robot teaching module, I will use the robot teaching module to learn.

"Facilitating Conditions" includes FC1. I anticipate/consider the learning system using the robot teaching module, and the quality of its service repairs is very important; FC2. I anticipate/consider that the use of robotic teaching modules in the course is accurate and reliable; FC3. I anticipate/believe that the best place to learn using the robotics module in the course is to make it easier to practice the internship; FC4. I anticipate/believe that the best thing about learning a robotic module in a course is that writing a course is easier.

"Behavioral Intention" includes BI1. I anticipate/plan to use the robotics teaching module in my field of study in the future; BI2. I expect/think that I will use the robot teaching module to learn in the course of learning-related robotics; BI3. I expect/think that I will enjoy using the robot teaching module to learn in the relevant robot course in the future; BI4. I expect/think that I would recommend other people (including younger siblings) to use the robot teaching module to learn.

"Personal Innovation" includes PI1. I expect/think that I like to try new technology products; PI2. I expect/think that when I heard a new technology, I would like to try it out.

There were 19 high school students who did not participate in the experiment conducted a reliability test to obtain high reliability of Cronbach's α value of .980, which proves the feasibility of the questionnaire.

3.6 Course Satisfaction

This questionnaire is mainly to explore the satisfaction of students after each PSI unit and adopted a five-point Likert scale according to 5, 4, 3, 2, and 1 score. The Course

Satisfaction has four dimensions including Course Content, Teaching Activity, Learning Outcome, and Learning Attitude. The questionnaire was tested by the 19 high school students who did not participate in the experiment. The reliability test showed that Cronbach's α value was .979, which proved the feasibility of the questionnaire.

4 Experiment Results

4.1 UTAUT Questionnaire Results

As shown in Fig. 2 that the average curves of the UTAUT experiment results of Traditional RSI and STEM-based RSI are very similar. The similarities are that both scored low on both Effort Expectancy and Behavioral Intention, indicating that some students feel that RSI still has some difficulty and does not want to recommend it to others.

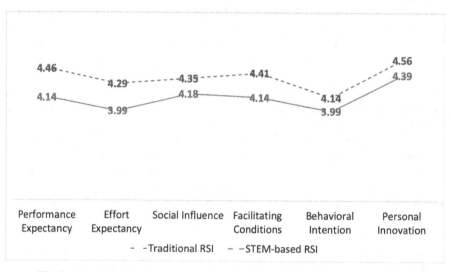

Fig. 2. The UTAUT experiment results of traditional RSI and STEM-based RSI

4.2 The UTAUT Pre-test and Post-test of the STEM-Based RSI

From Table 1, it can be found that the students have significant differences in the Performance Expectancy and Behavioral Intention ($*p < .05$) through the paired samples t-test. However, the three sub-items Effort Expectancy, Social Influence, and Facilitating Conditions More significant difference ($**p < .01$). This means that students feel better than expected for the "STEM-based RSI" arrangement, and there is no significant difference in their own "Personal Innovation" because it is always high.

4.3 Course Satisfaction Results

It can be seen from the average curve of Figs. 3 and 4 that although the first three units Course Satisfaction results of STEM-based RSI are not as high as that of the Traditional RSI, the satisfaction of the last two competition activities units has steadily increased,

Table 1. The paired samples t-test of STEM-based RSI

Item	Pre-test		Post-test		t
	M	SD	M	SD	
Performance expectancy	3.81	0.769	4.14	0.584	2.691*
Effort expectancy	3.61	0.716	3.99	0.567	3.481**
Social influence	3.85	0.751	4.18	0.61	2.714**
Facilitating conditions	3.85	0.694	4.14	0.508	2.783**
Behavioral intention	3.76	0.735	3.99	0.555	2.200*
Personal innovation	4.19	0.749	4.39	0.637	1.839

*$p < .05$ **$p < .01$

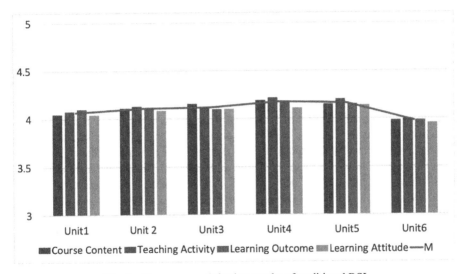

Fig. 3. The course satisfaction results of traditional RSI

but the Traditional RSI has declined. This result shows that the students of Traditional RSI have high satisfaction in each of the above four units because they only need to complete the learning of software and hardware. However, when the last two units need to use cross-domain knowledge to solve problems, they have learning difficulties. In contrast, STEM-based RSI is students feel very burdensome because each unit is integrated into science, technology, engineering, and mathematics, but in the last two competition activities units, they can use what they have learned to achieve satisfactory results. This result is similar to other studies, verifying that students have a positive attitude towards STEM model learning after participating in robotics activities [19]. In addition, if the participation in international competitions (such as Robo Cup Junior) is set as the goal of STEM courses, students will learn to solve complex problems through logical thinking in a teamwork manner [20].

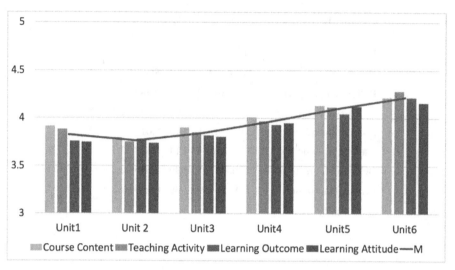

Fig. 4. The course satisfaction results of STEM-based RSI

5   Discussion and Conclusions

This study mainly compares the differences between the two methods of Robot-Subject Instruction (RSI) using traditional single subject teaching and STEM cross-disciplinary teaching. Through the UTAUT Questionnaire data, the study found that the six sub-item curves of the Traditional RSI and STEM-based RSI UTAUT are close, indicating that students have similar views on the acceptance of the two RSIs. The students' scores of the five sub-items (Performance Expectancy, Effort Expectancy, Social Influence, Facilitating Conditions, Behavioral Intention, Personal Innovation) of the STEM-based RSI UTAUT are significantly higher than the pre-tests, which means that the students' acceptance after class is significantly higher than the previous expectations of the course. Finally, in the Course Satisfaction questionnaire data after six units, we can find that the satisfaction of STEM-based RSI is low first and then high, and the traditional RSI is high first and then low. The key factor is that the Traditional RSI has a lower learning burden in the first four units, so the satisfaction is higher, but the Competition activities unit at the end of the period is prone to problems, causing a decline in satisfaction, while the STEM-based RSI students are the opposite. Taking the last unit as an example, the maze competition must promote systematic thinking and creativity through the logic of problem-solving. As the research results of [21], the learning process of STEM helps students control robots to complete tasks with more complex programming decisions and there is even a chance to promote the robot to other subjects such as informatics, mathematics, and physics [22, 23]. In addition, it is suggested that designing several competition units in the STEM-based RSI can increase students' teamwork and gain hands-on ability. Therefore, schools that are ready to promote RSI in the future can consider whether to use STEM-based RSI based on the analysis of this study.

References

1. Qi, B., Dong, Y., Chen, L., Qi, W., Okawa, Y.: The impact of robot instruction to education informatization. In: 2009 First International Conference on Information Science and Engineering, pp 3497–3500 (2009). https://doi.org/10.1109/icise.2009.1216
2. Fridin, M.: Storytelling by a kindergarten social assistive robot: a tool for constructive learning in preschool education. Comput. Educ. **53**, 53–64 (2013). https://doi.org/10.1016/j.compedu.2013.07.043
3. Chalmers, C.: Robotics and computational thinking in primary school. Int. J. Child-Comput. Interact. **17**, 93–100 (2018). https://doi.org/10.1016/j.ijcci.2018.06.005
4. Fridin, M., Belokopytov, M.: Acceptance of socially assistive humanoid robot by preschool and elementary school teachers. Comput. Hum. Behav. **33**, 23–31 (2014). https://doi.org/10.1016/j.chb.2013.12.016
5. Fonseca Ferreira, N.M., Araujo, A., Couceiro, M.S., Portugal, D.: Intensive summer course in robotics – Robotcraft. Appl. Comput. Inf. (2018). https://doi.org/10.1016/j.aci.2018.04.005. in Press
6. Zhong, B., Xia, L.: A systematic review on exploring the potential of educational robotics in mathematics education. Int. J. Sci. Math. Educ. **18**(1), 79–101 (2018). https://doi.org/10.1007/s10763-018-09939-y
7. Sharma, K., Papavlasopoulou, S., Giannakos, M.: Coding games and robots to enhance computational thinking: how collaboration and engagement moderate children's attitudes? Int. J. Child-Comput. Interact. (2019). https://doi.org/10.1016/j.ijcci.2019.04.004
8. Nag, S., Katz, J.G., Saenz-Otero, A.: Collaborative gaming and competition for CS-STEM education using SPHERES Zero Robotics. Acta Astronaut. **23**, 145–174 (2013). https://doi.org/10.1016/j.actaastro.2012.09.006
9. Kim, J.A., Kim, H.: Meta-analysis of researches of STEAM with coding education – in Korea. In: Misra, S., et al. (eds.) ICCSA 2019. LNCS, vol. 11623, pp. 82–89. Springer, Cham (2019). https://doi.org/10.1007/978-3-030-24308-1_7
10. Vega, A., Ramírez-Benavidez, K., Guerrero, Luis A.: Tool UTAUT applied to measure interaction experience with NAO robot. In: Kurosu, M. (ed.) HCII 2019. LNCS, vol. 11568, pp. 501–512. Springer, Cham (2019). https://doi.org/10.1007/978-3-030-22636-7_38
11. Davis, F.D.: Perceived usefulness, perceived ease of use, and user acceptance of information technology. MIS Q. **13**(3), 319–340 (1989)
12. Venkatesh, V., Morris, M.G., Davis, G.B., Davis, F.D.: User acceptance information technology: toward a unified view. MIS Q. **27**(3), 425–478 (1989). https://doi.org/10.2307/30036540
13. Ahmad, A.A., Love, S.: Factors influencing students' acceptance of m-learning: an investigation in higher education. Int. Rev. Res. Open Distance Learn. **14**(5), 83–107 (2013). https://doi.org/10.19173/irrodl.v14i5.1631
14. Fishbein, I., Ajen, M.: Attitude-behavior relations: a theoretical analysis and review of empirical research. Psychol. Bull. **84**(5), 888–918 (1977). https://doi.org/10.1037/0033-2909.84.5.888
15. Moore, G.C., Benbasat, I.: Development of an instrument to measure the perceptions of adopting an information technology innovation. Inf. Syst. Res. **2**(3), 192–222 (1991). https://doi.org/10.1287/isre.2.3.192
16. Agarwal, R., Prasad, J.: A conceptual and operational definition of personal innovativeness in the domain of information technology. Inf. Syst. Res. **9**(2), 204–224 (1998). https://doi.org/10.1287/isre.9.2.204

17. Pruet, P., Ang, C.S., Farzin, D.: Understanding tablet computer usage among primary school students in underdeveloped areas: students' technology experience, learning styles and attitudes. Comput. Hum. Behav. **55**(B), 1131–1144 (2016). https://doi.org/10.1016/j.chb.2014.09.063

18. Milošević, I., Živković, D., Manasijević, D., Nikolić, D.: The effects of the intended behavior of students in the use of M-learning. Comput. Hum. Behav. **51**(A), 207–215 (2015). https://doi.org/10.1016/j.chb.2015.04.041. Original Research Article

19. Ben-Bassat Levy, R., Ben-Ari, M.: The evaluation of robotics activities for facilitating STEM learning. In: Lepuschitz, W., Merdan, M., Koppensteiner, G., Balogh, R., Obdržálek, D. (eds.) RiE 2017. AISC, vol. 630, pp. 132–137. Springer, Cham (2018). https://doi.org/10.1007/978-3-319-62875-2_12

20. Wong, A.S.W., Jeffery, R., Turner, P., Sleap, S., Chalup, S.K.: RoboCup junior in the hunter region: driving the future of robotic STEM education. In: Holz, D., Genter, K., Saad, M., von Stryk, O. (eds.) RoboCup 2018. LNCS (LNAI), vol. 11374, pp. 362–373. Springer, Cham (2019). https://doi.org/10.1007/978-3-030-27544-0_30

21. Wongwatkit, C., Prommool, P., Nobnob, R., Boonsamuan, S., Suwan, R.: A collaborative STEM project with educational mobile robot on escaping the maze: prototype design and evaluation. In: Hancke, G., Spaniol, M., Osathanunkul, K., Unankard, S., Klamma, R. (eds.) ICWL 2018. LNCS, vol. 11007, pp. 77–87. Springer, Cham (2018). https://doi.org/10.1007/978-3-319-96565-9_8

22. Reich-Stiebert, N., Eyssel, F.: Robots in the classroom: what teachers think about teaching and learning with education robots. In: Agah, A., Cabibihan, J.-J., Howard, A.M., Salichs, M.A., He, H. (eds.) ICSR 2016. LNCS (LNAI), vol. 9979, pp. 671–680. Springer, Cham (2016). https://doi.org/10.1007/978-3-319-47437-3_66

23. Chi-Chieh, H., Fu-Yuan, C.: Examining the role of STEM in twelfth-grade robot subject instruction using the UTAUT model. In: Villalba-Condori, K.O., Adúriz-Bravo, A., García-Peñalvo, F.J., Lavonen, J. (eds.) Proceeding of the Congreso Internacional Sobre Educación y Tecnología en Ciencias - CISETC 2019, Arequipa, Perú, 10–12 December 2019, pp. 39–48. CEUR-WS.org., Aachen (2019)

Using DDMT Teaching Model to Cultivate Critical Thinking in a STEAM Classroom

Kee-Fui Turner Lam[1,2] ⓘ, Tzu-Hua Wang[1](✉) ⓘ, Yee-Shih Vun[1,3] ⓘ, and Ning Ku[1] ⓘ

[1] National Tsing Hua University, Hsinchu, Taiwan
tzuhuawang@mx.nthu.edu.tw, yeeshu@gmail.com,
kuning0917@gapp.nthu.edu.tw
[2] Edu-Aequitas Pte. Ltd., Singapore, Singapore
turner@edu-aequitas.com
[3] Affiliated Elementary School of National Tsing Hua University, Hsinchu, Taiwan

Abstract. In an environment disrupted by technology, critical thinking is a crucial 21st Century Skill that allows learners to stay intact when any number of organizations (corporate, political, educational and cultural) try to influence readers to think and act in ways that serve their purposes [1]. It has also been emphasized in the ATC21S [2] project as one of the desired outcomes under 'Ways of thinking'. In this paper, we aim to share about how Design Based Research and DDMT teaching model can shape a chemistry lesson on water for Grade 5 learners. The lessons will be shaped towards guiding the learners in understanding acidity/alkalinity as required by the national curriculum and also seek to provide an insight into how young learners showcase development of critical thinking in the learning process.

Keywords: Critical thinking · STEAM Education · Tsing Hua STEAM School · DDMT teaching model

1 Introduction

With the arrival of Industry 4.0, skills are gradually superseding knowledge as the number one criterion for work employment. While teaching of content is still much emphasized by many educators, the emergence of new technology has presented educators with a need to re-evaluate their teaching and assessment practices [3]. Young learners are redefining their learning styles and expectations; they want content to be delivered with more interactivity. Another challenge that educators faced is the integration of skills into the learning of content. Established and forwardlooking institutions such as OCED [4] and World Economic Forum have emphasized the importance of new skills critical for the young learners to be equipped before they can be work ready [5]. Program for International Student Assessment (PISA), a global academic benchmark will shift the test focus from reading, mathematics and science towards skills [6].

With skills becoming more important, STEM/STEAM Education has claimed number one spot for education innovation. Many educational companies are promoting Computer Science and Robotics as STEM/STEAM Education at major Educational Technology conferences such as ISTE and BETT, even big technology conglomerates such

© Springer Nature Switzerland AG 2020
K. O. Villalba-Condori et al. (Eds.): CISETC 2019, CCIS 1191, pp. 47–57, 2020.
https://doi.org/10.1007/978-3-030-45344-2_5

as Microsoft, Google and Apple are jumping onto the bandwagon with programs and applications regarding STEM Education. Yet, with all these external supports, a pressing question for educators is what is "STEAM Education" and how does it affect the way educators integrate into the Teaching and Learning process.

2 Related Work

2.1 Tsing Hua STEAM School

Tsing Hua STEAM school is an alliance of K-12 schools in Taiwan with the common vision of "Quality STEAM Education for All Learners". It has been advocated and promoted by Prof Tzu-Hua Wang and Prof Chi-Hui Lin since 2018. Educators on board the program aspire to write a STEAM curriculum based on solving daily issues revolving around the learners. Teachers teaching different disciplines are encouraged to partake in this program; but our goal is not about an inter-disciplinary project design, but rather a collaborative process of developing a learning process measuring not just academic content but also competencies [7]. The program started with 40 schools in one county but has since expanded to 80 schools from 3 countries.

There are numerous important elements in this program. The first element is constructivism. Constructivism is not a specific pedagogy, but rather a learning theory which suggests that humans construct knowledge and meaning from their experiences [8]. In addition, we believed that cognition is not located only located within the individual thinker but is a process that is distributed across the knower, environment in which knowing occurs and the activity in which the learner participates [9]. In today's classrooms, it is not uncommon to find many learners bored and disengaged from having to sit through long periods of lecture. One big reason is learners come into the classrooms with enormous amounts of knowledge. Yet many teachers 'ignored' the prior knowledge of these learners and proceed to teach them content as per required by Ministry of Education. Hence, in the process of designing curriculum, teachers need to role-play both the roles of a learner and a facilitator as they imagine how their activities would pan out in an actual classroom based on the prior knowledge of their learners entering the classroom. The teachers would need to develop excellent facilitating abilities to help learners 'connect the dots' (within their brain), help them see the relevance of their prior knowledge and how it is related to the curriculum requirement. This process would also require teacher facilitators to be fully prepared for class in order to help learners level up from the different 'entry levels' of the learners, a term we described as educational equity.

The second important element is empathy. For learners to better appreciate the problem-solving processes, it is important to begin with issues which learners can relate to in their lives. Empathy is also an important ingredient that distinguishes humans from robots. Humans who are empathetic can better understand the problems, indirectly leading to better problem-solving skills. At this point, technology should then be introduced to reinforce learners with the notion that technological solutions are built upon the ideas that humans have driven by empathy. This element will be elaborated in greater details in the following section under the 'Discover' and 'Model and Modelling' phases.

The third element is inquiry. Inquiry is a technique that encourages learners to discover or construct information by themselves instead of having teachers directly reveal the information [10]. Since the turn of the century, Science educators have repeatedly emphasized the importance of inquiry in the learning of Science, especially visible since 1950's and 60's [11] and Project 2061: Science for All Americans [12] instead of memorization and direct instruction [13].

The fourth element is hands-on learning, or maker-education. Digital fabrication and 'making' could be a new and major chapter in this process of bringing powerful ideas, literacies and expressive tools to children [14]. The framework for Making in STEM Education also showcases many qualities in alignment to 21st Century Skills [15].

Lastly, there is a need to connect the outcomes of the STEAM curriculum to the expectations of the national curriculum. After writing the curriculum and activities intended, teachers must now seek to find an alignment to what the national curriculum is advocating. This way, the STEAM curriculum would not be viewed as another meaningless project, but rather a project that complements the learning of content with skills. STEAM Education should also not be taken as a program heavily dependent on coding.

By practicing STEAM Education, educators would also be practicing the notion of teachers as 'agents of change' as suggested by OECD in their white paper for Education 2030, where change takes precedence in the way Teaching & Learning should evolve to help learners stay engaged and relevant within the classroom and eventually in work later on.

2.2   DDMT Teaching Model

The DDMT teaching model was first proposed by Prof Tzu-Hua Wang and Mr Turner Lam in early 2019. It consists of four phases; 'Discover', 'Define', 'Model & Modelling' and 'Transfer' with all four phases revolving around scientific inquiry, design thinking and maker practice [16]. The DDMT teaching model provides a scaffold for teachers to develop their competency-based and interdisciplinary STEM/STEAM teaching activities [7] and has been fine-tuned by the academic team of "Tsing Hua STEAM School" through the development of STEAM courses.

Discover
This phase requires learners to tap on their daily life experiences and identify problems based on their observation and empathy. This is done through 3 steps: Context awareness, Motivation and Core problem. During Context awareness, we set a boundary for learners to identify problems revolving around their lives. This way, the learners would be more motivated to brainstorm for solutions as they can better resonate with the problems. As the learners provide countless problems during brainstorming, we want the teacher to focus back on the core problem that aligns to the national curriculum for content learning. This may lead to a situation where learners feel that facilitators have a pre-conceived problem to solve. At this stage, the facilitator must explain to the learners that a good solution constitutes solving many different 'small problems'. No problem is prioritized to achieve a good solution, but rather the problem to be solved at that stage is dependent on the content to be learnt as stipulated by the national guidelines.

Define

In this phase, the learners must begin to undergo problem definition. The defined problem must be supported by collected or measured data. This portion strongly corelates to the Science and Mathematics theme. Based on their defined problem, learners must design experiments to gather data to support their hypothesis. The learners should also learn to identify variables and constants in testing their hypothesis. Technology becomes an enabler in this process as learners search the internet for information, present their findings, create graphs or questionnaires. Once they have concrete evidence to support their hypothesis, the learners must conceptualize a solution for their defined problem. Here, the teacher also plays an important role as he/she facilitates the learning of concept aligned to the solutions proposed by the learners.

Model and Modelling

The third phase is mainly the prototyping stage. In the design of a solution, each group would propose a viable problem-solving model (i.e., a plan containing words, diagrams, legends, equations, etc.) aligned to the concept identified in the Define phase. Apart from a theoretical model, the learners can construct a working prototype to demonstrate the viability of their model. Generally, this stage is when learners experience hands-on learning/making with technology. As the learners experiment with technology writing algorithm and constructing prototypes, they may encounter unforeseen challenges. A common challenge could be the program not performing the way it should. This can also be considered as the debugging stage as the learners must run the simulation and check for discrepancies between the actual code and their imagination. For many facilitators, they may not be comfortable leading this stage citing technical incompetence. At Tsing Hua STEAM school, we propose the use of Micro:Bit as a starting technology due to the low entry point and high ceiling. We hope that as learners progress through the years, there is also a learning progression as they skilled upwards in the different technologies; from block-code to Python and eventually to Big Data.

Transfer

Finally, the last phase would require learners to share their proposed model and final product. The value-added ness of this DDMT teaching model is also emphasized at this phase as learners are required to demonstrate their learning through different scenarios. A basic transfer of knowledge can occur between different subjects around a common concept (for example addition in Math and addition in Food Science). A higher order transfer would equip learners to internalize the concepts for use in a different context (for example traffic congestion due to cars and snow skis). Apart from highlighting the metacognition development in learners through deeper understanding, this phase also helps learners to build competencies such as critical thinking, communication and creativity. Please find below a graphical representation of the DDMT Teaching Model as seen in Fig. 1.

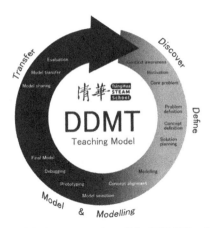

Fig. 1. A graphical representation of the DDMT teaching model

2.3   Critical Thinking

Critical thinking has been heavily emphasized as a core 21st Century Skill [17] in recent years and listed as one of five key learning outcomes [18] and in Assessment and Teaching of 21CC [2]. Furthermore, white papers by Organization for Economic Co-operation and Development (OECD) and World Economic Forum (WEF) has identified critical thinking as pivotal to future employment due to changing nature of jobs caused by advances in technology [19]. Although critical thinking has been emphasized countless times by researchers and employers, there has never been a tool that can accurately assess the critical thinking ability of any learner. On the other hand, there are however many avenues (technological toys) claiming to teach critical thinking in their curriculum. This brings to mind an important question: how does one determine critical thinking has been taught when there is no assessment tool for critical thinking?

Another important challenge brought about by technological advancements is the presence of fake news. Multiple countries have considered implementing rules to cope with fake news. Singapore for example has passed a "Protection from Online Falsehoods and Manipulation bill" (POFMA) to tackle "falsehoods, bots, trolls and fake accounts" [20]. This yet brings out another argument: What is false news and who determines the authenticity of the news? [21]. There is even a weekly summary by Yahoo on news which is not true [22].

Hence, critical thinking is a skill that allows learners to stay intact when any number of organizations (corporate, political, educational and cultural) try to influence readers to think and act in ways that serve their purposes [1]. It is equipping learners to reason and think objectively, using their knowledge and experience. While there have been increasing efforts to include critical thinking as an education outcome for K-12 learners, it was more common to find research regarding critical thinking for learners at higher education. Hence, it is imperative that more research is done at K-12 level in order to help younger learners develop the ability of critical thinking.

3   Research Methods

3.1   Design Based Research

Design Based Research [23] is "designing experiments that brings together two critical pieces in order to guide us to better educational refinement: a design focus and assessment of critical design elements". The assessment analysis comprises both qualitative and quantitative aspects [24].

There are a few differing factors between Design Based Research [23] from conventional design and traditional research. Firstly, when designers receive formative feedback, their intuition often leads to changes that may neither be grounded in theory nor be limited to enable comparative research across time. A big challenge we faced in education is the complexity of conditions for success required in effective interventions [25]. Secondly, Design Based Research emphasizes on adapting a design to its local context, a vital attribute for scaling up a successful innovation in one venue as compared to other venues with dissimilar characteristics [26].

Design Base Research provides a cycle that promotes the reflective and long-term foundation upon which research can be undertaken [27]. This process provides a richer understanding into how K-12 learners can develop critical thinking abilities.

3.2   Participants and Settings

The proposed study was carried out at The Affiliated Experimental Elementary school of National Tsing Hua University in East Division, Hsinchu City, Taiwan. This locale was chosen because of the following. Firstly, the school has been appointed as the experimental curriculum school of the national 12-year basic education policy. Furthermore, as the designated experimental school of National Tsing Hua University, the school serves as a good test ground for new STEAM initiatives from the university. Secondly, as an experimental school, conducting the lessons in English should not pose any problems to the learners. In addition, the stakeholders of the school (principal, directors of research and academic affairs, parents and learners) are very supportive of this research. The research studied 24 Grade 5 learners (who had no prior knowledge on acidity and alkalinity) over a 4.5 h (1.5 h per session) to verify their ability in critical thinking through DDMT teaching approach in STEAM Education.

4   Results

4.1   Lesson 1: Discover

In lesson 1, learners are given 2 activities to show how much they understood about water. The intention of this lesson was to look for any prior assumptions the learners have regarding the availability of water dispensers around them. Activity One was asking learners to identify the different sources of water around them. The learners are asked to list as many sources of water they can identify in their everyday lives in groups. Activity Two required learners to work individually to identify which source of water identified earlier was drinkable. The learners were also required to list down the reasons accounting for sources of water that is not consumable on post-it slips. Each student will then paste their slips to the teacher for collation. The teacher will then regroup the answers and lead learners towards the concept of acidity and alkalinity. Although learners gave many differing answers, this is the portion where the teacher will assume the role of a facilitator; to help learners navigate their learning towards acidity and alkalinity as this is the curriculum standards required of Grade 5 learners. For the other options given by the learners, the facilitator must also help the learners understand that alternative answers provided will be discussed at a later stage or till the time when learners have attained the expectations outlined by the curriculum. It could also be used as learning for higher order thinking at the discretion of the facilitators.

4.2 Lesson 2: Define

In lesson 2, learners were provided with 4 liquids (2 acids and 2 alkalis) and blue and red litmus papers. Their tasks were to use the litmus paper to check for the acidity and alkalinity of each liquid. All the learners were able to perform the task successfully. They were also able to identify that an acid turns blue litmus paper red while an alkali turns red litmus paper blue.

After completing the tasks, the facilitator checked with the learners if it was enough to just identify an acid or an alkali. All learners were able to identify from the experiments that identifying acids and alkalis with litmus paper is not enough. They wanted to have a more precise method of distinguishing between strong and weak acids/alkalis. Out of the 26 learners, 24 of them were able to suggest the use of a universal indicator as a preferred solution, despite the concept of universal indicator not being in the syllabus. The facilitator further introduced the concept of universal indicator to the class and learners were required to repeat the activity. At this point, the learners were comfortable matching the color obtained from the universal indicator to the pH scale provided. (Do note that pH is again not in the syllabus requirement).

To further stretch the learners, a question was posed to the learners. If milk has a pH color corresponding to orange, what can I do to change the final color to green? Again, the learners were able to display the concept of neutralization by pouring alkali to 'dilute' the acid. The final question was something which was made up on the spot because of the unanimous answer of 'universal indicator'. I wanted to test the learners' understanding of universal indicator [23].

4.3 Lesson 3: Model and Modelling

Based on the tasks in lesson 2, I got learners to write-down the steps undertook in arriving at the pH of the liquid. The learners were able to identify the processes involved:

1. Use a clean dropper to prepare a sample of the liquid to be tested into a testtube
2. Pour a few drops of universal indicator into the sample
3. Shake the test-tube
4. Repeat steps 1–3 for another 2 times
5. Find the average reading

The aim of lesson 3 was to get learners to design an automated pH monitoring device using the Micro:Bit. Apart from helping learners realize how technology can improve efficiency based on their thought processes, I also wanted to build upon the notion of STEAM Education mentioned earlier.

At the end of the lesson, learners were given a worksheet to obtain their feedback on the 3 lessons. The worksheet comprised of the following questions:

1. How do you feel about the 3 STEAM lessons which has just taken place?
2. Which aspect of the lessons did you enjoy? Which areas did you least enjoy?
3. Detergent can turn red litmus paper blue. Is detergent acidic or alkali?
4. When using a universal indicator, the obtained result is 2.5. Would you consider this value acidic or alkali?
5. What do you think are the advantages and disadvantages of litmus paper?
6. What do you think are the advantages and disadvantages of using a pH scale?
7. Do you think learning the Micro:Bit was useful? In which areas was it useful?
8. Which other aspects would you like to learn more about the Micro:Bit?
9. The average pH level of human blood lies between 7.35–7.45. It is considered slightly alkaline, thus drinking slightly acidic liquids aids in promoting wellness. It is common to find many mineral water suppliers promoting their water as slightly acidic. If you are tasked with the responsibility to measure pH, which method (litmus paper, universal indicator or Micro:Bit) would you choose?

4.4 Feedback Results

From the worksheet feedback, all 24 students expressed greater joy in learning acidity and alkalinity using STEAM approach [28] to learn in Question 1. Figure 2 shows the response of the learners, where the value of '1' corresponds to liking the lesson very much and '5' hating the lesson. For Question 2, as shown in Fig. 3, the learners preferred performing experiments to attending theory classes. Hands-on learning [14] is one of the core elements of Tsing Hua STEAM School.

Another important element is the alignment of STEAM activities to the national curriculum. As mentioned earlier, the expectations was to measure if the learners were able to identify acidity and alkalinity. Figures 4 and 5 showed that learners were able to

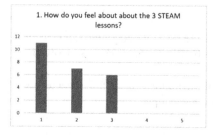

Fig. 2. Learners response to Question 1

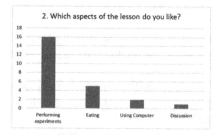

Fig. 3. Learners response to Question 2

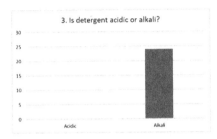

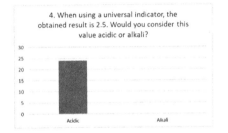

Fig. 4. Learners response to Question 3   **Fig. 5.** Learners response to Question 4

answer questions 3 and 4 correctly; indicating that content has been learned while they were engaging in activities.

For Question 5, 13 students were able to list all advantages and disadvantages of litmus paper versus universal indicator, demonstrating critical thinking in the ability to distinguish why using universal indicator is better than litmus paper. For Question 9, only one student suggested using the Micro:Bit. This learner pointed out that since the steps to determine acidity is repeated for different liquids, we should leverage on technology to automate the process, saving time and effort.

5   Further Considerations

Although the research was able to bring out evidences of critical thinking in Grade 5 learners, improvements could be applied to further improvements to the study. Firstly, we over-estimated the amount of time needed for the learners to learn the Micro:Bit. While many of the learners could appreciate the efficiency of algorithm, they needed more time to apply technology for the 'Transfer' phase. Owing to the lack of time and computers, many learners were stuck at the 'Model & Modelling' phase. While learners demonstrated great interest in learning technology, the allocated time of 45 min was not enough for the learners to integrate, apply and transfer the knowledge as it was the first time learners used the Micro:Bit.

Secondly, the lesson was intended to be conducted in Mandarin. However, due to a clash in schedules, the lesson was conducted partly in Mandarin and partly in English by a non-native Mandarin speaker. Generally, learners were able to understand the basic Mandarin used in delivering instructions. Some confusion arose when terminologies were delivered in English instead although the final survey showed that learners could deliver the outcomes highlighted at the start of the study, more could be done to make the data more reliable.

Thirdly, there was a mismatched in expectations in the initial knowledge domain of the learners. One of the research objectives was to use the DDMT Teaching Model to design a series of lessons regarding water to Grade 5 learners who had little or no prior knowledge of the topic. However, the learners came to class fully equipped with content knowledge. The accompanying teacher later revealed that the learners had learnt the content previously, so the lesson served as a revision.

For subsequent run, I would structure at least a 8 week lesson with 2 lessons (3 h) of technology time. Learners would have ample time to learn the basics of the Micro:Bit as well as additional sensors. In addition, I would want to have 2 classes for comparison. For both classes, the learners should not have any prior content knowledge of water and acidity.

6 Conclusion

From the study, it can be observed that learners thoroughly enjoyed the STEAM lessons comprising hands-on activities, technology-integration to construct knowledge. Although there were many impromptu changes brought about through Design Based research, the use of the DDMT teaching model has provided researchers with an ability to help learners delve deeper into learning of content which is beyond national curriculum requirements. This approach has also provided researchers with an ability to better bring out the critical thinking abilities of the learners in a formative way; using activities and questions to propel learners to explore the limitations of litmus paper and suggest alternatives to improve its reliability. More importantly, this short study has demonstrated that it is viable to identify and cultivate critical thinking in Grade 5 learners.

Acknowledgements. The authors would like to thank the following organizations and people for their invaluable contributions in piloting this research:

• Ministry of Science and Technology (Taiwan), Grant No. 106-S-007-003-MY3 (PI: Prof Tzu-Hua Wang)

• Ministry of Education (Taiwan), Project "Constructing Tsing Hua STEAM School Based on Inquiry, Design Thinking and Maker Practice" (PI: Prof TzuHua Wang)

• Huang Pei-Cheng, Director of Research Department, The Affiliated Elementary School of National Tsing Hua University

• Huang Hui-Hsien, Director of Academic Affairs, The Affiliated Elementary School of National Tsing Hua University

• Wang Qiang, Northwest Normal University

• Shao Yun-Xia, Zhejiang Normal University

• Liu Shu-Yu, National Tsing Hua University

References

1. Brookfield, S.: Teaching for Critical Thinking: Tools and Techniques to Help students Question Their Assumptions. Jossey-Bass, San Francisco (2013)
2. Griffin, P., Care, E.: The ATC21S method. In: Griffin, P., Care, E. (eds.) Assessment and Teaching of 21st Century Skills. EAIA, pp. 3–33. Springer, Dordrecht (2015). https://doi.org/10.1007/978-94-017-9395-7_1
3. Saettler, P.: The Evolution of American Educational Technology. Libraries Unlimited, Englewood (1990)
4. Future of Education and Skills 2030. http://oecd.org/education/2030-project/
5. The Future of Jobs. http://reports.weforum.org/future-of-jobs2016
6. Study International Staff: PISA to test more diverse range of skills in the future (2019). https://www.studyinternational.com/news/pisa-to-test-morediverse-range-of-skills-in-the-future/
7. Wang, T.-H., Lim, K.Y.T., Lavonen, J., Clark-Wilson, A.: Maker-centred science and mathematics education: lenses, scales and contexts. Int. J. Sci. Math. Educ. **17**(1), 1–11 (2019). https://doi.org/10.1007/s10763-019-09999-8

8. University of Sydney (n.d.). https://sydney.edu.au/education_social_work/learning_teaching/ict/theory/constructivism.shtml. Accessed 27 Jan 2020

9. Barab, S., Squire, K.: Design-based research: putting a stake in the ground. J. Learn. Sci. **13**(1), 1–14 (2004)

10. Uno, G.: Handbook on Teaching Undergraduate Science Courses: A Survival Training Manual. Thomson Custom Publishing, Independence (1999)

11. National Research Council: Inquiry and the National Science Education Standards: A Guide for Teaching and Learning. National Academy Press, Washington, D.C. (2000)

12. Rutherford, F.J., Alhgren, A.: Project 2061: Science for All Americans. Oxford University Press, New York (1990)

13. Duran, L.B., Duran, E.: The 5E instructional model: a learning cycle approach for inquiry-based science teaching. Sci. Educ. Rev. **3**(2), 49–58 (2004)

14. Blikstein, P.: Digital fabrication and 'making' in education: the democratization of invention. In: Walter-Hermann, J., Buching, C. (eds.) FabLabs: Of Machines, Makers and Inventors. Transcript Publishers, Bielefeld (2013)

15. Marshall, J.A., Harron, J.R.: Making learners: a framework for evaluating making in STEM education. Interdiscip. J. Probl. Based Learn. Tinkering Technol. Rich Des. Contexts **12**, 2 (2018)

16. Wang, T.H.: Effective Interdisciplinary STEM/STEAM Education: DDMT Teaching Model and WACEL system for e-Assessment (2019). http://trh.gase.most.ntnu.edu.tw/en/article/content/74

17. Griffin, P., McGaw, B., Care, E. (eds.): Assessment and Teaching of 21st Century Skills. Springer, Dordrecht (2012). https://doi.org/10.1007/978-94-007-2324-5

18. Hart Research Associates: It takes more than a major: employer priorities for college learning and student success, vol. 99, no. 2. Association of American Colleges and Universities (2013). http://www.aacu.org/leap/documents/2013_EmployerSurvey.pdf

19. Sternberg, R.J.: Giving employers what they don't really want. The Chronicle of Higher Education (2013)

20. Wong, T.: Singapore fake news law polices chats and online platforms, 9 May 2019. https://www.bbc.com/news/world-asia-48196985

21. Lam, L.: SDP fails in bid to have POFMA-linked case against Manpower Minister heard in open court, 20 January 2020. https://www.channelnewsasia.com/news/singapore/sdp-fails-in-bid-to-havepofma-linked-case-against-manpower-12266236

22. Dupuy, B., Lajka, A., Seitz, A.: NOT REAL NEWS: a look at what didn't happen this week, 31 January 2020. https://sg.news.yahoo.com/not-real-news-look-didnt204444038.html

23. Collins, A., Joseph, D., Bielaczyc, K.: Design research: theoretical and methodological issues. J. Learn. Sci. **13**(1), 15–42 (2004)

24. Choi, J., Lee, Y., Lee, E.: Puzzle based algorithm learning for cultivating computational thinking. Wireless Pers. Commun. **93**(1), 131–145 (2016). https://doi.org/10.1007/s11277-016-3679-9

25. Dede, C.: Why design-based research is both important and difficult. Educ. Technol. **45**(1), 5–8 (2005)

26. Dede, C.: If design-based research is the answer, what is the question? J. Learn. Sci. **13**(1), 105–114 (2004)

27. Amiel, T., Reeves, T.C.: Design-based research and educational technology: rethinking technology and the research agenda. J. Educ. Technol. Soc. **11**(4), 29–40 (2008)

28. Lam, K.F.T., Wang, T.H., Vun, Y.S., Ku, N.: Developing critical thinking in a STEAM classroom. In: Vilalba-Condori, K.O., Bravo, A.A., Garcia-Peñalvo, F.J., Lavonen, J. (eds.) Proceedings of the International Congress on Educational and Technology in Sciences 2019, Arequipa, Perú, 10–12 December 2019, pp. 82–90 (2019)

An Open Educational Game for Learning Fractions in the Brazilian Context

Josivan P. da Silva[1]([⊠]) [iD], Gabriel T. Rizzo[2] [iD], and Ismar F. Silveira[1,2] [iD]

[1] Mackenzie Presbyterian University, São Paulo, Brazil
josivan.engenharia@gmail.com, ismarfrango@gmail.com
[2] Cruzeiro do Sul University, São Paulo, Brazil
gabrielfox@hotmail.com

Abstract. The areas of Science, Technology, Engineering and Mathematics (STEM) careers, are important areas of knowledge for contemporary society. Among the basics subjects of these careers is Mathematics, but many young students present difficulty to understand basic mathematical concepts. This learning process is complex and demands a lot of motivation by part of the students. In this sense, educational games can act as a stimulating helping tool for them. In Brazil, the levels of proficiency on rational numbers in their fractional representation presented by students aged between 9 and 12 years, in general, are low. We present such a game, called Fracpotion, developed as an Open Educational Resource to teach about fractions to children guided by Didactic Situation theory. This game has been tested by a group of students in an elementary school at São Paulo city, Brazil, and the preliminary results were positive.

Keywords: Open educational resources · Open educational games · Fractions · Didactic situations

1 Introduction

Professions are very important for society so people study and specialize in specific areas to play roles they like, and think it's important, in the job market. In this context, the STEM (Science, Technology, Engineering and Mathematics) careers are become each time more important for contemporary society [1].

Some of basic skills of STEM careers are on Math, but many young students present difficult to understand very fundamental Mathematical concepts [2]. If the student present difficulties in fundamentals of Mathematics still in his childhood or youth and choose to avoid of Mathematics and similar areas, probably they will be increasingly unmotivated through the years and will also avoid STEM careers in the future.

If we want to prepare our children and teenagers to have possibilities of work in future STEM careers, we should offer more didactical and motivational tools and challenges to them. According to [3] we should not to force young students to learn with same methods their grandparents have been exposed to, because traditional school learning based on predefined sequential curricula cannot completely meet requirements for the 21st century children, so modern tools (like digital games, for example) should be applied

K. O. Villalba-Condori et al. (Eds.): CISETC 2019, CCIS 1191, pp. 58–72, 2020.
https://doi.org/10.1007/978-3-030-45344-2_6

to complement and demand a big amount of motivation by students. Thus, naturally motivating tools like educational games can be interesting as vectors of stimuli for students [1].

Mathematics has many sub-topics that makes impossible to develop a digital game to cover all subjects once, so it is appropriate to select a specific topic to guide the design and application of educational game.

In Brazil the mean level of proficiency in Mathematics, in general, presented by students aged between 9 and 12 years, is low; this situation is more serious when they comes to learn some topics that are not common in their daily activities, like rational numbers in their fractional representation. Different from its neighbors in Latin America, in Brazilian culture the fractional representation is not a commonplace – even ½ is often represented in its decimal form (0,5 – with comma).

The learning of fractions is a complex process for students; difficulties can arise when students try to apply the properties of natural numbers to fractions, without understanding the differences between the two sets [4].

[5] claims that fractional numbers are avoided by students, because they do not like it or do not feel familiar with it. [6] clarify that when students are encouraged to solve problems using acquired knowledge and able in their daily activities and with symbolic representations, they can gradually evolve and use the daily knowledge to solve more complex problems and learn new skills, but it is not the case to fractional representations in Brazil's culture.

On the other hand, digital games are each more common in the daily activities of the young people, including students, so the development of a game about fractions would be of great value to complement the learning of this topic, especially if the game offers some facility of adaptation by teachers. Therefore, in this paper we present an Open Educational Game [7] called FracPotion to help students about fractions. The game was applied to 18 students of an elementary school at São Paulo, Brazil, and the results were positive.

The paper is organized as follows: Sect. 2 describes the panorama and difficulties in teaching fractions in Brazil; Sect. 3 explains Guy Brousseau's theory of Didactic Situations; Sect. 4 demonstrates an overview of educational games for mathematics teaching; the fifth section presents the proposal of the paper; Sect. 6 presents the experiment and results, and Sect. 7 completes the paper.

2 The Brazilian Reality on Learning of Fractions

This section will describe the panorama about learning fractions at elementary schools since 1980s to 2015, according some important national and international educational assessments; and will show some difficulties in teaching fractions.

2.1 Panorama According Important Educational Assessments

According to [8], among 1980s and 1990s, official assessment reports, such as the National Basic Education Assessment System (SAEB), the Programme for International

Student Assessment (PISA) and the National Student Performance Exam (ENADE), confirm the consensus pointed out in Brazilian and international studies on the difficulties of students and teachers in dealing with the concept of rational number.

The SAEB of 2001 [9] reveals that only 35% of Brazilians students were able to solve simple problems involving fractions; many of those that failed had problems with the part-whole relation, which is considered the most basic concept in this topic. The São Paulo State Performance Assessment System (SARESP) in 2005 [10] revealed that only 37% of students answered simple questions regarding such a topic. The results of the PISA (2012) [11] showed that two out of three students do not know how to work with simple operations involving fractions.

A survey recently conducted by the International Student Assessment Program in (2015) [12] showed a drop in scores in the three areas assessed: Science, Reading, and Math. The drop in scores also reflected Brazil's drop in the world ranking: the country ranked 63rd in science, 59th in reading and 66th in Mathematics. The Fig. 1 shows the results of proficiency in Sciences, Reading and Mathematics of the Brazilian students in elementary schools, according to OCDE and PISA 2015 [12].

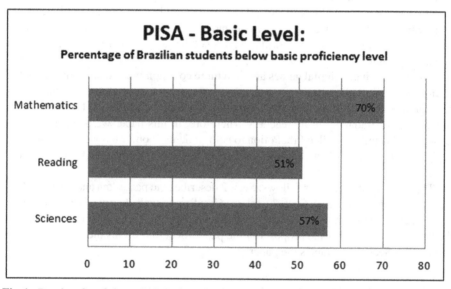

Fig. 1. Results of proficiency in Sciences, Reading and Mathematics of the Brazilian students in elementary schools, evaluated by OCDE and PISA 2015 (Source: adapted of [1]).

As we can see in Fig. 1, of the three areas evaluated in the assessment the Mathematic is the area with the worst performance of the Brazilian students.

2.2 Difficulties in Learning and Teaching Fractions

The teaching and learn of fractions is one of the most difficult areas in elementary school mathematics; is believed that failure to learn fraction arithmetic hinders children to learn more advanced math and difficult their success in careers that use math [13].

Children who have not yet understood fractions generally believe that the properties of whole numbers are the same for all type numbers [14].

Among children misconceptions of fraction are: fraction equivalence, common denominators and fractions arithmetic operations.

In the set of natural numbers, each number has a single representation, but when working with fractions, the same number can be represented by infinite fractions; And when multiplying a natural number by another natural number (except for the values 0 and 1) the result will be greater than the numbers used in the multiplication, this does not always happen with the multiplication between fractions [4].

There is a high rate of difficulties presented by students in understanding the concept of rational number and thinking about multiplication; a survey of 4th to 8th graders of elementary school showed that even students with good performance in mathematics generally achieved poor performance on issues with the whole part, quotient and multiplier operator in work with fractions; These same students performed well in multiplying natural numbers [15].

Based on [16] and [8] we found four important aspects to the practice and learning of fractions [10]:

- First (I), the practical aspect, in which fractions in their different representations appear, often in several situations related to the expression of measures and quantities – this fact highlights the need for extension of the set of natural numbers.
- Second (II), the psychological aspect, since working with fractions appears as a privileged opportunity to leverage and expand mental structures necessary for intellectual development.
- Third (III), the mathematical perspective aspect, since it will be precisely the first studies with the fractions that will ground more complex ideas such as operations.
- Finally (IV), order of numbers in their fractional representations.

We believe that an Educational Game that presents fractions and give player the task of reorganize and perform arithmetic operations with fractions them can offer experiences that address the four aspects mentioned by [16] and [8].

As we can see in (I) different representations of number in fractional form should be presented to the students in a more natural as possible way; in (II) the Brousseau's theory of didactic situation can guide the educational game application (because helps to expand the knowledge and achieve at target knowledge); in (III) and (IV), about the third and fourth aspect explained by [10], many authors show different approaches to the mathematical perspective in the teaching of fractions, as examples we can cite, according to [12] the focus of mathematical programs should be on fractions as quantities, to allow students to make a correlation with their previous knowledge of natural numbers as quantities, and [13] suggests that teachers need to introduce a variety of fractional interpretations for students, as students whose fraction learning was previously focused on regular fractions of tend to have an impoverished understanding of the rational numbers.

According to [8] young students often process numerator and denominator as two separated whole numbers, because it is uncommon to them, and it can cause errors like:

- $1/4 + 1/2 = 2/6$, what is incorrect and refers to III; And
- $1/5 > 1/3$, refers to ordering the fractional numbers as showed in IV.

Still according to [8], to overcome these errors young students have to interact with rational numbers, experiment, modify and compare results to get familiar with fractions and understand the rational number set as a distinct set of whole number set and accept that this new set has his own rules and functioning; here we make a relatives with de Didactic Situation theory by Guy Brousseau and the application of educational games to teach fractions, because the main idea of Didactic Situation and usage of educational games is also allows the student experiment, modify and compare results to learn in a less intimidating and more independent way.

3   Didactic Situation Theory by Guy Brousseau

Guy Brousseau proposed the Didactic Situation theory that consists, basically, of three elements: knowledge, divided in the knowledge that the student already owns and the knowledge that student have to learn (the target), teacher and student. These three elements relate to affect the pedagogical relationship that takes into account professor, student, knowledge (of the student and of the professor), rules, informations, environment and the resources (objects of study or tools) [17]. The Fig. 2 illustrates the Didactic Situation.

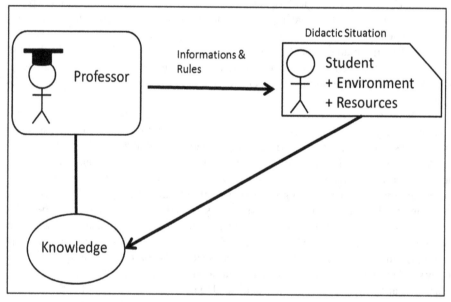

Fig. 2. Brousseau's Didactic Situation illustration: pedagogical relationship (Source: authors).

In the Didactic Situation theory, the professor must provide favorable situations to encourage the students, so that students can transform information and data into knowledge. The role of the student is to experiment, observe concepts, construct hypotheses and strategies, follow theories, follow rules and build models. The role of knowledge in the Didactic Situation is to anticipate theory and provide information to guide the student on their experiments [18].

The Didactic Situation theory defines that the teacher, in order that the student reaches the knowledge to which he intends to reach, must create didactic situations to motivate the student to learn the content independently, without intimidation and understanding the process of building that knowledge.

According Silva, Ferreira and Tozetti [19], the teacher must be an educator-researcher and the student must be a student-researcher; The difference is in the degree and difficulty of the content that the teacher can research and the problems that the teacher can solve, being that the teacher is a totally independent researcher (in the subject/discipline in question) and able to formulate the problems to be solved.

The didactic situation is an activity that must be dosed so that the teacher does not create challenges for the student, which are too difficult, to the point of discouraging him, or too easy to the point of compromising the student's dedication in building his knowledge, independently.

In the context of the Didactic Situation, an Educational Game fits well, because a game provides independence to the student, the possibility of experiment actions, observing and learning from errors, build strategies to meet the challenges of the game and the game's own rules can provide theory and information to the Student.

4   Digital Educational Games to Teach and Learn Mathematics

This section will be describes the educational games overview in practical perspective in the teaching of mathematics; and will show some related works.

4.1   Educational Games Overview and Applications to Teach Mathematics

Today we live in a world that offers many technology tools for children and young people; usually these young people's first contact with electronic equipment happens through Digital Games [3]. These can be defined as engaging, interactive environments that capture player attention by offering challenges that require increasing levels of dexterity and skills [20, 21].

Many teachers believe that regardless of whether a digital game has or not some educational purpose, it could contribute to psychomotor skills, development of analytical skills and computational skills of the player. This is mainly due to the difficulties faced during the game, the need to create new strategies (when strategies used before are no longer good), the pressure to develop strategic thinking, among other common aspects.

Educational games could be effective learning resources, mainly when applied to courses such as Mathematics or Science, often considered as difficult, abstract courses. They also have the potential of influencing students' social and daily life, affecting their behavior with colleagues [22]. However, many authors – like [23] and [24] suggest that educational games need more empirical evidence of effectiveness, requiring more evidences in this field. According to [25] the research field of educational games still has a limited quantity of empirical evidence about the effectiveness of games, especially in the domain of Mathematics. Some other works, like [26], bring stimulating results regarding to the use of digital games in the specific topic of fractions.

4.2 Related Works

Educational games could be effective learning resources, mainly when applied to courses such as Mathematics or Science, often considered as difficult, abstract courses. They also have the potential of influencing students' social and daily life, affecting their behavior with colleagues [22]. However, many authors – like [23] and [24] suggest that educational games need more empirical evidence of effectiveness, requiring more evidences in this field. According to [25] the research field of educational games still has a limited quantity of empirical evidence about the effectiveness of games, especially in the domain of Mathematics. Some other works, like [26], bring stimulating results regarding to the use of digital games in the specific topic of fractions.

In [27], an educational game called "Animo Math" was developed to help 5–7 years old children to learn Mathematics. The game has five levels with different difficulties, beginning with calculus that uses only single digit numbers (0–9) to teach/reinforce addition and subtraction operations; the other levels present more digits and different difficulties in calculus. In this work, there were expected the following four benefits in his game:

1. Make children more interested in positive learning in Mathematics.
2. Gain more of children's attention by using cartoon animations and fun sound effects.
3. Enable children to see the fun of Mathematics.
4. Parents perceive how to use modern digital technology and computers for children in mathematical learning.

In [25] an educational game was developed to teach about decimal numbers. In this game the students are introduced to a group of some fantastic characters that act as guides to Decimal Point Game and encourage students to play, congratulating them when they correctly solve problems. The game is composed by several mini-games inside a kind of Amusement Park. However, the game does not present numbers in factionary format. After playing a mini-game and correctly solving the problem, the student was prompted to explain his or her solution, by choosing possible pre-listed explanations from multiple-choice options available.

5   The Proposal: FracPotion Educational Game

FracPotion is a 2D educational game that was created for elementary school students. It is expected to evaluate whether students find the game funny and whether they can better identify, practice and understand educational content about fractions.

For the game to be better accepted by students, a narrative was created that justified the need to work with fractions in the game. In this sense, a wizard is proposed as a character since he employs fractions to combine potion ingredients that allow player to have progress in the game, when potions are properly created with the correct fractional quantity calculations. The background history to support the narrative follows:

"The game takes place in a kingdom called Camelot, ruled by Arthur. This kingdom is being threatened by a wicked witch named Morgana who, along with an army of wizards is heading toward Camelot to defeat Arthur and rule over humanity, but with the help of Merlin and his apprentice Arthur intends to defeat her with Magic potions.

For the creation of potions, it is necessary to define the right dose that is in the form of fraction and thus create the potion to defeat Morgana and save the kingdom from destruction."

5.1 The Open Digital Educational Game Overview

The game FracPotion is a simple adaptation of the classic history of King Arthur and his knights, where to defeat the villain Morgana, the player (as an apprentice) will have to hit the right amount of ingredients to complete the potion represented by fractions. This kernel of the game is explained (in Portuguese) on screen of game illustrated in Fig. 3.

Fig. 3. Game title screen with options; Play, Instructions, About and Exit (Source: the authors)

Players are not punished for their mistakes; they only earn stars according to the number of attempts they used to reach the required amount of ingredient that was thrown into the cauldron. Figure 4 is an exhibition of the first level of the game. Contains a question the player must answer to complete the potion. In Fig. 4 we can see the score markers, error markers and the elapsed time. The character is the wizard in the lower right corner of the screen and the alternatives A, B, C and D are the possibilities to complete the potion in the cauldron.

Fig. 4. Screenshot of gameplay at first level of the FracPotion game (Source: [1])

It must be noted that, even though the game was conceived in Portuguese language, it can be easily translated to any other language, as well as it is possible to modify most of its aspects, given that it was designed as an Open Educational Resource Source code is available (https://github.com/josivanSilvaCodes/FracProc) and is made available under open source license.

5.2 Design and Development of the Game

The Game uses a 2D view and was developed in JavaScript and WebGL to facilitate the visual work that forms the look-and-feel of the game. Game's target audience is composed by students who want to discover or review contents about basic fractions.

Cocos2D-x is a multi-platform framework for developing games and graphic applications [22] – the "x" letter in the name of the framework means that it can be changed by one between several languages supported; in our case, the chosen language was JavaScript (JS). This framework is a branch of another framework with a similar name called Cocos2D, which is focused on development for Apple devices running the IOS operating system. The big advantage of Cocos2D-x was to bring improvements to the then Cocos2D:

- It has a simple but also very powerful phase creator.
- Accessible through all major operating systems.
- Make it possible to publish games, for various platforms such as Windows, Mac OS, Linux, Android, iOS and also to the Web, in any HTML5-supported browser.

- Possibility to create your applications through various programming languages, such as C++, Lua, JavaScript, Objective-C, Swift, C#. Figure 5 exposes de Cocos2D-x framework used in this paper.

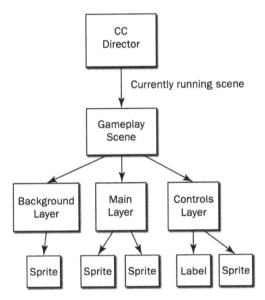

Fig. 5. Cocos2D framework hierarchy (Source: [1])

The Fig. 5 illustrates the Cocos2D framework hierarchy, the concept evolve a hole of Director that runs a Scene that contains several elements, as: background layer, controles layer and etc.

The way the framework works is by using the concept of a director and scenes, being each object on the screen a node in a component tree. Everything that will be drawn is controlled by a class called CCDirector, where it has the ability to modify the order of how components will be drawn and also change the game scenes, being responsible for defining the initialization of the components that are requested by the framework calls. The Cocos Creator tool tends to hide most of this complexity.

Cocos Creator is an editor that works on top of the Cocos2D-JS framework, assisting in the development of the graphical application whatever it is, showing the properties of the components, also providing a preview of what the game scene will be at the moment that it is loaded and a way to graphically manage the files and scripts that will be within the game. The main structure of Cocos Creator can be seen in Fig. 6.

The scenes within Cocos2D-x are the most basic component of each game window, within each scene, will be all the components, effects, texts and images of the game being then managed by the Director. The Cocos Creator offers a Scene View and a Game Preview to facilitate the development the game and provides fast feedback to the developers; it can be seen in the illustration of Fig. 6. The Fig. 7 shows the UML Class Diagram of the game.

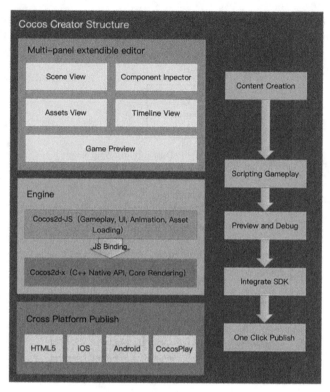

Fig. 6. Cocos Creator main structure: about cocos creator framework structure (Source: [28])

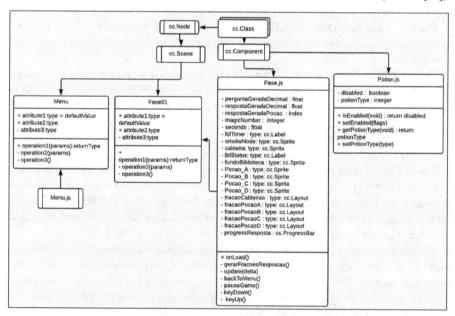

Fig. 7. UML Class Diagram of the FracPotion game (Source: the authors)

In the Class Diagram of the Fig. 7, we can see the composition of the game with the relationships of the classes, mainly between the Fases and Potions to be completed.

6   Evaluation of the Game and Educational Content

For the evaluation of the game FracPotion, an experiment was carried out with elementary school students. As we wanted to evaluate the experience of the children under a qualitative approach, we studied two different frameworks in the evaluation process. The first one was the generic ITU BT500 assessment (https://www.itu.int/rec/R-REC-BT.500) –and the other one was the MEEGA+ model [29]. After we have analyzed these two assessment models, we have chosen the second one, so the MEEGA+ model was used to evaluate the quality of the game and educational content, since it is directly focuses in educational game evaluation instead the generically approach of the ITU BT 500 for all type of software.

6.1   The Experiment

The experiment was carried out with elementary school students. The participants of the research were 18 students and the criterion of choice was that they already knew the basic concepts of fractions learned in the classroom. The profile of the students of the experiment presented a mean age of 12 years, there was a balance with respect to gender, but the girls slightly predominated on boys; 92% of volunteers make regular use of digital games - 47.6% on a daily basis and 9.5% weekly. Players first had an experience of interacting with the game, without the help of any instructor. Soon after, they answered a survey about the aspects of the game, involving the visual characteristics of the game, the interface, the easiness that the game possibly presents and other aspects of usability of the game. In addition, the survey had extra questions about the educational content presented and its relationship with the game, as a way to verify if the game met the educational purpose regarding fractions. The students answered the questions using five possible responses in a Likert-like scale (Too little, Little, Neutral, Very, and Very much).

The questions to evaluate the educational content of the game were:

(1)   How motivated did you feel to learn about fraction with this game?
(2)   Did you learn about fractions with this game?
(3)   Would you recommend this game to a friend?
(4)   Would you rather learn fractions using this Game?
(5)   Did you feel challenged by this Game?

6.2   Results of the Work

The combination of texts, colors and sources were pointed out as good combination and consistency by 61% (11 students) of the interviewees and the other almost 17% (3 students) answered neutrally (neither agree nor disagree). As for the game being intuitive and easy to adapt approximately 28% (5 students) agreed with this aspect and approximately 44% (8 students) responded with neutrality. As for the easiness to understand rules 50% (9 students) judged them easily understandable and the other almost 28% (5 students) responded with neutrality.

About the questions regarding the educational content, the students have answered to the question (1) positively or neutral 61% (11 students); question (2) have 56% of positive answers (10 students); third question (3) had 94% of positive or neutral answers (17 students); question (4) had 78% of positive answers (14 students); and question (5) had 67% of positive or neutral responses (12 students). The Table 1 was created to simplify this visualization.

Table 1. Evaluation of the game by students in 1 to 5-scale based on MEEGA+.

Characteristics of the game and questions to evaluate	(1) Too little	(2) Little	(3) Neutral	(4) Very	(5) Very much
(1) Motivation	3 (16.66%)	4 (22.22%)	3 (16.66%)	4 (22.22%)	4 (22.22%)
(2) Learn fractions	1 (5.55%)	2 (11.11%)	5 (27.77%)	6 (33.33%)	4 (22.22%)
(3) Recommend to others	1 (5.55%)	0 (0%)	7 (38.88%)	7 (38.88%)	3 (16.66%)
(4) Prefer this game against traditional methods	1 (5.55%)	1 (5.55%)	2 (11.11%)	9 (50.00%)	5 (27.77%)
(5) Feel challenged	3 (16.66%)	3 (16.66%)	5 (27.77%)	2 (11.11%)	5 (27.77%)

7 Conclusions

The teaching and learning processes in the field of Mathematics require an important effort on building knowledge over a very abstract body of knowledge, but with many practical applications in real-world situations. Fractions, for instance, tend to represent an extremely abstract concept, mainly when local culture do not make regular use of this kind of representation in common situations – which is the case for Brazilian culture, which have adopted the floating point decimal representation in detriment of the fractional one. Tools that help to stimulate students to keep motivational aspect when learning such subjects are potentially useful to these process.

This paper presented a game designed to support students to learn or revise some basic fraction concepts. Regarding the group to which this game was applied, the players/students showed interest in game's subject and they reported to have enjoyed the learning process supported by the game. However, the results point out that more research is needed in order to improve the game itself and to apply it in other study groups. Further work includes the development of other games for different subjects in Mathematics and other STEM areas. The current game is in its beta version; as improvements, new phases are to be developed with other types of fractions and operations, as well as the translation and adaptation capabilities of the game as an Open Educational Resource are to be tested.

Acknowledgements. This work was supported by Mackenzie Presbyterian University (UPM) and its Electrical Engineering and Computer Postgraduate Program, also known as PPGEEC, under grant #509 as a full scholarship for the first author, we want to thank both.

References

1. Silva, J.P., Nogueira, R., Rizzo, G., Silveira, I.F.: FracPotion: an open educational game to teach fractions in Brazil. In: International Congress on Education and Technology in Sciences – CISETC 2019, Arequipa, Perú, 10–12 December 2019, pp. 301–311. CEUR-WS.org, Aachen (2019)
2. Drigas, A.S., Marios, A.: On line and other game-based learning for mathematics. Int. J. Online Biomed. Eng. (2015)
3. Darwesh, A.M.: Serious Games in Adaptive Learning (2016)
4. Monteiro, A.B., Groenwald, C.L.O.: Dificuldades na Aprendizagem de Frações: Reflexões a partir de uma Experiência Utilizando Testes Adaptativos. ALEXANDRIA Revista de Educação em Ciência e Tecnologia **7**(2), 103–135 (2014). ISSN 1982-5153
5. Justulin, A.M., Pirola, N.A.: Um estudo sobre as relações entre as atitudes em relação à Matemática e a resolução de problemas envolvendo frações (2008)
6. Nunes, T., Bryant, P.: Crianças Fazendo Matemática. Artmed, Porto Alegre (1997)
7. Silveira, I.F., Villalba-Condori, K.O.: An open perspective for educational games. J. Inf. Technol. Res. (JITR) **11**(1), 18–28 (2018)
8. Fávero, M.H., da Silva Pina Neves, R.: A divisão e os racionais: revisão bibliográfica e nálise. Zetetike (2012)
9. Neto, J.B.G.: Sistema Nacional de Avaliação da Educação Básica - SAEB: matemática. Brasília, DF (2002). (in Portuguese)
10. São Paulo (Estado). Secretaria de Estado da Educação: Boletim de Resultados do SARESP: anual (2005). (in Portuguese)
11. Ministério da Educação. Pisa: Programme for International Student Assessment. Organização para a Cooperação e Desenvolvimento Econômicos – OCDE. Brasília (2012). (in Portuguese)
12. OCDE. PISA 2015 Results in Focus, PISA in Focus, no. 67. OECD Publishing, Paris (2016). https://doi.org/10.1787/aa9237e6-en
13. Kor, L.K., Teoh, S.H., Mohamed, S.S.E.B., Singh, P.: Learning to make sense of fractions: some insights from the Malaysian primary 4 pupils. Int. Electron. J. Math. Educ. **14**(1), 169–182 (2019)
14. Gabriel, F., Coché, F., Szucs, D., Carette, V., Rey, B., Content, A.: A Componential View of Children's Difficulties in Learning Fractions (2013)
15. Okuma, É.K., Ardenghi, M.J.: Fraction of teaching and learning: a comparative study and teaching intervention. Universitári@ - Revista Científica do Unisalesiano – Lins – SP, ano 2, n. 3, jan/jun de 2011
16. Santos, A.: O conceito de fração em seus diferentes significados: um estudo diagnóstico junto a professores que atuam no Ensino Fundamental. Dissertação (Mestrado em Educação Matemática) – Pontifícia Universidade Católica de São Paulo, São Paulo (2005). (in Portuguese)
17. Pommer, W.M., Pommer, C.P.C.R.: Uma Situação a-didática em Sala de Aula para introduzir a noção de multiplicação. In: II Encontro da rede de professores, pesquisadores e licenciandos de Física e de Matemática (2010)
18. Brousseau, G.: Introdução ao Estudo das Situações Didáticas: Conteúdos e métodos de ensino. Ática, São Paulo (2008). 128 p.

19. Silva, N.A., Ferreira, M.V.V., Tozetti, K.D.: Um estudo sobre a situação didática de Guy Brousseau. In: V Seminário Internacional Sobre profissionalização Docente - SIPD (2015)
20. Reese, D.D., Tabachnick, B.G., Kosko, R.E.: Video game learning dynamics: actionable measures of multidimensional learning trajectories. Br. J. Edu. Technol. 46(1), 98–122 (2013)
21. Paul Albert, A.: Digital games – a magical learning tool for slow learners. Int. J. Res. Granthaalayah 6(5), 407–412 (2018). https://doi.org/10.5281/zenodo.1285245
22. Chizary, F., Farhangi, A.: Efficiency of educational games on mathematics learning of students at second grade of primary school. J. Hist. Culture Art Res. 6(1), 232–240 (2017). https://doi.org/10.7596/taksad.v6i1.738
23. Ahmad, S.M.S., Fauzi, N.F.M., Hashim, A.A., Zainon, W.M.N.W.: A study on the effectiveness of computer games in teaching and learning. Int. J. Adv. Stud. Comput. Sci. Eng. 2(1), 1 (2013)
24. De Freitas, S.: Are games effective learning tools? A review of educational games. J. Educ. Technol. Soc. 21(2), 74–84 (2018)
25. McLaren, B.M., Adams, D.M., Mayer, R.E., Forlizzi, J.: A computer-based game that promotes mathematics learning more than a conventional approach. Int. J. Game-Based Learn. (IJGBL) 7(1), 36–56 (2017). https://doi.org/10.4018/ijgbl.2017010103
26. Aluan, B.B.: Increasing Mathematical Performance Among Grade Six Pupils of San Roque Elementary School Using Game-Based Learning for the School Year 2016–2017. Sariaya, Quezon (2018)
27. Sukstrienwong, A.: Animo math: the role-playing game in mathematical learning for children. TEM J. 7(1), 147–154 (2018). https://doi.org/10.18421/tem71-17. ISSN 2217-8309
28. Cocos Creator: About Cocos Creator: Framework Structure. Cocos Creator v1.9 User Manual. https://docs.cocos.com/creator/1.9/manual/en/getting-started/introduction.html. Accessed 10 Feb 2020
29. Petri, G., Wangenheim, C.G.V.: How to evaluate educational games: a systematic literature review. J. Univ. Comput. Sci. 22(7), 992–1021 (2016)

An Architectural Model
for the Production of Virtual
Reality Learning

Héctor Cardona-Reyes[1]([✉]) [iD], José Eder Guzman-Mendoza[2] [iD],
Gerardo Ortiz-Aguiñaga[3] [iD], and Jaime Muñoz-Arteaga[2] [iD]

[1] CONACYT Research Fellow, CIMAT Zacatecas, Zacatecas, Mexico
hector.cardona@cimat.mx
[2] Autonomous University of Aguascalientes,
Av. Universidad #940, Cd. Universitaria, 20131 Aguascalientes, Mexico
{eder.guzman,jaime.munoz}@edu.uaa.mx
[3] Center for Research in Mathematics, Quantum: Knowledge City,
Zacatecas, Mexico
gerardo.ortiz@cimat.mx

Abstract. Learning environments integrate multiple technology platforms allowing people to meet learning objectives through available content, resources, and integrated services. Learning environments allow users to cover learning objectives in different subject areas, such as social skills development, health, etc. This article presents a development model of Learning Environments through Virtual Reality (VR). This model incorporates new forms of interaction for learning, such as immersion in simulated scenarios that support users in attaining learning objectives. A VR tour of a university is presented as a case study, where distinct users, such as teachers, students, and general public interact with content, resources available and services to achieve the specific learning objectives.

Keywords: Virtual environments · Learning model · Immersive learning

1   Introduction

The design of learning environments involves a multidisciplinary work in which specialists participate in the generation of content, pedagogical design, in addition to technologists for the design and programming of digital platforms and content [1]. Learning environments allow to learner acquires knowledge through elements that are presented in the environment, these elements can be physical or cultural and involve the way in which people interact with the environment, other people and other organization ways towards achieving learning [2].

Supported by CONACYT.

There are several ways to represent a learning environment, currently there is a wide variety of accessible devices to support the learning process, such as websites that offer courses at low cost, interactive books where the learner solves in a didactic way problems to reinforce knowledge and video games that allow a degree of interaction allowing the apprentice to meet goals.

This work proposes a model for the production of virtual reality learning environments, in the proposed model design and interaction artifacts are presented, also the inclusion of several available services and the existence of different user roles that can meet their learning objectives [3]. This work is composed of seven sections, in the following section related works to the proposal are presented, theoretical foundations section presents some conceptual elements of learning environments that are the basis for the proposed model. Next, problem outline section presents the challenges when producing learning environments in virtual reality. A production of virtual learning environments section shows the elements of model proposed, after, a case study section with a proposed solution in high education and finally conclusions a future works section are presented.

2   Related Work

This section presents a literary review of the state of the art of works that propose learning environments, these works refers to diverse approaches, platforms and several application contexts, as presented in the Table 1.

Table 1. Literature review of learning environments

Author	Approach	User centered	Feedback	Platform	Services	User roles	Interaction type
Yang et al. [4]	Physical interaction system	•	•	Video	•	-	Semi immersive
Pan et al. [5]	Game-based	•	•	VR	-	-	Immersive
James et al. [6]	Object recognition	-	-	VR	-	-	Immersive
Goulding et al. [7]	Game-based training	•	•	Web 3D	•	-	Semi-Immersive
Proposal	Game-based virtual map	•	•	VR	•	•	Immersive

As a first criterion, several approaches are presented such as video-games based [5,7], object recognition by the user [6] or even a combination of real elements with virtual approach is included [4]. A second criterion presented is the user-centered approach [8], that is, if the learning environment considers the facility to determine what actions are possible at any given time, besides being able to represent a conceptual model of the system and evaluate your state. A third criterion presented is the feedback provided by the learning environment, that is, it shows information of importance for the reinforcement of the learner and educator. Goulding et al. [7] shows simulation scenarios for training in the industry. The platform is the criteria that help us to identify the devices used for the learning environment, among the literature, specialized devices for object recognition to web platforms and virtual reality. The user role is the criterion that allows the learning environment to offer content and services according to the user role, finally the type of interaction of the learning environment is presented, as you can see most of the works have a type of interaction immersive or semi-immersive [9], in the first one the users are completely isolated from the real environment and respond to the actions of the existing virtual elements in the scene presented to them, in the second the users perceive and can respond to both environments, real and virtual. Next section presents some conceptual elements of learning environments that are the basis for the proposed model.

3   Theoretical Foundations

Virtual reality is a technology that has become increasingly accessible to users and has begun to take part in various fields, science, health, education and entertainment. In the context of education it allows learning environments offer a range of possibilities in which the learner can interact with simulated elements that lead to the acquisition of knowledge. According to LaValle and Shin [10,11], virtual reality allows to induce the directed behavior of a person through the use of artificial sensory stimulation while the person has little or no awareness of interference.

3.1   Reasons to Use Virtual Reality in Education

In the literature we can find that different authors present positively the use of virtual reality in education. Pantelidis [12] describes the use of virtual reality as a natural evolution of computer-assisted instruction (CAI) or computer-based training (CBT). Bowman et al. [13] and Wickens [14] agree that virtual reality gives increased learning and retention of the learner, since cognitive effort required load and activities related to the tasks and activities related to the system. Other authors such as Chen et al. [15] and Dede [16], propose strategies for the design and evaluation of virtual reality learning environments to determine in which situations it can be adopted or not. Pantelidis [12] mentions a series of advantages and disadvantages that we can take into account when adopting virtual reality in learning environments.

- Advantages
  - Virtual reality can more accurately illustrate some features, processes, and so forth than by other means.
  - VR allows extreme close-up examination of an object and gives the opportunity for insights based on new perspectives.
  - Virtual reality can change the way a learner interacts with the subject since active participation is required instead of passivity.

- VR allows a learner to learn by doing, a constructivist approach.
- VR provides a way for some objectives to be taught via distance education which were previously impossible to teach in that way.
- Disadvantages
  - The costs associated with the adoption of virtual reality.
  - The time required to learn how to use the hardware and software of virtual reality devices.
  - Possible health effects that may be caused to the user, such as vertigo, dizziness, sickness virtual reality, etc. [17].

Como se puede observar, la realidad virtual puede ofrecer una gran aporte al contexto educativo, y es necesario indicar que su uso en el aprendizaje se debe ver como una herramienta y resaltar las ventajas de su uso.

3.2   Virtual Reality in Leaning Environments

Shin and Huang [11, 18], agree that virtual reality oriented learning environments allow learners to interact with others while carrying out a set of tasks. [11] in his model presents key elements when designing virtual educational environments, as presented in Fig. 1.

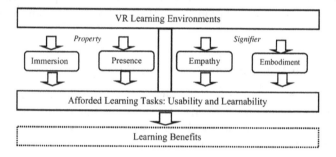

Fig. 1. Virtual learning environment approach by Shin et al. [11].

The model in Fig. 1 is based on the concept of affordance [11], for learning environments represents a characteristic of the environment that, when perceived, provides an opportunity for some action [19]. In the case of virtual reality learning environments affordances they are divided into technological and affective, technological represent how users perceive the technology and affective affordance of user's perceived technological property. In other hand signifiers help how people discover the possible actions that can be performed [20].

3.3   Virtual Reality in Constructivism Context

Virtual reality has a great adoption of the constructivist approach to learning since it allows learners to build their own knowledge from meaningful experiences [21].

This applied to a learning environment, allows the apprentice to control the way in which he acquires knowledge, in an exploratory way avoiding any possible consequences [22].

In general, the theory of constructivism mentions that humans generate knowledge by interacting with the environment and acquire knowledge by establishing a relationship between acquired experiences and ideas [23–25].

There are learning environments such as Edugames, dedicated to supporting collaboration and learning in education in a safe and meaningful way [26]. An example which may be mentioned of such learning environments with constructivist approach is Minecraft[1].

According to Schifter and Cipollone [27], Minecraft is seen as a tool that offers students (or players) the ability to gain knowledge through experimentation in the constructivist sense. Basically it is an open world construction game that allows the user the freedom to represent a world through the use of blocks that present various structures such as elements of nature, minerals, etc. It presents various game modes such as survival, adventure, creative, among others.

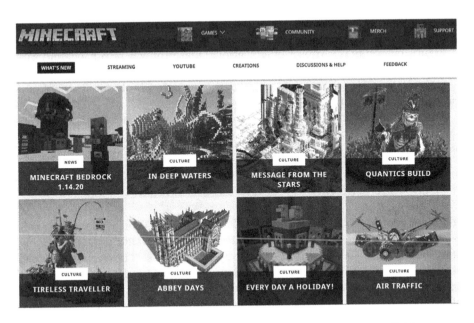

Fig. 2. Minecraft community website, with many resources available

---

[1] https://www.minecraft.net.

As shown in Fig. 2, Minecraft[2] has a large community in which various types of contents are provided, ranging from representations of historic sites, vehicles, buildings, etc.

In addition, Minecraft has an educational version, this presents a safe environment where the teacher can have control without losing the essence of the game is creativity and freedom. In addition to offering specific functionality for teachers and ready scenarios for specific activities and adapted for classroom use.

Fig. 3. Minecraft education edition; main page with some lessons *(left)* and math lesson example about 3D fractions *(right)*

Figure 3 presents the Minecraft educational platform, where you can find various resources that can be support for teachers and apprentices. These resources range from lessons, science, math, programming, etc. Tools for learners and teachers to adapt, edit and create content.

The use of such virtual environments under the constructive approach allows trainees to acquire knowledge themselves to interact with the virtual environment [26].

4 Problem Outline

This work proposes a model for the production of virtual reality learning environments that considers a user-centered design, virtual reality aspects, learning strategies and the incorporation of educational services. The proposed model allows the generation of content for various user roles, under a constructivist [28] learning approach, in which the learner (user) can select and transform the information for their decision-making, in addition to this can build their own processes to solve situations to various problems within a virtual reality environment [29–31]. Therefore, developing a learning environment that can solve these points is a complicated task that requires consider the following:

---

[2] https://www.minecraft.net/en-us/community.

- Establish a user-centered design for the creation of software oriented to learning needs and thus achieve the highest satisfaction and user experience.
- Develop digital scenarios based on a virtual reality-based learning strategies.
- Allow the adaptability of virtual reality learning environments to multiple contexts of use, platforms, available services and ways to acquire knowledge.
- Identify and define the various user roles within the virtual reality learning environment.
- Provide feedback information to the various user roles.

The following section presents in detail the design of the proposed model.

5   Production of Virtual Learning Environments

Virtual reality is a technology that has recently entered the field of education and is currently accessible at low cost [32]. In the educational context it can be used so that trainees can have an inverse experience in the learning process, this generates the need to propose models that help integrate virtual reality to produce applications according to learning needs [28]. Figure 2 shows a production model of learning environments is presented, this model shows elements comprising virtual reality and using educational services to produce applications that can be a support for learners, educators and other roles associated with the educational process. This model is based on the constructivist [30,33] approach and includes basic principles for understanding learning, these principles involve the exploration and discovery of artificial worlds and technological features that support learning [28]. Next, elements of model proposed in Fig. 4 are described.

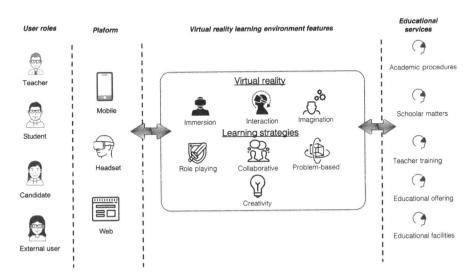

Fig. 4. Proposed architectural model for virtual reality learning environments

5.1 User Roles

The model proposes support for several roles within the learning environment, these roles define the actions of the user and their learning process, in the reverse part of virtual reality determines the type of interaction and content available and its associated educational services [34–36]. Table 2 describes each of these user roles.

Table 2. User roles description in virtual reality learning environment model.

User	Description
Teacher	- Provide student orientation services
	- Provide content for pedagogical activities
	- He is an expert who dominates the contents
	- Share learning experiences with students
	- Encourage student participation
	- Facilitate the understanding of the basic contents and encourage self-learning
Student	- It generates its own knowledge
	- It is characterized by being interactive
	- It is related to the learning process
	- Guided by the teacher while building their own knowledge
	- Plans the learning activities
Candidate	- It has access to educational offering services
	- Interact with the contents academic procedures and educational facilities
	- It has access to some school matters
External user	- It has access to content public, and limited access to content and services

5.2 Platform

Virtual reality learning environments produced can be built on different platforms according to the needs of the user, the available platforms ranging from mobile devices, web applications and desktop applications that require a virtual reality headset such as Oculus Rift[3] or HTC Vive[4]. The platform selection also determines the degree of interaction and content that can be presented to the user within in virtual reality learning environments.

5.3 Virtual Reality Learning Environment Features

The objective in virtual reality learning environments is that users achieve their learning objectives through a transfer of immersive learning based on virtual reality to the real world with real situations through practice by interacting with objects and events in the simulated world [28,37]. The following describes two important features for the design of virtual reality learning environments under the proposed model.

---

[3] https://www.oculus.com/.

[4] https://www.vive.com/us/product/vive-virtual-reality-system/.

Virtual Reality

- Immersion technology aspects are considered to offer the user the feeling of presence in an artificial environment as if he were in a daily learning situation [10].
- According to Huang and Burdea [28,38], interaction considers the strategies for the user to interact with the virtual reality learning environment, user inputs and feedback with the system are defined. Also it refers to strategies to take into account that the user is engaged in the virtual environment [39].
- Imagination refers to how the learner uses his problem solving skills and his ability to perceive and creative sense to interact with simulated elements [28].

Learning Strategies

- Role-playing allows the learner representation or simulation of roles for a given situation or event that occurs within the virtual environment, which encourages the learner to think creatively and solve situations [28,40].
- Collaborative refers to the strategy where users exchange ideas and experiences to gain knowledge within the virtual reality environment [28].
- Problem-based is based on the methodology of problem-based learning where the user faces real situations using their own strategies using the tools offered by the virtual environment [41].
- Creativity refers to strategies for the user through new ideas and concepts develop their ability to solve problems [28].

5.4   Educational Services

Educational services within the virtual reality learning environment complement the virtual content offering support to academic institutions processes. Educational services of the proposed model are described below.

- **Academic Procedures:** Service available for users to perform management or diligence management or diligence that is performed to obtain a result regarding an academic process.
- **Scholar Matters:** Service responsible for administrative tasks and validation of study programs also register and validate information derived from the educational process of students and provide academic and administrative support to the teaching staff.
- **Teacher Training:** Service responsible for policies and procedures to prepare teachers in the field of knowledge, attitudes and skills [42].
- **Educational Offering:** Service refers to the different opportunities of education degrees, these are offered by the university to future students.
- **Educational Facilities:** Service to find out the educational infrastructure.

6 Case Study

This section presents a virtual reality learning environment called "UAA Virtual tour and services", is designed to be used to offer learning content and educational services for the Autonomous University of Aguascalientes (UAA). The UAA is an institution of higher education that has an approximate of 20,128 students distributed in postgraduate, undergraduate and high school. Currently, the UAA has 89 plans and programs of study, 25 of which are postgraduate programs in masters and doctorates, 64 undergraduate 1 and a high school plan [43].

6.1 Virtual Learning Environments in Higher Education

According to Cuadro et al. [44], learning environments represent a series of steps towards teaching allowing a reduction in time and space making it possible for a large number of people to have access to content while attending their daily activities. The "UAA Virtual tour and services" (VRUAA) is intended to people who attend a higher education institution can cover their learning needs in an immersed way where the user interacts with 3D elements and make use of simulated educational content, In addition to having available services offered by institutions of higher education, such as, consulting kardex, class content, teachers information, etc. Among the advantages that we can mention when incorporating VRUAA are [45]: Provide elements for learning in an understandable way that is not limited to the classroom or the educational institution; having a platform accessible from a mobile device to a virtual reality device; Allow interaction of different types of roles such as students, academics, etc. Integrate different resources and services to enhance the way of teaching.

6.2 Collaborative Work

Figure 4 shows a model of a virtual reality based learning environment, which in other words, is a scenario of consumers of educational services based on virtual reality learning strategies. However, for the case study, it is also necessary to describe the model of collaborative work that has been carried out to describe the process of creating educational services. In other words, there cannot be a service consumption scenario without a scenario where those services are being produced. For this reason, Table 3 describes the roles involved in the design and production of educational services in the virtual reality model.

In Fig. 5, the collaborative work carried out by the different roles to create the virtual reality environment is shown through a use case diagram. According to Fig. 5, the RV-UX Designer is responsible for designing the user research strategy, where he uses quantitative and qualitative user research methods to discover the insights that will become the inputs to define the virtual reality experiences. The RV-UI Designer is responsible for transforming the insights into Virtual Reality based user interfaces. When the RV-UI-Designer finishes the UI designs, the RV-QA takes care of applying various usability tests.

Table 3. Role description for design and development of virtual reality learning environments.

Role	Description
RV-UX Designer	- Applies quantitative and qualitative methods of User Research to detect features (insights) - Analyze the usability tests and proposes improvements - Design learning strategies based on VR services
RV-UI Designer	- Define low and high level VR wireframes - Design the prototypes of educational services UI - Design the prototypes of 3D objects
RV-Developer	- Develop the objects in 3D - Develop the scenarios based on VR Services
RV-QA (quality assurance)	- Define the instruments and metrics of Usability - Applies the Usability tests - Generate the reports of the Learning Analysis

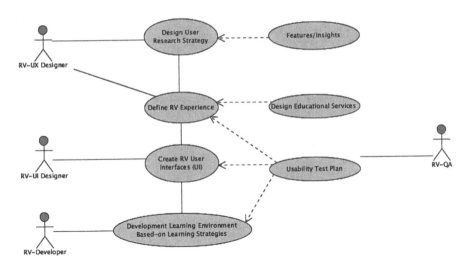

Fig. 5. Use case diagram of collaborative work.

The results obtained are analyzed by the RV-UX-Designer with the purpose of finding improvements in the UI features. When all UIs have been validated, they are sent to the RV-Developer who is responsible for transforming the UI-RV into the VR Educational Services. The VR-UX-Designer and the VR-Development work together so that the development process is adjusted to the creation of the learning environment and the strategies.

6.3   Participants

The launch of the VRUAA includes the participation of 20 students on average graduate aged 25 to 30 years, of which 15 are men and 5 women. The procedure for launch was that each participant used a virtual reality headset (HTC Vive System) in which the VRUAA presents content and the user has an immersive experience, as shown in Fig. 6. The following subsection the results of the information obtained from the launch of the VRUAA are presented.

Fig. 6. VRUAA environment learning launching.

6.4   Results

The data for this study were gathered by means of an online survey based on Davis et al. [46]. The survey is divided into two sections with six questions and answers on a scale of 1 (unlikely) to 7 (likely). The purpose of the survey is to measure in user experience in terms of perceived usefulness and ease of use of VRUAA. The chart in Fig. 5 presents the result of the survey of perception of utility and ease of use applied to the group of participants that used the VRUAA. The objective is to know the degree of perceived usefulness, that is, to what extent the user believes that using the VRUAA can improve their performance and take advantage of their learning activities. Perceived ease of use, refers to degree to which a person believes that using the VRUAA can be free of

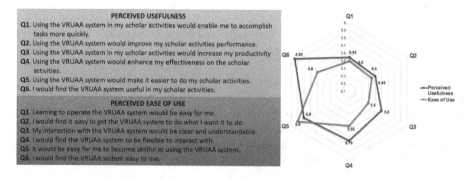

Fig. 7. Perceived usefulness and ease of use survey (left) and results chart (right) of VRUAA launching.

effort into their learning activities [46]. As shown in the chart in Fig. 7 for both aspects greater value 5 is obtained, indicating that there is a good acceptance in perception generates usefulness and ease of use of the learning environment VRUAA.

7   Conclusions and Future Works

The work presented in this article proposes a method to produce virtual reality learning environments. The main objective is to integrate multiple technological platforms that allow people to meet learning objectives through available content, resources, service integration and various user roles. In the proposed model, each of its elements is described in order to have a base and design to produce virtual reality learning environments to support the needs of higher education institutions.

The case study presents the implementation of VRUAA, which is an immersive virtual reality system composed of 3D simulated content and services associated with the purpose of offering support to various users who attend a higher education institution. An evaluation is also presented showing the degree of perception of utility and ease of use of the system, allowing users to know the acceptance in general. The future work of this research includes new strategies for the design and production of virtual reality educational environments, new forms of interaction, new usability evaluation techniques and user experience focused on supporting new learning needs through virtual reality.

References

1. Núñez, M.E.C., et al.: Entornos de aprendizaje digitales (2004)
2. Salinas, J.: Cambios metodológicos con las tic. estrategias didácticas y entornos virtuales de enseñanza-aprendizaje. Bordón **56**(3–4), 469–481 (2004)
3. Ortiz, G., Cardona, H., Guzman, E., Arteaga, J.: Production model of virtual reality learning environments. In: Proceeding of the Congreso Internacional Sobre Educación y Tecnología en Ciencias - CISETC 2019 (Arequipa, Perú, 10–12 December 2019), Aachen, Germany, 319-328. CEUR-WS.org. (2019)
4. Yang, J.C., Chen, C.H., Jeng, M.C.: Integrating video-capture virtual reality technology into a physically interactive learning environment for english learning. Comput. Educ. **55**(3), 1346–1356 (2010)
5. Pan, Z., Cheok, A.D., Yang, H., Zhu, J., Shi, J.: Virtual reality and mixed reality for virtual learning environments. Comput. Graph. **30**(1), 20–28 (2006)
6. James, K., Humphrey, G., Vilis, T., Corrie, B., Baddour, R., Goodale, M.: "Active" and "passive" learning of three-dimensional object structure within an immersive virtual reality environment. Behav. Res. Methods Instrum. Comput. **34**(3), 383–390 (2002)
7. Goulding, J., Nadim, W., Petridis, P., Alshawi, M.: Construction industry offsite production: a virtual reality interactive training environment prototype. Adv. Eng. Inform. **26**(1), 103–116 (2012)

8. Abras, C., Maloney-Krichmar, D., Preece, J., et al.: User-centered design. Bainbridge, W. (ed.) Encyclopedia of Human-Computer Interaction, vol. 34, no. 4, pp. 445–456. Sage Publications, Thousand Oaks (2004)

9. Alqahtani, A.S., Daghestani, L.F., Ibrahim, L.F.: Environments and system types of virtual reality technology in stem: a survey. Int. J. Adv. Comput. Sci. Appl. (IJACSA) 8(6), 77–89 (2017)

10. LaValle, S.: Virtual reality (2016)

11. Shin, D.H.: The role of affordance in the experience of virtual reality learning: technological and affective affordances in virtual reality. Telematics Inform. 34(8), 1826–1836 (2017)

12. Pantelidis, V.S.: Reasons to use virtual reality in education and training courses and a model to determine when to use virtual reality. Themes Sci. Technol. Educ. 2(1–2), 59–70 (2010)

13. Bowman, D.A., Hodges, L.F., Allison, D., Wineman, J.: The educational value of an information-rich virtual environment. Presence: Teleoperators Virtual Environ. 8(3), 317–331 (1999)

14. Wickens, C.D.: Virtual reality and education. In: Proceedings of 1992 IEEE International Conference on Systems, Man, and Cybernetics, vol. 1, pp. 842–847, October 1992

15. Chen, C.J.: The design, development and evaluation of a virtual reality-based learning environment. Australas. J. Educ. Technol. 22(1), 39–63 (2006)

16. Dede, C.: Introduction to virtual reality in education. Themes Sci. Technol. Educ. 2(1–2), 7–9 (2010)

17. Lee, J., Kim, M., Kim, J.: A study on immersion and VR sickness in walking interaction for immersive virtual reality applications. Symmetry 9(5), 78 (2017)

18. Huang, H.M., Liaw, S.S., Lai, C.M.: Exploring learner acceptance of the use of virtual reality in medical education: a case study of desktop and projection-based display systems. Interact. Learn. Environ. 24(1), 3–19 (2016)

19. Van Raaij, E.M., Schepers, J.J.: The acceptance and use of a virtual learning environment in china. Comput. Educ. 50(3), 838–852 (2008)

20. Norman, D.A.: Affordance, conventions, and design. Interactions 6(3), 38–43 (1999)

21. Sharma, S., Agada, R., Ruffin, J.: Virtual reality classroom as an constructivist approach. In: 2013 Proceedings of IEEE Southeastcon, IEEE, pp. 1–5 (2013)

22. Bailenson, J.N., Yee, N., Blascovich, J., Beall, A.C., Lundblad, N., Jin, M.: The use of immersive virtual reality in the learning sciences: digital transformations of teachers, students, and social context. J. Learn. Sci. 17(1), 102–141 (2008)

23. Tobias, S., Duffy, T.M.: Constructivist Instruction: Success or Failure? Routledge, New York (2009)

24. Kirschner, P.A., Sweller, J., Clark, R.E.: Why minimal guidance during instruction does not work: an analysis of the failure of constructivist, discovery, problem-based, experiential, and inquiry-based teaching. Educ. Psychol. 41(2), 75–86 (2006)

25. Kintsch, W.: Learning and constructivism. In: Constructivist Instruction. Routledge, pp. 235–253 (2009)

26. Callaghan, N.: Investigating the role of minecraft in educational learning environments. Educ. Media Int. 53(4), 244–260 (2016)

27. Schifter, C.C., Cipollone, M.: Constructivism vs constructionism: implications for minecraft and classroom implementation. In: Isaías, P., Spector, J.M., Ifenthaler, D., Sampson, D.G. (eds.) E-Learning Systems, Environments and Approaches, pp. 213–227. Springer, Cham (2015). https://doi.org/10.1007/978-3-319-05825-2_15

28. Huang, H.M., Rauch, U., Liaw, S.S.: Investigating learners' attitudes toward virtual reality learning environments: based on a constructivist approach. Comput. Educ. **55**(3), 1171–1182 (2010)
29. Piaget, J., Vigotsky, L.: Teorías del aprendizaje. Materia (2012)
30. Bermejo, V.: Aproximación al concepto de aprendizaje constructivista. Revista Candidus **3**(16) (2001)
31. Calzadilla, M.E.: Aprendizaje colaborativo y tecnologías de la información y la comunicación. Revista Iberoamericana de educación **29**(1), 1–10 (2002)
32. Chittaro, L., Ranon, R.: Web3d technologies in learning, education and training: motivations, issues, opportunities. Comput. Educ. **49**(1), 3–18 (2007)
33. Kohlberg, L., DeVries, R.: Constructivist Early Education: Overview and Comparison with Other Programs. National Association for the Education of Young Children, Washington, DC (1987)
34. Contreras, P.A.R., González, B.M., Paniagua, P.M.M.: El rol del estudiante en los ambientes educativos mediados por las tic. Revista Lasallista de investigación **12**(2), 132–138 (2015)
35. Pérez, F.O., Álvarez, F.J.A.: Los nuevos roles en entornos educativos extendidos en red: La experiencia de diseño de un entorno virtual de aprendizaje colaborativo orientado al desarrollo de proyectos colectivos en educación superior. REDU: Revista de Docencia Universitaria **11**(2), 353 (2013)
36. Llamozas, B.M., Fernández, M.P., Llorent-Bedmar, V.: Roles del docente y del alumno universitario desde las perspectivas de ambos protagonistas del hecho educativo. REDHECS: Revista Electrónica de Humanidades, Educación y Comunicación Social **9**(18), 273–293 (2014)
37. Council, N.R., et al.: Virtual Reality: Scientific and Technological Challenges. National Academies Press, Washington, DC (1995)
38. Burdea, G.C., Coiffet, P.: Virtual Reality Technology. Wiley, Hoboken (2003)
39. Sherman, W.R., Craig, A.B.: Understanding Virtual Reality: Interface, Application, and Design. Morgan Kaufmann, Amsterdam (2018)
40. McSharry, G., Jones, S.: Role-play in science teaching and learning. Sch. Sci. Rev. **82**, 73–82 (2000)
41. Bueno, P.M., Fitzgerald, V.L.: Aprendizaje basado en problemas problem-based learning. Theoría: Ciencia, Arte y Humanidades **13**, 145–157 (2004)
42. Parveen, S., Mattoo, M.I.: Teacher education in the age of globalization. Commun. **21**(2), 137 (2012)
43. Universidad Autonoma de Aguascalientes: Agenda Estadistica (2017). http://dei.dgpd.uaa.mx/agenda/index.php. Accessed 15 Oct 2019
44. Cuadro, E.I.D.: Uso de entornos virtuales de aprendizaje en la educación superior. Pro Sci. **1**(2), 12–14 (2017)
45. Robles, A.S., Vigil, M.Á.G.: Entornos virtuales de aprendizaje: Nuevos retos educativos. Revista científica electrónica de Educación y Comunicación en la Sociedad del Conocimiento **13**(2), 260–272 (2014)
46. Davis, F.D.: Perceived usefulness, perceived ease of use, and user acceptance of information technology. MIS Q. **13**, 319–340 (1989)

Developing Teachers' Didactic Analysis Competence by Means of a Problem-Posing Strategy and the Quality of Posed Mathematical Problems

Carlos Torres$^{(\boxtimes)}$ (iD)

Pontificia Universidad Católica del Perú, Lima, Peru
ctorresn@pucp.pe

Abstract. The study was designed to improve teachers' didactic analysis competence by means of problem-posing tasks and evaluate the quality of mathematical problems posed by them. For this purpose, a problem-posing strategy has been implemented which sample consisted of in-service mathematics teachers. This strategy involves a reflection stage that is very close to mathematical practices and it encourages to develop didactic analysis competence. The quality of the mathematical problems was evaluated through qualitative criteria. Some findings of the research are related to didactic analysis competence and it means that the posers could formulate better problems with educational purposes.

Keywords: Problem posing · Didactic analysis competence · Quadratic function · In-service mathematics teachers · Quality of mathematical problems

1 Introduction

Problem posing has long been recognized as a critically important intellectual activity in scientific investigation [1]. This importance has been reflected in the development of empirical investigations, where those whose focus of study is the didactic analysis competence in the teaching of mathematics based on problem posing (PP) tasks are more significant [2–4].

Problem-posing tasks demand a person to expose his mathematical knowledge. However, if the posed problem is aimed at contributing to the student's knowledge – or more specifically, to understanding and solving other more complex problems – then the teachers' didactic-mathematical knowledge must also intervene. This aspect is closely related to the teachers' didactic analysis competence, which has been broadly studied within the onto-semiotic approach of cognition and mathematics instruction (OSA) [5].

In the literature on mathematics education research, several studies analyze the relationship between the mathematics teachers' competence and the mathematical tasks for the learning of mathematics. For instance, [6] presented a review of the empirical research done on mathematics teachers, and it concluded that these researches show teachers have difficulties to analyze the mathematical tasks (and their educational potential) that their

© Springer Nature Switzerland AG 2020
K. O. Villalba-Condori et al. (Eds.): CISETC 2019, CCIS 1191, pp. 88–100, 2020.
https://doi.org/10.1007/978-3-030-45344-2_8

students propose. In order to overcome these difficulties, it is fundamental for teachers to have the ability to analyze their own mathematical tasks and we consider that our research provides specific means to do so, through problem-posing strategy with a phase of didactic reflection.

On the other hand, the quality of a mathematical problem is a subjective concept that cannot be measured in an objective way. However, it is mandatory to deep into this concept by means of quality criteria and suitability to have a picture of what are the indicators that a problem should have to be considered as a *good* problem from a didactic perspective. In this study, some theoretical tools from OSA framework are considered to approach to this concept through the notion of didactical suitability.

2   Theoretical Framework and Methodology

In this study, we consider two theoretical frameworks, which gave us some tools to analyze the data.

2.1   Onto-Semiotic Approach of Cognition and Mathematics Instruction (OSA)

We adopt the OSA as framework because we are interested in teachers' competences when analyzing the mathematical activities that they develop. Likewise, we believe it is relevant to use an approach that provides us with categories to analyze both teachers' mathematical knowledge and didactic knowledge. In this framework, didactic-mathematical knowledge is understood as the deepest knowledge of mathematics and its teaching, which a mathematics teacher must have to design, implement and assess the complex processes of mathematics teaching. In addition, important OSA theoretical constructs for the analysis of mathematical objects, such as concepts, procedures, propositions and arguments, are the epistemic and cognitive configurations, which we will explain next.

According to [7], when a person carries out a mathematical practice and assesses it, he or she has to activate a mixture composed by some or all of the mathematical objects, that is to say: problem situations, languages, propositions, definitions, procedures and arguments. These objects will be interrelated, making configurations defined as webs of objects that intervene and emerge from the systems of practice (Fig. 1); such configurations are *epistemic configurations* (EC) when they are webs of objects considered from an institutional perspective, and they are *cognitive configurations* (CC) when they are webs of objects considered from a personal perspective. Analyzing these configurations allows us to obtain relevant information about a problem and its solution. We call it *anatomy of the problem* because it can give us the different objects, which is involved in a mathematical problem, so the teachers could modify them according their educational purposes.

The Quality of a Mathematical Problem (A Didactic Perspective)

The quality of a mathematical problem can be understood from several perspectives. For instance, the analysis of the problem can be carried out from a qualitative perspective that focuses on its cognitive demand [8]. Or even more, this aspect can be deepened by restricting our analysis in the treatment of the mathematical objects that are immersed into the solution to the problem [4, 9]. This kind of research allows us to clarify the

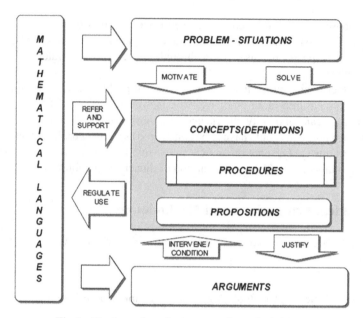

Fig. 1. Configuration of primary mathematical objects

quality of the problem based on its intentionality. Another approach implies a cognitive framework which could face the quality of the problem taking into consideration the cognitive load that requires its resolution. The cognitive load theory [10] explains it in greater depth. The notion of complexity could be another approach to analyze the quality of a mathematical problem. Thus, the complexity of the problem is determined by the conceptual density into the problem, which comprises the number of concepts and properties essential for its solution [11]. All of these perspectives involve some aspects related to the meaning of quality. However, we must focus our analysis in a general view to study this quality. It means to adopt an eclectic posture which should be closed to educational perspective.

In our study, we want to focus this quality on didactic perspective for the teaching and the learning of mathematics. According to [12], the characterization of the quality of a mathematical problem requires tools of description and explanation. This scholar presents a proposal, which takes into consideration the notion of didactical suitability of the OSA framework. This suitability can be subdivided into six specific categories [13]:

- Epistemic Suitability refers to the teaching of "good mathematics". In order to achieve this, in addition to considering the approved curriculum, the intention is to refer to institutional mathematics that have been incorporated into the curriculum.
- Cognitive Suitability refers to the extent to which applied/desired learning is within the parameters of the students' potential development, as well as the correlation between what the students indeed learn and the applied/desired learning.

- Interactional Suitability is the extent to which the means of interaction allow conflicts of meaning to be identified and resolved and how interaction methods favor autonomous learning.
- Mediational Suitability is the degree of availability and aptness of time and material resources necessary for the development of teaching-learning processes.
- Affective Suitability refers to the degree of the students' involvement (interest, motivation) in the study processes.
- Ecological Suitability is the extent to which the process of study is adapted to the center's educational project, the curricular norms and the social environment etc.

As we mentioned before, [12] uses these six specific categories to formulate some property indicators and describe the quality of a mathematical problem. Here we present these indicators related to a "good" mathematical problem from a didactic perspective:

- The difficulty is not too great and it is perceived by the student that the solution is achievable. (Cognitive Suitability)
- It favors to an intuitive way to obtain the solution or to conjecture a solution. (Interactional Suitability, Affective Suitability and Cognitive Suitability)
- It favors making some verifiers, eventually with the help of a calculator or computers for maintaining or rejecting the conjectures. (Interactional Suitability and Mediational Suitability)
- It is perceived by the student that it is interesting or useful to solve the problem. (Affective Suitability and Ecological Suitability)

Taking in mind those six categories that contain the didactic suitability, we highlight the epistemic, cognitive and ecological suitability. This choice is justified in the conception taken from [14], because the importance of the cognitive aspect of problem posing activities for a curricular design that considers these activities as a means to improve the learning and the teaching of mathematics. Moreover, it implies stronger cognitive demand. Likewise, [14] state that the problem posing tasks allow developing more elaborate and advanced problem solving strategies. This last aspect, we think, corresponds very well with the epistemic and ecological suitability.

2.2 Problem Posing and Mathematics Teachers' Didactic Analysis Competence

It is worth mentioning that there are different positions in terms of what researchers understand by engaging in problem posing activities [1]. In our study, we adopt the proposal from [15], according to which problem posing is a process through which a new problem is formulated. Moreover, in this proposal, if the new problem is obtained by modifying a given problem, it is said that the new problem was obtained by *variation*. At the same time, if the new problem is obtained from a given situation or from a specific requirement, whether mathematical or didactic, it is said that the new problem was obtained by *elaboration*. Taking into consideration our research goals, we focus in the first one, it means getting new problems by variation. Likewise, these scholars consider that problems have four fundamental elements: information, requirement, context and mathematical environment; in that sense, problem posing by variation entails quantitative or qualitative modifications of one or more of these elements in a given problem. We analyzed these elements in problem posed by in-service teachers.

Additionally, [3, 15] implemented a strategy in workshops with in-service teachers in order to stimulate their ability to pose problems by variation. This is the EPP strategy since it stands for Episode, Pre-problem and Post-problem, by considering the problem posing by variation, where there were evidences that mathematics teachers lack didactic analysis competence to pose problems with didactical purposes. In this sense, given the importance that mathematics teachers must develop this competence, especially when they pose mathematics problems with emphasis on teaching, in our study we implement the EPP strategy for problem posing by considering a phase (R) of metacognitive and didactic reflection; therefore, the strategy name would be ERPP. In the new strategy ERPP, there is a phase where the teachers must elaborate a CC of their solutions to the problem presented in the episode (episode problem (EP)) and – based on it – reflect on their practices. In the next lines, we propose some phases for implementing this new strategy.

3 Method

In this research, we used a multiple case study with 16 in-service high school mathematics teachers who participated in a problem-posing workshop. Our study is exploratory, descriptive and analytical, taking as unit of analysis the problems posed by the teachers participating in the workshop. We analyse these problems using OSA tools, it means EC and CC for solving and posing practices. The use of EC and CC is a methodology previously used in some researches done in the OSA framework [2, 16], with the aim of examining the mathematical solutions of pupils. In addition, we evaluate the quality of the mathematical problem using the expert triangulation, which qualifies it by means of the four indicators.

3.1 Problem-Posing Workshop on Quadratic Function

In our study, we implemented the ERPP strategy in the *Problem-Posing Workshop on Quadratic Functions* that purpose goes on to stimulate the development of the ability to pose problems by varying a given problem. We focused our attention on pre-problem posing, since it requires didactic criteria from the person proposing the problem, so it should have the characteristic to facilitate the comprehension and resolution of a previously given problem.

In the next lines, we summarize the dynamics of the problem-posing workshop.

- *First session*: a test on quadratic functions was applied which purpose was to go deep into participants' mathematical competence. In addition, a class episode on affine function that we designed in a previous research [3] was presented. Indeed, this episode includes an EP on affine function. Moreover, in this session an EC associated to EP of this class episode was discussed which objective was to initiate the participants on their CCs elaboration.

- *Second session*: Based on their solution for the EP on affine function, the participants elaborated their CC associated to it, later they reflected on their mathematical practices of solving through a previously elaborated questionnaire. At the end of this session, some CC were socialized.
- *Third session*: Another class episode was presented. The participants solved the EP that is involved in this episode and elaborated their CC based on their solution to episode problem (CCPe). Then, the EP solution and some CCPe were analyzed in detail between all of the participants. Subsequently, they were asked to pose and solve a pre-problem (P1) considering the student's reactions to the EP, as well they were asked to elaborate the CC of the solution to P1 (CCPp1). Afterward, each participant reflected individually about his or her mathematical practices related to problem posing. To reinforce the didactical reflection, the participants formed pairs to discuss the pre-problems posed and their CCPp1. For digging into this reflection, it was conducted by the researchers taking into account a comparison between CCPe and the CCPp1 for each participant. Next, some P1 and the results of their reflection process were socialized with the intention of broadening the problems analysis with didactical emphasis among the assistants.
- *Fourth session*: The participants were asked to pose another pre-problem (P2) associated to the reflection made on P1 and its CCPp1. After a specified time, the participants, working individually and then in pairs, reflected on the P2. As the culmination of the workshop, some P2 were socialized.

Considering teachers' didactic experiences in teaching functions in high school, the research team selected the following episode, in order to present it to the teachers participating in the workshop. This episode includes some comments from students whom aged between 14 and 15 years old and they were exposed to the episode problem:

Mr. Pérez proposed the following problem to eighth-grade students in a mathematics class on functions:

Find a pair of numbers whose sum is 43 and their product is the maximum possible. Solve the problem and explain your procedure in detail.

After a few minutes, some students commented:

Pedro: The numbers are 21 and 22.

Isabel: You cannot know the maximum product.

Santiago: What good does it do for me to solve this problem?

An expert solution was adopted for the problem, and the EC of such solution was made in order to have it as a reference to analyse and compare it to the CC of the participants' solutions (CCPp1).

3.2 Expert Solution and EC of the Episode Problem (ECPe)

The expert solution to this problem implies defining a function that allows us to obtain a pair of numbers which sum is known and which product must be the maximum. In this way, the function $f(x) = x(43 - x)$ is defined, where *"x" and "43 − x"* are numbers

Table 1. Epistemic configuration of the solution to the episode problem (ECPe).

Languages
• **Expressions:** First number, second number, maximum, product function, completing squares, concave, function, product, first component, vertex, abscissa, parabola, represents, sum.
• **Verbal representations:** Number, function, maximum, product, parabola, vertex.
• **Symbolic representations:** 43, x, 43-x,, =, 2, /, 1849, 4, f (x), 43/2, (;), 0
• **Graphic representations**

Problem-situation
• **Information:** The sum of two numbers is 43.
• **Requirement:** Find two numbers that meet the given information, whose product is maximum.
• **Context:** Intramathematical
• **Mathematical environment:** quadratic functions, linear equation

Concepts
Function, vertex, graph of a quadratic function, linear equation

Propositions
• Since the product of two numbers must be the maximum, the function is defined $f(x) = x(43 - x)$
• Since f is a concave quadratic function it will have maximum for $x = \dfrac{43}{2}$
• The abscissa of the parabola's vertex is the maximum value that f can take.
• The maximum is at the top of the inverted parabola and corresponds to the point $\left(\dfrac{43}{2} ; \dfrac{1849}{4}\right)$

Procedures
• The information behind of the problem is identified.
• The variable "x" and function f are defined: $f(x) = x(43 - x)$.
• Complete the square is applied to find the maximum of the function.
• The result is interpreted considering the concavity of the parabola that represents the function under the conditions of the problem.
• The linear equation $x - \dfrac{43}{2} = 0$ is posed to obtain the abscissa that maximizes the function.
• The graph of the product function is outlined and interpreted to respond to the problem.

Arguments
Thesis
The product function $f(x) = x(S - x)$ would have maximum if $x = \dfrac{S}{2}$
Argument
Using complete square technique, we can represent product function in another algebraic expression: $$f(x) = -\left(x - \frac{S}{2}\right)^2 + \frac{S^2}{4}$$ Now, since the function is a quadratic function, the graph for this will be a concave parabola. So the maximum is when $x = \dfrac{S}{2}$.

which product must be maximum. Therefore, both numbers are equal to 43/2 and their product is 1849/4. On the other hand, this answer can also be found by associating the number to the value of the abscissa that maximizes the function f. Another strategy for solving this problem, entails relating the vertex of the parabola that represents f, so the vertex would be the coordinates of the point (43/2, 1849/4). This last strategy makes use of the graphic representation of the function.

While elaborating the EC of the solution to the episode problem (see Table 1), we could recognize different mathematical objects whose area involved in the mathematical practices. They are the languages used (verbal, symbolic and graphic representations); the information, requirement, context and mathematical environment; the concepts involved (quadratic function, linear equation, the maximum of a quadratic function, vertex, parabola, graphs of functions). Also, the emerging proposition (the function given by $f(x) = x(S - x)$ will have a maximum for $x = S/2$, where S is the sum of the two numbers), the procedure which follows to the solution and the arguments explained to tell the truth about the given proposition, which derives in the conclusion. All of them are explicitly stated.

4 Analysis of Data

In relation to the solutions of EP, it was observed that most of the teachers consider the quadratic function as an object associated with the problem and this is closer to what was posed in the expert solution. From the sample, only 12 of the participants solved the problem correctly. In addition, it is significant that, even though 10 participants define a variable for solving the problem, 6 of them make explicit the function to be maximized. On the other hand, in order to find the maximum value of the function, 5 use the completing square strategy, while 5 do it by using the algorithm to find the vertex of the quadratic function and, as a result, to study its corresponding maximum. Three participants solved the problem with the support of a table of values. However, a teacher used the table partially. It gave us an idea to state that he or she recognized the numeric sequence related to the problem. Precisely, the use of the tables led some teachers (4) to make their analysis in the set of natural numbers and to fail the correct answer.

By analyzing in a qualitative way the CCPe made by the teachers, it was observed that most of them recognized the mathematical objects, at least partially. However, only some of the participants were able to elaborate with greater certainty the objects so-called propositions and arguments. In the same way the lack of robustness in their propositions and/or arguments, correspond to a lack of practice in the analysis of their mathematical chore, and by extension we can say that they lack or they do not show the competence of the didactic analysis.

On the other hand, the P1 were categorized by using the analysis of content and the methodology of expert triangulation. From this categorization, based on the ECPp1 and CCPp1, we can say that most of the participants have an idea of function typified by an epistemic configuration focused in formalist approach instead of empiricist approach [17]. This tendency is showed in posed problems as well, where intra-mathematical environment prevails.

4.1 Case of Study: Teacher T11

Because of space limitations, in this paper we only present the case of a teacher that hereinafter we will call T11 and in this section, we analyze ECPe and ECPp1.

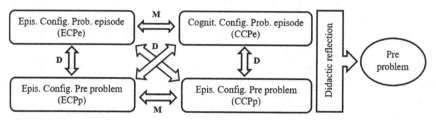

Fig. 2. Scheme to compare configurations

For the analysis of the configurations and the reflection on the mathematical practices of solving and posing for this case, we used a scheme (Fig. 2) according to the strategy ERPP. In this scheme it is shown the interaction among different configurations, whether epistemic or cognitive, in order to study the mathematical competence (M) or didactic analysis competence (D) of the teacher. In this context, looking forward to our interests, we focus on studying the interactions involving the competence in didactic analysis (D).

As an example of the pre-problem posing task, we present the first pre-problem posed by T11 (associated to CCPp1):

Determine the pair of numbers whose sum will be, respectively, 1, 2, 3, ..., 10; but in such a way that the product of that pair's components will be the maximum possible. (a) On the basis of what was observed, could you indicate which are the features that, in each case, the pair of numbers must meet? (b) If you must formulate each product as a mathematical function, express it.

Along with the problem posed, T11 showed a possible solution to his problem and it allowed us to move into not very explicit aspects of the problem (Fig. 3). Likewise, the teacher elaborated the CCPp1. Finally, he answered the questionnaire about the mathematical practice of posing.

4.2 Analysis: ECPe and ECPp1

From the analysis of ECPe and ECPp1, it was observed that the information is similar and that it was only modified quantitatively. Even though it is true that the amount of pairs of numbers is greater, these are more manageable numbers for a high school student. In the same way, the requirement suffered a change, since in the P1 there are two questions that invite the student to reflect on his/her procedures and solution.

In addition, the problems keep up the intra-mathematical context. In order to answer the requirement of the EP it becomes necessary to use algebraic expressions, however, in P1 posed by T11, it is not necessary to use this resource, except in part "b" in which the notion of generalization using functions is a request. This would be an advantage from the didactic point of view in order to solve the EP, without using the quadratic function.

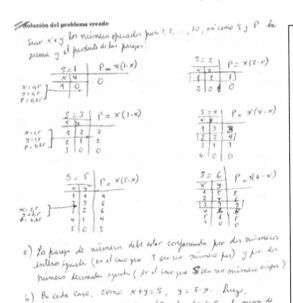

Translation:

Let us call "x" and "y" the possible numbers which sum and product are S and P respectively, so...

a) The pair of numbers should be two equal integers numbers (if S is an even number) and equal decimal numbers (if S is an odd number).

b) In each case, x+y=S and y=S-x. Then, P(x)=x(S-x), where S is the sum of the numbers.

Fig. 3. Solution to PP1 proposed by T11

Based on an expert solution to P1 and the solution proposed by T11, we state the following: for the language, in general terms, the use of graphical representations is highlighted: the parabola for EP and the table of values for P1. Likewise, in EP and P1 the requirement of maximum is evident. Thus it becomes explicit the use of the quadratic function in P1 regarding EP. Unlike P1, in EP it is necessary to use linear equations to formalize and give rigor to the problem solution. For the considered concepts in both configurations, it is easy to see the coincidence in many of them, like the case of the concepts of function, product of function, the idea of maximum of a function, completing squares, among others.

The propositions and arguments in the EP are more formal and rigorous. In P1, the fundamental feature of the propositions and arguments has a lower level of formality, in such way that allows using the inductive and deductive reasoning easily. As a sample to highlight this reasoning, T1 suggests a table of values in order to recognize a pattern that will allow solving the EP easily.

Talking about the procedures, the use of similar strategies is emphasized, in the sense that both problems require the identification of the main information and requirements. However, in P1, the situation becomes more intuitive, since it is not required to formulate a correspondence rule to solve it, except for the explicit requirement. Certainly, in EP there is no need of this, but due to reasons of effectiveness.

The arguments of the EP are more rigorous and formal, since they use concepts that are closer to the quadratic function, for example: concavity, vertex of a quadratic function. Moreover, in P1 the arguments are closer to an inductive reasoning, since the plan is to elaborate a strategy that makes the solution to the EP. For this last case, the use of a value table will permit to guess the practical rule that emerges as consequence of the analysis of the given values and that is one of the purposes of the problem.

4.3 Approaching to a Didactical Problem Posed by Quantitative Variation

The teacher T11 was asked to reformulate his pre-problem (P1), considering a didactic analysis of the problem posing process through the comparison between CCPe and CCPp1. Thus, T11 posed a second pre-problem (P2) that was analyzed by expert triangulation taking into consideration the four indicators explained in the Sect. 2.1. Next comes the problem P2:

> Determine the pair of numbers whose sum will be, respectively, 5 y 6, in such way that the product of the pair's components will be the maximum as possible. Elaborate a table for the next cases: (a) For the case whose sum is 6, which are the components of the pair of numbers whose product is maximum? (b) For the case whose sum is 5, is there just one pair of numbers whose product is maximum? Explain your answer. (c) If we consider that there is just one pair of non-natural numbers whose sum is 5 and whose product is maximum and it is not a natural number, which are those numbers? (d) Elaborate a strategy in order to obtain the maximum product, in case of the sum of the pairs' components will be an even number. Is this strategy different in case of the sum will be an odd number? Explain your answer. (d) Formulate the product of the numbers whose sum is 5 as a mathematical function.

From the expert triangulation, there is evidence to say that the P2 posed by T11 has the features of a pre-problem, since it makes easier to conjecture a pattern that allows to solve the EP. It is also observed that it was well conceived and detailed in order to achieve subsequently a solution of the EP easily. Thus part "c" fosters an intuitive solution, against the part "d" that invites to the generalization. The section (e) would be a simple exercise that helps a lot to think about how to solve the EP. In addition, we claim that the problem posed has a closer approach to cognitive, interactional, affective and epistemic suitability. This statement is made based on the experts' opinion under the indicators proposed for evaluating the quality of a mathematical problem from a didactic perspective. Moreover, following the answers given by T11 in the post-workshop questionnaire, it is observed that he makes an explanation of the benefits of his problem, using the elements of his configuration and considering its didactic emphasis. Precisely, these aspects are highlighted by the experts when they analyzed the pre-problem posed by T11.

5 Final Consideration

At this time, in the mathematical education field, there are several theories and theoretical approaches for researching. A reason for the existence of different theories and theoretical approaches is the complexity of the topic of research itself [18]. We belief that with our study, we contribute in a way to use different theories for analyzing the mathematical practices of solving and posing problems. Indeed, our proposal to use theoretical notions from OSA and the conception of problem posing tasks gave us evidence for promoting the didactic analysis competence. This competence is crucial and its core represents an advance in teacher education.

Our study proposes a new problem-posing strategy that includes EC and CC tools taken from the OSA framework to analyze the teacher's mathematical practices. Because of this implementation, we have evidence to state that in-service teachers' didactic analysis competence shows to be incipient and urge to develop it. Certainly, our position about the conception of the didactic analysis complements that proposal of [19, 20], it implies *the subject–didactical competence* and the *competence of reflection*, since we consider a strategy for problem posing which includes individual and group reflections taking into account the posed problem using a phase of didactic reflection. Therefore, there is a need of going deeper in our study.

The use of indicators to evaluate the mathematical problems from a didactic perspective is important and relevant, in such a way that it collaborates with the decision-making process for didactic reflection before or after the problem posing process. We can state, based on the data analysis, that the reflection stage is more enriching and profound for education of prospective teachers.

References

1. Cai, J., Hwang, S., Jiang, C., Silber, S.: Problem-posing research in mathematics education: some answered and unanswered questions. In: Singer, F.M., Ellerton, N.F., Cai, J. (eds.) Mathematical Problem Posing. RME, pp. 3–34. Springer, New York (2015). https://doi.org/10.1007/978-1-4614-6258-3_1
2. Torres, C., Malaspina, U.: Improving in-service teachers' problem posing skill by means of didactic reflection. In: Berqvist, E., Österholm, M., Granberg, C., Sumpter, L. (eds.) Proceedings of the 42nd Conference International Group for the Psychology of Mathematics Education, vol. 5, p. 176. PME, Umeå (2018)
3. Malaspina, U., Torres, C., Rubio, N.: How to stimulate in-service teachers' didactic analysis competence by means of problem posing. In: Liljedahl, P., Santos-Trigo, M. (eds.) Mathematical Problem Solving. IM, pp. 133–151. Springer, Cham (2019). https://doi.org/10.1007/978-3-030-10472-6_7
4. Malaspina, U., Torres, C.: Teaching of discontinuous functions of one or two variables: a didactic experience using problem posing and levels of cognitive demand. In: Jankvist, U.T., van den Heuvel-Panhuizen, M., Veldhuis, M. (eds.) Proceedings of the Eleventh Congress of the European Society for Research in Mathematics Education. Freudenthal Group & Freudenthal Institute, Utrecht University and ERME, Utrecht (2019)
5. Breda, A., Pino-Fan, L., Font, V.: Establishing criteria for teachers' reflection on their own practices. In: Csíkos, C., Rausch, A., Szitányi, J. (eds.) Proceedings of the 40th Conference of the International Group for the Psychology of Mathematics Education, vol. 1, pp. 283. PME, Szeged (2016)
6. Stahnke, R., Schueler, S., Roesken-Winter, B.: Teachers' perception, interpretation, and decision-making: a systematic review of empirical mathematics education research. ZDM Int. J. Math. Educ. **48**(1), 1–27 (2016)
7. Godino, J.D., Batanero, C., Font, V.: The onto-semiotic approach to research in mathematics education. ZDM Int. J. Math. Educ. **39**(1–2), 127–135 (2007)
8. Smith, M.S., Stein, M.K.: Selecting and creating mathematical tasks: from research to practice. Math. Teach. Middle Sch. **3**(5), 344–350 (1998)

9. Gutierrez, A., Benedicto, C., Jaime, A., Arbona, E.: The cognitive demand of a gifted student's answers to geometric pattern problems. In: Singer, F.M. (ed.) Mathematical Creativity and Mathematical Giftedness. IM, pp. 169–198. Springer, Cham (2018). https://doi.org/10.1007/978-3-319-73156-8_7

10. Sweller, J.: Cognitive load during problem solving: effects on learning. Cogn. Sci. **12**, 257–285 (1988)

11. Silver, E.A., Zawojewski, J.S.: Benchmarks of Students' Understanding (BOSUN) Project: Technical Guide. University of Pittsburgh, Pittsburgh (1997)

12. Malaspina, U.: Intuición y rigor en la resolución de problemas de optimización. Un análisis desde el Enfoque Ontosemiótico de la Cognición e Instrucción Matemática. [Intuition and rigour in the solving of optimization problems. Analysis based on the ontosemiotic approach to mathematical cognition.] Unpublished Doctoral dissertation. Pontificia Universidad Católica del Perú (2008)

13. Breda, A., Pino-Fan, L.R., Font, V.: Meta didactic-mathematical knowledge of teachers: criteria for the reflection and assessment on teaching practice. EURASIA J. Math. Sci. Technol. Educ. **13**(6), 1893–1918 (2017)

14. Cai, J., Moyer, J.C., Wang, N., Hwang, S., Nie, B., Garber, T.: Mathematical problem posing as a measure of curricular effect on students learning. Educ. Stud. Math. **83**(1), 57–69 (2013)

15. Malaspina, U., Mallart, A., Font, V.: Development of teachers' mathematical and didactic competencies by means of problem posing. In: Krainer, K., Vondrová, N. (eds.) Proceedings of the Ninth Congress of the European Society for Research in Mathematics Education (CERME 9), pp. 2861–2866. ERME, Prague (2015)

16. Badillo, E., Font, V., Edo, M.: Analyzing the responses of 7–8 year olds when solving partitioning problems. Int. J. Sci. Math. Educ. **13**, 811–836 (2015)

17. Font, V., Godino, J.D.: La noción de configuración epistémica como herramienta de análisis de textos matemáticos: Su uso en la formación de profesores. (The notion of epistemic configuration as a tool for the analysis of mathematical texts: Its use in teacher preparation). Educaçao Matemática Pesquisa **8**(1), 67–98 (2006)

18. Bikner-Ahsbahs, A., Prediger, S. (eds.): Networking of Theories as a Research Practice in Mathematics Education. AME. Springer, Cham (2014). https://doi.org/10.1007/978-3-319-05389-9

19. Tichá, M., Hošpesová, A.: Developing teachers' subject didactic competence through problem posing. Educ. Stud. Math. **83**(1), 133–143 (2013)

20. Torres, C., Malaspina, U.: Developing teachers' didactic analysis competence by means of problem-posing. In: Villalba-Condori, K.O., Adúriz-Bravo, A., García-Peñalvo, F.J., Lavonen, J. (eds.) Proceeding of the Congreso Internacional Sobre Educación y Tecnología en Ciencias - CISETC 2019, Arequipa, Perú, 10–12 December 2019, pp. 234–243. CEUR-WS.org, Aachen (2019)

Enhancing Local Environmental Education in Schools in Arequipa by Means of an Environmental Atlas

Carlos Zeballos-Velarde[1]([⊠]) [iD] and Jonathan Quiroz Valdivia[2] [iD]

[1] Universidad Católica San Pablo, Urb. Campiña Paisajista s/n, Arequipa, Peru
crzeballos@ucsp.edu.pe
[2] Universidad Católica Santa María, Urb. San Jose s/n, Yanahuara, Peru

Abstract. Faced with the palpable effects of climate change among many other environmental situations, many governments have put emphasis on environmental education in schools, in order to raise awareness in youth about the importance of these problems. However, there is a gap between the knowledge imparted in school texts developed in a national level, and the real knowledge and awareness of the local situation by students. This article seeks to identify this breach by conducting research on university students in Arequipa, Peru. Subsequently a methodological framework for the development of the Environmental Atlas of Arequipa is devised, as an educational tool to complement local environmental education. Finally, strategies are proposed for the dissemination and use of such atlas as a massive instrument for urban environmental education in Arequipa.

Keywords: Environmental education · Environmental awareness · Environmental atlas · Arequipa

1 Introduction

Citizen participation at all levels is key for the development of successful environmental management, as well as for the commitment of the population to solve environmental problems and to increase resilience in society [1]. Education is very important and effective way to foster participation and in raising awareness about increasing resilience, especially when it is based on knowing and solving local problems through interactions between learners and their biophysical environment [2]. Both an integral education and an effective environmental management need access to systematized, accessible and understandable information: however, in countries of the Global South, this information is usually inaccessible, dispersed, is very technical or simply does not exist. It is also necessary to give a new approach to environmental education, by incorporating local issues into the discussion on global environmental issues that are typically taught in schools. This approach will allow to modify attitudes and collective behaviors [3], which will be easier and more effective by the use of massive communication tools [4].

Environmental education in Peru has made significant progress through the implementation of the National Environmental Education Plan (PLANEA), designed to

© Springer Nature Switzerland AG 2020
K. O. Villalba-Condori et al. (Eds.): CISETC 2019, CCIS 1191, pp. 101–113, 2020.
https://doi.org/10.1007/978-3-030-45344-2_9

encourage the discussion of problems such as climate change, health, risk management and environmental efficiency in schools throughout the country. This has motivated awareness and even youth activism on environmental issues.

However, local environmental problems are much less known by the community, given the lack of available information or simply the absence of it. In particular, many university students, although they have empathy for matters concerning ecology, are unaware of both the characteristics, the magnitude and the location of the environmental problems of their locality, particularly in the case of areas away from the capital. This is due, partially, because school texts used for learning are developed mainly in Lima and do not address situations at the regional, provincial or metropolitan level, and also because of the lack of systematized and organized information that can be easily known by the community.

The lack of an integral knowledge of the local problems has important effects on the city's environmental deterioration and its low resilience. Given this situation, this research aims to establish the degree of awareness, in terms of attitudes and behaviors, as well as the spatial knowledge of environmental problems, by university students in Arequipa.

Subsequently, a methodology is proposed to create a mass education tool such as an environmental atlas, as well as to develop a strategy to disseminate this document among the community, particularly in the city's schools.

2 An Overview of National and Local Environmental Education

In 2015 the UN defined 17 global objectives as part of the new sustainable development agenda, which seeks to eradicate poverty, protect the planet and ensure the prosperity of all its inhabitants in a period of 15 years [5]. Although the Sustainable Development Goals (SDGs) are interrelated, "Sustainable Cities" seeks "to make cities and human settlements inclusive, safe, resilient and sustainable" [6].

In this regard, environmental education is key to achieve sustainable development. However, there is a difference between education about and education for the environment. While education about the environment is driven by contents, education for the environment enables students to think critically about environmental issues and take measures to address such situations [7]. Similarly, it is suggested that education can not only be about resilience as a concept, but can also guide students to build resilience within their own local surroundings, their neighborhood, their school or any other social-ecological system where they live. Critical thinking and the proactive attitude of action inherent to education for the environment, as well as skills that address resilience qualities such as the capability to include multiple sources of knowledge and perceptions in managing decision making, would be important in an education that is designed to build resilience [2].

In Peru, the development of the National Environmental Education Plan (PLANEA) has been promoted through collaboration between the Ministry of Education and the Ministry of Environment [8]. This process was carried out in a participatory fashion and was validated in several workshops and meetings with a large attendance of stakeholders from public entities (ministries, regional and local governments, etc.), private institutions (companies, universities, NGOs, etc.) as well as civil society organizations (rural and indigenous communities, environmental volunteer networks, etc.).

PLANEA is composed of four themes: (a) Climate change education, aimed at increasing awareness and capacity to adapt to climate change, (b) Health education, which aims at improving healthy lifestyles in the educational community, (c) Eco-efficiency education, to develop skills in research, business participation and applicability of progressive control of environmental impacts and (d) Education in risk management, in order to promote a culture of prevention and adaptation.

Among the most effective methods to foster local education and environmental management at various levels are the environmental atlases, which are specialized compendiums that address, define and discuss the main characteristics of a given place. One of the first experiences of developing an environmental Atlas was in Porto Alegre, Rio Grande do Sul, Brazil [9], a city where several environmental and participatory policies had already been developed. Published in the year 2000, the Atlas systematized the city's environmental information, becoming an important instrument for city planning. At the same time, the atlas became an effective means to disseminate local environmental information among citizens, particularly teachers and schools in Porto Alegre, promoting active citizen participation [10]. Over the course of 2 decades, the atlas has contributed to the construction of an environmental identity in schools, building concepts of value of its communities, improving the knowledge of the city's problems and contributing to the conception of solutions by its citizens [11]. After 20 years of its publication, the Environmental Atlas of Porto Alegre has been digitized and is available for consultation on the web for free, although it does not have the characteristics of a geo-digital platform, and it is only an online book, it is a reliable source reachable by anyone [12].

After this successful experience, the Education Program for Urban Management in Peru (PEGUP) [13], in agreement with the IHS and ITC institutes from the Netherlands, developed Environmental Atlases in Arequipa, Lima, and Trujillo, having as a counterpart to the municipalities of these cities. An atlas draft was developed in Arequipa, but for political reasons, it was never published by the municipality. However, it served as a model for the environmental atlases of Lima (on a provincial scale) [14] and Trujillo (on a provincial and metropolitan scale) [15], which were indeed published. These publications served used as a reference in various research projects of these cities. In the case of the environmental atlas of Lima, citizenship education and awareness were encouraged, for which it was distributed freely to several universities, to several public schools and to the district municipalities [16]. This atlas was a high-quality technical tool, but unfortunately, its dissemination was not continued again for political reasons.

3 Materials and Methods

Several methods have been used in order to address each of the research questions.

3.1 Characteristics of School Textbooks

Various school textbooks on Science and Technology were reviewed, verifying their content on environmental issues and their degree of specificity at national, regional or local level. Students were also interviewed about the importance of these books in developing their awareness of environmental problems.

3.2 Knowledge of University Students About Environmental Problems in Arequipa

(a) Evaluation of attitudes and behaviors on environmental issues

An electronic data collection sheet was created using a Google form (https://forms.gle/vK7KGiy92ryjk6ob9). The instrument evaluated sociodemographic variables such as age, academic training, attitudes and behaviors on environmental issues by the population surveyed.

Questions such as: "I am concerned about the amount of waste produced in Peru". "More land should be reserved for wild habitats" or "I think I can contribute to the solution of environmental problems" were included for evaluating attitudes. Questions such as "I strive to reduce the number of products I consume", "I avoid buying products that have a negative impact on the environment", or "I recycle paper, glass and/or metal waste products at home or at school" were included for the evaluation of behaviors. Subsequently, a sum of every graded question was made according to attitudes and behaviors. The survey was distributed through the use of social networks. Likewise, the evaluation of the results was carried out using the Excel software and SPSS Statistics.

The Likert scale was used to calculate the results, which were then converted into percentages and analyzed under the following ranges; group A, including percentages greater than 60, which indicates a highly developed environmental culture. Group B comprised percentages between 50 and 60, representing a moderately developed environmental culture and group C involved percentages lower than 50 indicating very little awareness on environmental issues.

(b) Evaluation of the spatial situation of the environmental problems of Arequipa

A graphic survey was carried out with 4 maps requesting the identification and graphing of points or areas of (a) risk of disasters (b) environmental problems in the Chili River (c) urban heat islands (d) loss of green areas. Although in recent years the massive use of geographic applications such as Google Maps and others based on maps has developed a lot of spatial knowledge, especially in young generations, a group of first-year architecture students from different realities and socioeconomic strata were chosen for the survey. Architecture students receive training in spatial knowledge and thus the potential cartographic illiteracy was not an obstacle to express their ideas on a map.

Subsequently, the maps were digitized into ArcGIS, converted to raster format and then, overlaid through map algebra, in order to identify which were the areas that most students perceived as problematic. Finally, these maps were contrasted with official ones produced by the municipality.

3.3 Methodological Framework of Environmental Atlas of Arequipa

In order to compile and systematized different types of information, Geographic Information Systems were used as a powerful analysis and modeling tool [17] that promotes research and a better understanding of several environmental issues [18, 19]. After defining cartographic base maps at a provincial and metropolitan level, the different themes were compiled in a geodatabase, which was standardized and georeferenced in the WGS84 Projected Coordinate System and the 18S zone. According to the kind of information, 2 types of maps produced:

1. **Cartographic representation:** obtained from primary sources, whether national, international or self-produced.

   (a) Vector maps: Made up of a georeferenced vector graphic component (points, lines or areas) and a database [20].
   (b) Satellite photographs: were obtained from various international sources such as USGS /NASA's Global Explorer, and used as background for contextual reference.
   (c) Creation of ortho-mosaics: Historical aerial photographs have been ortho-referenced and re-projected because they have a photographic distortion as they approach the edge of the image, due to the angle generated by the surface photographed with the aircraft [21].

2. **Scientific analysis based on GIS:** In these cases where new information was produced through a GIS operation.

   (a) Statistical analysis: made of the combination of vector maps or raster image analysis.
   (b) Point density maps: characterize the pattern of point distribution and its agglomeration variations with respect to the study area [22], simplifying a large amount of information and show the trends of a given point map, based on its concentration or dispersion.
   (c) NDVI multispectral analysis: For the analysis of Landsat 8 satellite images, the ENVI program has been used, which allows the study of the different bands that make up a multispectral image. A map algebra correction, a radiometric correction, and an atmospheric correction were made by the FLAASH method. Finally, spectral indexes were used to generate the NDVI image.
   (d) MODIS multi-temporal vegetation change analysis. Images from the same month of two different years are used, using the MOD13Q1 product of the MODIS satellite. Map algebra was used to subtract the most recent image from the oldest and later reclassified to determine the gains and losses of the vegetation cover.

(e) Temperature maps based on satellite imagery and drone survey: allows verifying the surface temperature and urban heat islands. The TIR (Thermal Infrared) image of Landsat 8 was selected, the respective projection, the radiometric, and atmospheric corrections and finally the conversion of Kelvin degrees to Celsius were made in order to show the location of heat islands on a macro scale. For a microanalysis a Flir Duo camera mounted on a drone has been used, in order to determine the air temperature, humidity, atmospheric conditions and emissivity.

4 Results

4.1 Characteristics of School Texts

For this research, books of the Science, Technology and Environment course, produced by Bruño Publishing and Santillana Publishing were reviewed. The texts addressed environmental issues in a graphic and didactic way, but their scope was global and their specificity level was general. The texts are aimed at creating environmental awareness in the student, but not to develop a critical and proactive attitude towards problems. In conversation with the students, they referred to some activities carrying within the course, such as classifying products for recycling, activities that are important but are applicable to any reality, and not developing an understanding of the real problems of the locality. The revised materials referred to environmental issues globally and, very occasionally, at a national level at most.

4.2 Perception Surveys

(a) Evaluation of attitudes and behaviors on environmental issues

Data were collected from 282 people, which were processed and systematized according to their professional background [23–25]. They were distributed as follows; 45.65% corresponds to university and college students, and 54.3478% corresponds to graduates and professionals (Table 1).

Table 1. Data analysis.

Educational level	Component	Average	Standard deviation
University/college students	Attitudes	48.8%	6.893
	Behaviors	58.9%	15.832
Graduates/professionals	Attitudes	47.6%	6.474
	Behaviors	62.5%	15.339

Universities and college students are placed in category C regarding their attitudes and B as for their behaviors, with a medium to low environmental awareness (Fig. 1).

UNIVERSITY STUDENTS

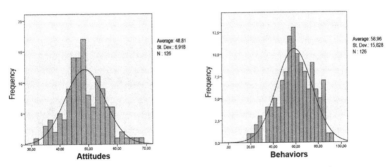

Fig. 1. Attitudes and behaviors in university and college students

Also, most professionals belong in category A regarding behavior, which means that in their actions demonstrate positive behaviors with the environment, but they have less positive attitudes, as they fall into category B (Fig. 2).

PROFESSIONALS

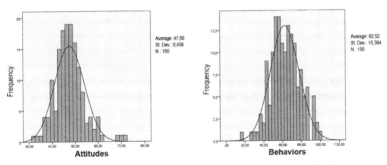

Fig. 2. Attitudes and behaviors in graduates and professionals

The results indicate that among the interviewees there is an interest and empathy for environmental issues. However, there is a lack of knowledge about the environmental problems that afflict the city. Bad practices are also evidenced in terms of environmental awareness. Having small improvement in these behaviors by large numbers of people can have a great positive impact on society.

(b) Evaluation of the spatial situation of the environmental problems of Arequipa

The surveyed students have had a different level of certainty in their answers. For example, in the question "locate the areas of greatest risk", the answer has been in general terms, close to reality, placing the areas of greatest risk in the foothills of the volcanoes and near the river. Without the responses, the creeks were not included, which when activated in the rainy season are flood areas that produce the greatest number of material and human losses (Fig. 3A and B).

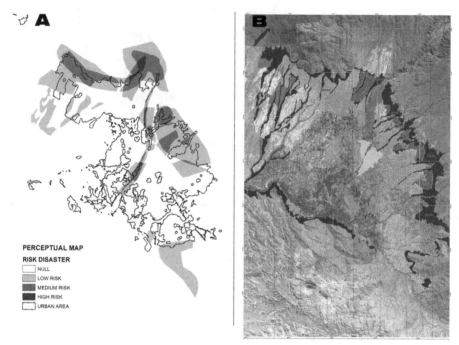

Fig. 3. (A) Summary map of the perception of disaster risks drawn by interviewed students. (B) Disaster risk map made by the author based on official risk map by the Planning Institute of Arequipa. IMPLA.

The rest of the questions have had answers mostly away from reality. For example, when faced with the question "locate the areas of agricultural land loss" the answers were very far from the real situation, even if the agricultural areas were plotted on the map provided to the students (Fig. 4A and B). A similar case has resulted in the resulting maps to the questions related to pollution and heat island, which shows a poor spatial knowledge of the position of local environmental problems.

4.3 The Development of the Environmental Atlas of Arequipa

In order to contribute to the improvement of the deficiencies of environmental education evidenced in both surveys, an environmental atlas has been developed that has had the participation of more than 20 professionals from different fields, giving it a multidisciplinary and transversal approach. For the first edition, a printed version was chosen instead of a digital one, since in Arequipa the reading of electronic books on tablets or computers is not widespread among school students and the general public, due to technological and economic constraints. On the contrary, a printed book can be easily read and shared between users who do not have a computer available or who are not familiar

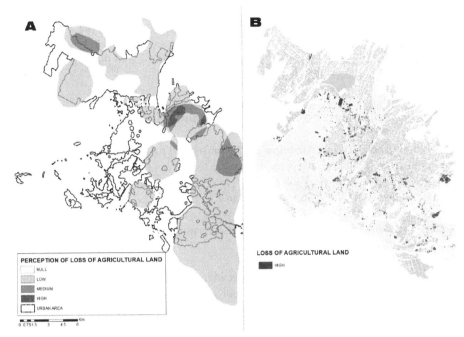

Fig. 4. (A) Summary map of the perception of loss of agricultural land drawn by interviewed students. The darkest spots identifies and area where there is not and has never been agriculture. (B) Loss of agricultural land map made by the author based on official risk map by the Planning Institute of Arequipa. IMPLA.

with certain digital technologies at the time of reading. Although the development of an interactive digital atlas is the natural next step of the project, the most important thing is the construction of a consistent and systematized content through a geodatabase, which can be used in both printed and digital formats.

The atlas is based on the systemic approach, which is the study of the ecosystems that make up our habitat as well as the relationships and flows of matter and energy that co-exist in them. An ecosystem is composed of two elements: the **Biotope**: which is the "territory or living space whose environmental conditions are adequate for a specific community of living beings to develop in it" [26] and the **Biocoenosis**: which is formed by "all the interacting organisms that live together in a specific habitat or biotope, forming an ecological community" [27]. However, the systemic approach also focuses on the ecosystems' interrelations [28].

For educational purposes, emphasis has been given to certain themes, grouped into three main areas: (a) **The natural environment**: which addresses the study of ecosystems and their two main elements: biotopes (the territory, soils, hydrology, climate, and temperature) and biocoenosis (flora and fauna); (b) **The built environment**: it centers on the city's constructed habitat, its urban evolution, the monumental heritage (as Arequipa's city center is a UNESCO heritage site), the main land uses, the road infrastructure and the agricultural and recreational green areas; and (c) **The social-cultural**

environment: it focuses on the relationship between the society and the environment: the demographic configuration of the community, its activities towards risks, resilience building and environmental culture.

Despite this classification, several topics are interrelated, using the multi-thematic analysis capabilities accessible by GIS.

5 Strategies for Spreading the Atlas Among School Students

The Environmental Atlas of Arequipa will be introduced to schools after March 2020, therefore it is not feasible at this point to measure the impact that it will produce among the community, particularly school students. However similar surveys will be conducted in 2022 to understand if this publication had an effect in the improvement environmental education and awareness as well as spatial knowledge among young university students.

However, some approaches may allow better acquirement of the atlas content.

(a) Massive atlas dissemination

The Universidad Católica de Santa María which has published the atlas, might play an important role in incorporating the content of the atlas into the environmental education of Arequipa students, through two concrete measures:

(1) The donation of a number of books to public libraries and schools organizing, along with other universities, several diffusion workshops.

(2) The inclusion of the atlas content in the university entrance exam. This will encourage pre-university students to read and discuss local environmental problems to be readily prepared for the exam.

(b) Development of an interactive digital version

After the printed version the production of a digital atlas is planned. The advantages of the digital format include its periodical update in an easy way, the interactivity with the user, the friendly navigation between superimposed layers, the possibility to carry out verification in situ, the opportunity of zooming in and out maps to a larger scale and the exchange of various types of information.

A web-based version will be a platform that will allow interaction with the user combining and comparing different levels of information. Additionally a mobile application version will display concrete layers, such as land use, risk areas, watercourses, natural areas, etc. in order to promote in-situ learning activities.

The expected results after the publication of the Environmental Atlas of Arequipa in its physical and virtual stages are (a) the reinforcement of the knowledge and awareness of local environmental issues to enrich the citizens environmental culture, particularly the young population and (b) its contribution in decision making as well as a model for capacity building focused around the environmental culture. Additionally, it can encourage the creation of new environmental atlases related to other districts, provinces or other cities in Peru, based on the Environmental Atlas of Arequipa.

6 Conclusions

- Environmental education is considered to be one of the pillars of sustainable development in cities, being transversally and closely linked to environmental culture [29, 30]. In order to transform young people's environmental culture, it is central to combine general knowledge with local environmental awareness.
- According to this study, there is no evidence to indicate that the school texts contributed to local environmental education since they have a very general approach and content.
- This is associated to the fact that many young university students have moderate to low environmental behaviors and attitudes. However, a small percentage of professionals showed good environmental behaviors, as they got higher results compared to the group of students; therefore, it can be deduced that university education contributes positively but not significantly to the improvement of environmental culture.
- This is related to the fact that many young university students have moderate to low environmental behaviors and attitudes. However, a small percentage of graduated professionals show developed environmental behaviors as they afford higher results when compared to the group of students; therefore it can be inferred that university education contributes in a positive but not significant way to the improvement of environmental culture.
- The shortcomings in spatial knowledge of local environmental problems are obvious. The dissemination of the environmental characteristics and problems of a city must be an important aspect of environmental management among decision-makers and a powerful instrument of environmental education at different levels.
- Environmental atlases have become effective instruments to promote both environmental management and education, being resources for the acquisition of new knowledge, providing a framework for citizen participation.
- Universities can play a role in disseminating the content of the atlas, encouraging the discussion of local problems and envisioning of possible and well-documented solutions.

Acknowledgments. We would like to thank the Universidad Católica de Santa María, for financing the printed version of the Environmental Atlas of Arequipa, especially to Dr. Gonzalo Dávila del Carpio, Vice-Rector of Research, for his constant support in the development of this project. We also thank the collaborators of various institutions that contributed to the atlas, particularly to Milagros Álvarez Huamaní, Sarelia Castañeda Alejo and Christian Málaga Espinoza, for their participation and assistance in that publication.

References

1. PNUD: Objetivos del Desarrollo Sostenible. PNUD (2017)
2. Krasny, M., Tidball, K., Sriskandarajah, N.: Education and resilience: social and situated learning among university and secondary students. Ecol. Soc. **14**(2) (2009). www.jstor.org/stable/26268335. Accessed 19 Jan 2020
3. Martínez Castillo, R.: La Importancia de la educación ambiental ante la problemática actual. Revista Electrónica Educare **14**(1), 97–111 (2010)

4. El Tiempo: Falta de Conciencia Ambiental, El Tiempo, 14 Septiembre 1998
5. UN: Objetivos de Desarrollo Sostenible (2015). https://www.un.org/sustainabledevelopment/
   es/objetivos-de-desarrollo-sostenible/
6. ONU: Objetivo 11: Lograr que las ciudades y los asentamientos humanos sean inclu-
   sivos, seguros, resilientes y sostenibles (2015). https://www.un.org/sustainabledevelopment/
   es/cities/
7. Fien, J.: Education for sustainable living. An international perspective on environmental
   education. South. Afr. J. Environ. Educ. **13**, 7–20 (1993)
8. MINEDU: Decreto Supremo 016-2016 MINEDU. Aprueban Plan Nacional de Educación
   Ambiental 2017–2022. Ministry of Education, Government of Peru, Lima (2016)
9. Menegat, R.: Atlas ambiental do Porto Alegre, Universidade Federal do Rio Grande do Sul,
   Prefeitura Municipal de Porto Alegre and Instituto Nacional de Pesquisas Espaciais, Porto
   Alegre (1998)
10. Menegart, R.: Participatory democracy and sustainable development: integrated urban envi-
    ronmental management in Porto Alegre. Environment & Urbanization, Brazil, vol. 14, no. 2,
    pp. 181–206 (2002)
11. JA: Atlas Ambiental inspira ecologia nas escolas municipais, 20 November 2007. http://www.
    jornalja.com.br/atlas-ambiental-inspira-ecologia-nas-escolas-municipais/
12. UFRGS: Versão digitalizada do Atlas Ambiental de Porto Alegre, Universidade Federal do
    Rio Grande do Sul, 30 November 2018. http://www.ufrgs.br/editora/news/lancada-versao-
    digitalizada-do-atlas-ambiental-de-porto-alegre
13. Steinberg, F., Miranda, L.: The Peru urban management education programme (PEGUP)—
    linking capacity building with local realities. In: Habitat International, pp. 417–431 (2000)
14. PEGUP & ITC: Atlas Ambiental de Lima, Municipalidad Provincial de Lima (2000)
15. PEGUP & ITC: Atlas Ambiental de Trujillo, Municipalidad Provincial de Trujillo, Trujillo
    (2002)
16. S. C. G. &. F. L. Villacorta: Atlas Ambiental de Lima metropolitana: Mapas de Susceptibilidad
    en el Ordenamiento Territorial. XIII Congreso Peruano de Geología. Resúmenes Extendidos.
    Sociedad Geológica del Perú, Lima (2006)
17. Selby, D., Kagawa, F.: Archipelagos of learning: environmental education on islands. Environ.
    Conserv. **45**(02), 137–146 (2018)
18. Mitchell, A.: The ESRI guide to GIS analysis. ESRI, E.E.U.U, vol. 1 (1998)
19. Dent, B.: The ESRI Guide to Cartography: Effective Map Design and GIS, ESRI, Redlands,
    EEUU (2002)
20. Universidad de Alcalá de Henares: SIG vectoriales (2008). http://www.geogra.uah.es/gisweb/
    1moduloespanyol/IntroduccionSIG/GISModule/GIST_Vector.htm
21. FAO: Las fotografías aéreas y su interpretación. http://www.fao.org/3/t0390s/t0390s08.htm
22. Guimond, M.: Chapter 11 Point pattern analysis (2019). https://mgimond.github.io/Spatial/
    point-pattern-analysis.html
23. Courtney, N.: An analysis of the correlations between the attitude, behavior, and knowledge
    components of environmental literacy in undergraduate university students, EEUU, University
    of Florida, Florida (2000)
24. Sosa, S., Issac Márquez, R., Eastmond, A., Ayala, M., Arteaga, M.: Educación superior y
    cultura ambiental en el sureste de México, Universidad y Ciencia, pp. 33–49 (2010)
25. Tikka, P., Kuitunen, L.: Effects of educational background on students' attitudes, activity
    levels and knowledge concerning the environment. J. Environ. Educ. **31**(3), 9–12 (2000)
26. RAE: Diccionario Jurídico (2019). https://dej.rae.es/lema/biotopo
27. Biology Dictionary: Biocenosis (2019). https://www.biology-online.org/dictionary/Bioco
    enosis
28. Arce Rojas, R.: El enfoque sistémico en la gestión ambiental, 6 Set 2010. https://www.servindi.
    org/actualidad/30913

29. Zeballos-Velarde, C., Álvarez Huamaní, M., Quiroz Valdivia, J., Catañeda Alejo, S., Málaga Espinoza, C.: An environmental atlas as a tool for improving local environmental education and awareness in Arequipa. In: Villalba-Condori, K.O., Adúriz-Bravo, A., García-Peñalvo, F.J., Lavonen, J. (eds.) Proceeding of the Congreso Internacional Sobre Educación y Tecnología en Ciencias - CISETC 2019, Arequipa, Perú, 10–12 December 2019, pp. 191–201. CEUR-WS.org, Aachen (2019)
30. Severiche Sierra, C., Gómez Bustamante, E., Jaimes Morales, J.: La educación Ambiental como base cultural y estrategia para el desarrollo sostenible. Telos **18**(2), 266–281 (2016)

Emergency Evaluation of Obstetric Hemorrhage (Red Key) Through a Web Application

Jannet Escobedo-Vargas[1]([⊠]) (iD), Elfer Arenas-Alarcón[2] (iD), Luis Cabrera-Diaz[2] (iD), and José Sulla-Torres[2] (iD)

[1] Facultad de Obstetricia y Puericultura, Universidad Católica de Santa María, Arequipa, Peru
jescobed@ucsm.edu.pe
[2] Escuela Profesional de Ingeniería de Sistemas, Facultad de Ciencias e Ingenierías Físicas y Formales, Universidad Católica de Santa María, Arequipa, Peru
elfer@fotovoltaicosperu.com, andrec393@gmail.com,
jsullato@ucsm.edu.pe

Abstract. Aim: Allow online training, evaluation and feedback of Obstetrics students in emergency care: obstetric haemorrhage (red key). Methods: an analysis of the current state of the teaching of emergency obstetric haemorrhage was performed, the basic requirements, functionalities and deliverables were based in the SCRUM methodology. A web server, a "Somee" database management system, SqlServer and Visual Studio application development environment were required. The database model was designed based on the emergency learning requirements identifying all the entities, standardization techniques of the tables originated from the entities were applied; the user interfaces were designed. Conclusion: The GEO web application provided the feedback of knowledge to the Obstetrics student after its use and evidenced in the results an improvement in the qualification (p <0.05). The use complements the teaching that is currently practiced in the classrooms, promoting the improvement of the quality of teaching through the integration of a new self-learning model.

Keywords: Emergency · Hemorrhage · Obstetric · Web application · Submit · Visual studio · SqlServer

1 Introduction

According to the World Health Organization (WHO), "complications of pregnancy, childbirth and the puerperium are the first cause of disability, disease and death in reproductive age" [1]. The WHO report indicates that dealing with the situation described above is not complicated, if simple measures are taken, such as the application of accessible, affordable services and quality and trained professional staff in the mother and child area. Several studies show that there is no adequate emergency obstetric care (COE) and that this is mostly due to the absence of properly trained obstetric personnel [2, 3].

© Springer Nature Switzerland AG 2020
K. O. Villalba-Condori et al. (Eds.): CISETC 2019, CCIS 1191, pp. 114–127, 2020.
https://doi.org/10.1007/978-3-030-45344-2_10

1.1 Description of the Problem

Scientific evidence allows obstetric professionals to perform essential obstetric functions and procedures, it is a cost-benefit strategy to improve maternal and child health. However, it happens that cases of obstetric emergencies happen very sporadically, so that specialized obstetric personnel are not in constant practice of the unique procedures established to apply in these scenarios [4, 5].

Within the emergency entities of obstetric hemorrhage, postpartum hemorrhage (PPH) that is commonly defined as a blood loss of 500 ml or more within 24 h after delivery, while severe PPH is defined as a loss of blood of 1000 ml or more within the same time frame. PPH affects approximately 2% of all women in labor: it is associated not only with almost a quarter of all maternal deaths worldwide, but also the leading cause of maternal mortality in most countries Low income PPH is a significant factor that contributes to severe maternal morbidity and long-term disability, as well as a number of other serious maternal diseases generally associated with considerable blood loss, including shock and organ dysfunction [6].

Attention of Obstetric Emergencies in Real Scenarios. At national and regional level there is a health system by levels of care in order to attend EMERGENCIES in this case OBSTETRIC; In Arequipa there are Hospitals level II and level III that receive the references of peripheral establishments such as Health Center level I-4 that attend normal deliveries and in case of any complications refer to the hospitals; and Health Centers and Posts that attend 12 h that attend normal obstetric conditions that, in any event, are also referred to CS level I-4 or Hospitals [7].

In the Arequipa region, 80% of normal (eutocic) births are attended by obstetric professionals with the appropriate capabilities to provide obstetric care under normal conditions and to be able to identify or detect the presence of any pathology to be able to refer timely [7].

This system has some flaws in both the attention process and geographical and cultural accessibility.

Maternal health continues to be one of the priority public health issues at the international and national levels. The events related to pregnancy, childbirth and the puerperium are considered as preventable deaths, which must be measured meticulously, because they have sub registration and problems in the quality of the diagnosis, so the possibilities of addressing mortality in pregnancy, childbirth and puerperium using other data sources and not only death certificates, are very relevant [8].

The reason for maternal death in Peru for 2015 was 68 x 100,000 live births. According to estimates of the maternal mortality ratio (1990 to 2015) made by WHO, UNICEF, UNFPA, the World Bank and the United Nations Population Division, Peru reached an RMM of 68 maternal deaths per 100,000 born alive, for the year 2015; Therefore, our country is considered to have made progress towards improving maternal health and achieving the MDG [4]. In 2015, 443 cases of maternal death were reported in Peru, 63% directly during the puerperium, 63% and 9% birth, with obstetric hemorrhage being the first direct cause of maternal death [9].

MATERNAL MORTALITY due to direct causes (pregnancy, childbirth and the puerperium) is still average in the Arequipa Region (15 maternal deaths × 100,000 nv in 2015), that is, they have died from obstetric hemorrhage, pregnancy-induced hypertension and obstetric sepsis such as First causes, all preventable but that, because they were not treated properly or too late, ended in maternal death [7]. To reduce maternal mortality, there must be health services that offer quality essential obstetric care and that these are used by pregnant women either in simple alerts or for emergencies, which is where more misfortunes occur [10, 11]. Regional medical professionals and obstetricians at the Ministry of Health (general practitioners 1123 and obstetricians 542 between hospitals and peripheral establishments) [7], some hired and others appointed carry out their activities with great dedication and responsibility, the Ministry of Health constantly trains to its professionals but it does not have universal coverage since those chosen to go to a training must make replicas in their establishment of origin that almost always does not occur in the same conditions as the original. It is necessary to make a global refreshment of the obstetric emergencies permanently to the staff so that they are expedited to act in case of any emergency and have the necessary instruments to achieve this cooling when required starting from the undergraduate.

The Faculty of Obstetrics and Childcare (FOP) of the Catholic University of Santa María-Arequipa was created in 1977 and since then (38 years ago) has been training professionals whose profile is aimed at training professionals in obstetrics and childcare of high academic level, scientific and humanistic, identified with the country's health problems with a focus on Family and Community Health at different levels of care, especially the most vulnerable mother-child group and throughout the process of Women's Sexual and Reproductive Health, Family and Community (FOP Mission 2015) [12].

Throughout the operation of the Faculty, there have been 4 curricular restructuring opportunities based on the scientific and technological advances of the current obstetrics, making it increasingly clear that it tends to have a modern and competence-based curriculum. In V, VI, VII and III semesters there are specialized training subjects with theoretical and practical classes of the Physiological Obstetrics and Pathological Obstetrics Courses where knowledge is imparted, it is possible to promote skills and abilities with practical sessions and favorable attitudes towards Obstetrics. Currently there are 2 subjects related to the teaching of Obstetric Emergencies the Pathological Obstetrics I and Pathological Obstetrics II courses by gynecological obstetricians, the theoretical classes of these Courses of 2 h per week and the practical classes of 2 h per week in clinical fields Hospitals Level II and III of the Ministry of Health and Health.

The theoretical evaluation is through the application of several instruments such as written tests, seminars, exhibitions. The practical classes are evaluated in the clinical fields with real patients in the application of standardized care protocols through the International JHPiego Guidelines of the John Hopkins University (EU) [13] and the Ministry of Health (Care Standards) [14, 15]. In 2000 the Jhpiego Corporation donated to the FOP Anatomical models for teaching in Reproductive Health that is used by teachers and students in the different subjects of the specialty.

It has been observed on several occasions and as stated by graduates of the FOP, that the training in Pathological Obstetrics was limited by access to patients with some risk that limits professional practice but that there may be emergency cases that must be resolved is that new ways of approaching the teaching of these topics are required. To date there is NO teaching based on the use of computer technologies of these subjects which could be a very valuable instrument in the field to promote and deepen the forms of action in scenarios that could arise.

The implementation of continuing education programs that impact public health policies and active participation within the interdisciplinary group that attends to the mother-child binomial in public health surveillance activities and development of management guides in the area of perinatology can contribute within reach of these national and global goals. Several studies showed that adequate emergency obstetric care (COE) was not available and that it was mostly related to the absence of adequately trained personnel [8, 11].

Competency-based training was introduced at MINSA 8 years ago, covering evidence-based practices for normal delivery as well as COE. For skills-based training, skill modeling, the use of standard protocols and evidence-based practices are essential, particularly for the initial management of obstetric emergencies are essential to ensure the survival of a woman. Current evidence-based practices, including the practice of clinical skills in anatomical models, followed by the practice of initial competencies under supervision, first, and then independently at training sites. The courses focus attention on the specific knowledge, skills and attitudes necessary to conduct normal deliveries and perform COE functions in a standardized manner, as well as the skills for interpersonal communication [13].

1.2 Main problem

For the aforementioned, there is a problem that goes beyond the preparation of the professional and is that there is no automated, visual and interactive solution at your fingertips, to guide you in these emergency scenarios, which must be solved in a matter of minutes because of the high risk of damage to the patient or the fetus and in the worst case the risk of losing one's life. There is a gap in terms of having a positive and permanent feedback on learning achieved in cases of emergency obstetric hemorrhage and that is not really applicable daily, but only when the obstetric emergency arises.

Against this background, a question has been raised in order to know if it is possible to develop an application based on information technologies [16], which can contribute to the performance of the Obstetrics student and consequently to their performance in the face of these situations so critics. As a result of globalization, there is currently a growing and almost widespread, convenience of having access to the Internet through any type of device and in most places where we are. This reality makes the vision of developing an efficient and complete solution for this need translate into the development of web technology [17–19].

In this way you have the option to carry out the implementation and put into practice the solution so that it can be used by teachers and students of Obstetrics and thus obtain the indicators that demonstrate the usefulness of the project. Currently, the necessary tools and/ or support are not available, such as in hospitals or clinics where often if they are not adequately treated through the single protocol established according to Emergency Obstetric Care (COE) [13]. Similarly, the Obstetric Emergency web solution (GEO Web), serves for the evaluation and feedback of professionals specialized in Obstetrics, in order to optimize their skills and improve their performance. An influential factor in the performance of the obstetrician professional in relation to the real scenarios of obstetric emergencies is that they do not have the feedback of the information continuously, generating a gap between their knowledge acquired during their years of study and the implementation of the same.

To produce a competent professional in services, it is required that you handle modern tools such as mobile devices that are intended to simplify everyday tasks with simple processes, or the web platform, which is a tool accessible by all [13, 18, 19]. It is necessary to readjust and strengthen some specific activities in these tasks, because there are lives involved. Nowadays, it is taking fortifications of services offered in health centers as well as project development, training, replicas and health internships. Develop a methodology with the help of technology that is orderly and systematic that guarantees reducing perinatal maternal mortality by providing comprehensive care for women and children by health personnel, this is one of the solutions being proposed.

Justification: There is an urgent need to contribute through a web solution that integrates standardized procedures for obstetric emergency care to help reduce the response time of professionals. Likewise, it is necessary to provide feedback to the obstetric staff through evaluations, which place them in scenarios that resemble reality or that could arise in their professional life [20].

Importance: Allow obstetric specialists to have a web-based solution that helps them perform in the face of obstetric emergencies, and at the same time provide feedback on their knowledge acquired in their years of study, by using the system continuously.

Limitations of Research: At present, there are few applications oriented to the field of obstetrics, so this work does not consider any previous work that could have served as a basis for development; furthermore, the web solution arises based on our own research and with the contribution of knowledge and experience of a specialist in the field.

2 Materials and Methods

Type of applied research. Quasi experimental research level.

Units of Study: students of the VIII Semester of the Faculty of Obstetrics and Childcare of the UCSM, Semester Par 2015 preparing for the Internship in obstetric centers.

The GEO Web application was created using the SCRUM methodology [21]. To carry out the project, an analysis of the basic requirements, the desired functionalities, previous information and professional interests was carried out, through meetings and deliverables based on this methodology. Scrum is an agile methodology for the development of projects that require greater speed and adaptability in their results.

The executives who apply it in their organizations have two main objectives: to provide greater value of final products for their consumers and to enhance flexibility in their processes. The Scrum is based on sprints, established intervals that arise to generate a deliverable product. In each of them mini projects are developed that serve to improve the effectiveness of the main project. The main stages of the Scrum are: Sprint planning where a meeting between the team and the project manager is held to explain how each point in the interval will be developed. Here, changes, decision making, improvements and more factors will be evaluated. 2. Development stage where compliance with the deadlines established for its term is ensured. 3. Sprint review to analyze and evaluate the results. The following points are included: Collaboration between teams, supervisors, managers and product owners, external analyzes are allowed as a form of complementation. The work team responds what has been developed and what shortcomings they have had. Based on this, you can return to the planning stage to evaluate how to improve the next sprint. The review includes how, so far, the product could generate more value. The capabilities of the team, the timeline, among other details, are analyzed to know what to boost. And the feedback where the results can be delivered to receive feedback not only from the professionals within the project, but also from the people who will directly use what they want to achieve; that is, potential customers. The lessons learned during this stage will allow the next sprint to be much more effective and agile.

Subsequently, a technology selection process was carried out in order to identify the most appropriate to the requirements of the need. The proposed solution has required a web server, a database management system and an application development environment. In this order Free server called "Somee", SqlServer and Visual Studio development environment were selected. The development of work in three major stages. First, the database model was designed based on the requirements raised by identifying all the entities and as part of the data processing it was necessary to apply the standardization techniques of the tables originated from the entities. Information needed for the records in the tables was also collected. Second, the user interfaces were designed, an identification page was developed at a first level that controls access to the system and differentiates functions according to the type of user, then a search tool that provides the user to obtain a list of obstetric emergencies with keywords. Finally, an evaluation module was developed to analyze the performance of obstetric personnel. To provide the functionality required to the application, a set of routines were developed that include querying and updating at runtime the information shown in the interface, consulting and downloading external files in PDF format.

Software Engineering or software engineering process is defined as: "a set of partially ordered stages with the intention of achieving an objective, in this case, obtaining a quality software product" [20].

This process is also called the software life cycle that comprises four major phases: conception, development, construction and transition, viewed in the context of a methodology called traditional, classical or predictive.

- Conception: Defines the scope of the project and develops a business case.
- Preparation: Defines a project plan, specifies the characteristics and the foundation for the architecture.
- Construction: Creates the product.
- Transition: Transfers the product to users. To carry out this software development life cycle in which the development phases are defined, it is necessary to establish the most suitable models, depending on each type of project [21]. In this Case the choice was: Cascade Model: Linear life cycle, although it supports iterations. It is defined as a sequence of phases in which at the end of each of them the documentation is gathered to ensure that it meets the specifications and requirements to move on to the next phase: requirements, design, implementation, verification and maintenance. The progress flows from top to bottom, in a cascade fashion. To carry out this software development life cycle in which the development phases have been defined, the Logical Architecture of the System "architecture of 3 or more layers" [21] was used.

This architectural style logically separates and in some cases physically, the presentation aspects of the interface layer, the application layer and the storage layer. The interface layer contains the graphical user interface that allowed users to interact with the system. This layer was implemented using JavaScript, HTML, CSS3, AJAX and all its menus. The application layer contains the logic and rules for storing data in the database layer and also for retrieving these according to the needs of the users. Finally, the storage layer saved the data required by the system [16].

Interface Design: The interaction with the system is through a Web browser; specifically, the system interfaces are Web pages generated by the GEO Web system hosted on a cloud server. The programming language used to elaborate the pages is HTML which, despite being a standard, is interpreted differently by some Web browsers. For this reason, techniques were used that allowed to anticipate these situations, such as Cascading Style Sheets CSS) whose use in Web pages minimizes the risk that the interface alters its appearance when using Web browsers different from the traditional ones. On the other hand, for the design of the interface it was also taken into account that users with different levels of knowledge will employ the system; this requires an interface that is scalable, intuitive and easily accessible to the user. For the development of the interfaces, the main sections or areas contained in the interface adopted will be indicated through a numerical identifier to be explained later.

Database Manager, an analysis and selection were carried out taking into account the main characteristics of each database manager, as well as its advantages, disadvantages and other criteria, which helped us to choose the most appropriate manager according to the needs of the draft. In addition, it was necessary to take into account which tool is associated with the greater knowledge and usage, since it is a criterion with higher priority. The database manager chosen was Microsoft SQL Server, mainly because of its query processing power, and for allowing us to control, through its security features, the instance in which the database is located. In addition, it offers a very simple way to save backup copies and restore them to another server, which is necessary for the migration to the cloud that this project required.

SQL is a language of access to databases that exploits the flexibility and power of relational systems allowing a wide variety of operations in the latter. It is a declarative language of "high level" or "non-procedural", which thanks to its strong theoretical basis and its orientation to the handling of record sets, and not to individual records, allows high productivity in coding and object orientation. In this way, a single sentence can be equivalent to one or more programs that are used in a low-level record-oriented language [21].

To feed the content of the issues of the red key emergency obstetric haemorrhage, the manuals and teaching guides of the Ministry of Health and the Jhpiego Corporation [13, 24] were taken as a reference. It was used Scenarios or Clinical Cases. A clinical case is the orderly description of both the events that occur to a patient in the course of a disease and the complementary data provided by the diagnostic procedures, the course of clinical reasoning, the diagnostic conclusion, the treatment used and the evolution of the patient. A clinical case is hence a detailed presentation of the symptoms, medical signs, diagnosis, treatment and follow-up of a patient.

Processes for the analysis of Use Cases were executed: Use Case Development, Start User Session, Start Administrator Session, User Management, Evaluation Management, Emergency Process Management, Surrender of Evaluations - See Results, Search and Review of Emergencies, Generation of Evaluation Reports.

The following Fig. 1 shows the sections of the visual interface of the Care Guide-Basic user.

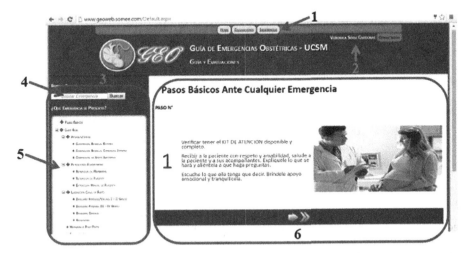

Fig. 1. Visual interface of the emergency care guide - basic user.

Section 1: Top Menu, shows during all the navigation of the system so that it allowed to move through all the main modules.

Section 2: User options, shows the name of the user who entered the system and is currently in use, as well as the option to end the session.

Section 3: Search Panel.

Section 4: Search Box, is intended to allow the user to enter keywords through which they can find emergencies accurately.

Section 5: Search Tree, allows the user to find emergencies according to a standardized classification across categories.

Section 6: Emergency Assistance Guide, is the core of the system since it is here that the user can move step by step for the correct attention of the required emergency.

We used frequency tables to show descriptive analysis. Chi-square test was used to compare categorical variables. We considered a significance level of 5% ($p<0.05$). Data processing was performed using SPSS software.

3 Results

Prior to entering the Geo Web Platform, students were evaluated with a written test with the same parameters as the evaluation of the application, where a third of the students had a result of 10 to less than a disapproving note. And a satisfactory note only 16.2% (14 or more), as seen in Table 1.

Table 1. Writing assessment of Emergency Obstetric Hemorrhage

Writing assessment	No. Of students	Percentage
Less than 11	8	32.4
11–13	13	51.4
14–15	4	13.5
16–20	1	2.7
Total	**26**	**100.0**

Source: Written evaluation

After registering and entering the system where through the applications they studied and resolved clinical cases of the emergency, they entered the online evaluation where the majority of students had a satisfactory evaluation 14 to more: 57.7%; as seen in Table 2.

Table 2. GEO Web evaluation of Emergency Obstetric Hemorrhage

GEO Web evaluation	No. of students	Percentage
Less than 11	7	26.9
11–13	4	15.4
14–15	6	23.1
16–20	9	34.6
Total	**26**	**100.0**

Source: GEO Web

The GEO web evaluation interface is shown below (Fig. 2).

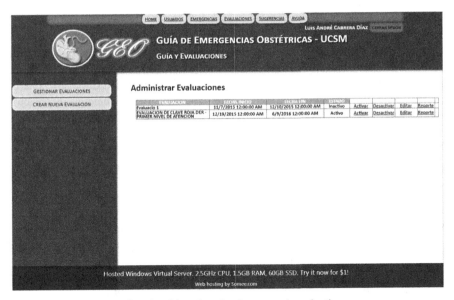

Fig. 2. Visual interface for the geo web evaluations.

Figure 3 shows the evaluation through the application GEO Web improved the performance in the evaluations being the results in the platform superior to the written evaluation that had the same parameters as that of the platform, these being significant differences (p <0.05).

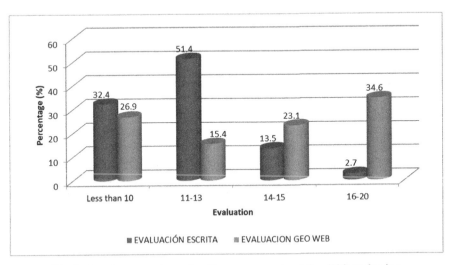

Fig. 3. Results comparison of written assessment and Geo Web evaluation.

4 Discussion

Given the need for a system that uses information and communication technologies, in December 2015, the official launch of Geo Web v 1.0 was carried out, with the concurrence of students, authorities of the Faculty of Obstetrics and Childcare, and the Teacher in charge of implementing the content of the GEO Web for emergency obstetric haemorrhage in the facilities of the Santa María Catholic University, with the aim of publicizing the correct way to use and interact with each of the application modules web, it is worth mentioning, that the use of the evaluation module was highlighted as it would be the fundamental piece to measure both their knowledge and the added value generated by the system.

Post-Production Scenario, once the system was presented, there was a considerable time interval for student training using the emergency care guide module obstetric hemorrhage (red key) [13, 24]. In this way it was useful both for users to improve their knowledge and for the system to have real access records in order to keep more sought emergency controls and frequency of access to the system by users.

At the same time, the results of the evaluation rendered were obtained, which are compared with the results of the written evaluation developed prior to the use of the application, with the objective of determining whether the use of the interactive Geo Web system with a friendly interface, emergency search engine and classified information and standardized.

Nowadays there are studies that are carried out in the stage of pregnancy, childbirth and postpartum by means of technology multimedia computer tools, to be able to show in a real dimension, phenomena that are usually studied theoretically by students of medicine and obstetrics [19]. The Medical Sciences Review [25], published an article about educational software for the development of practical- professional skills in the subject of gynecology and obstetrics that is constituted by three fundamental parts that include contents of obstetrics, gynecology and self- assessment questions with your answers The designed software provides students with continuous learning and self-evaluation with a useful methodological and didactical approach to reinforce the theoretical and practical learning of the subject. Its creation responds to a real need that is satisfied with the use of this teaching medium. The GEO Web only prioritized the management of the emergency obstetric hemorrhage as a fundamental aspect that an obstetrician should know how to apply the immediate action measures. Hipolito Breijo Madera et al. [26] carried out an investigation of the technological innovation type in the Pedro Borrás Astorga University Polyclinic in Pinar del Río, from September 2005 to June 2006, deciding to prepare software to quickly show the main parameters of the Prenatal Care consultation, according to the gestation time Interesting application but that only involves care during pregnancy with the most important milestones to have quality care, the methodology used is similar to ours but the issue is obstetric but we prefer to cover the first cause of maternal death nationwide and Thus, in the future, it is possible to implement for the most important cases of obstetric emergency, such as the red code, the blue code (pregnancy-induced hypertension) and the yellow code (puerperal sepsis).

The universe of this research was made up of all the students of Medical Sciences who attended the Polyclinic Library mentioned during this period. The sample was those students (214) who used the simulator for some reason and voluntarily decided to answer the applied survey. In the realization of this medium, a 600 MHz Celerón microcomputer was used with the Windows XP operating system and the Flash 5 Macro media software, using Spanish as a language and creating a Prenatal Care (ATENPRE) consultation simulator with multimedia sequences, which a Through a series of links they lead the user to recognize the search query. Among the main results is more than 90% of acceptability, efficiency and utility, concluding that educational software (ATEN-PRE) is another tool to be used by undergraduate students in the active search for information.

Arturo Atria et al. [27] argues that the current obstetric medical field must rely on computer resources, not only oriented to the processing of information in databases or search and consultation of scientific information, but in the use of computational and computer tools that complement the actions diary. Under this context, a comprehensive software oriented to the obstetric medical environment has been developed. This software is developed for personal digital assistant (PDA: Personal Digital Assistant) of the Pocket PC type. It allows the calculation and management of information concerning gestational age, fetal and embryonic biometrics, estimation of fetal weight and national and international benchmarks, quickly, safely and effectively.

Our work has an impact on the management of obstetric emergencies, given that in our country these entities can appear at any time and place and in the preparation of undergraduate there are few opportunities to intervene in these high-risk cases that endanger the life of the mother and fetus and/ or newborns, which is why the JHpiego Corporation of Johns Hopkins University [13, 28] trains, prepares and has teaching materials and manuals available to everyone that help staff to train as is the case of the Faculty of Obstetrics of the UCSM teachers who attended the Courses and gave replicas to the rest of the staff but we see the need to also use an application such as the one created called GEO Web whose use is complementary to what JHpiego offers.

Regarding the completeness of the system, all the information of standardized emergency processes was integrated into a tree view data structure, which for the end user becomes a category tree interface, which helps navigation effective for it. Complementing the development of the completeness of the system, a data structure was implemented, which serves as an emergency container for Red Key obstetric hemorrhage and its entire procedure segmented in care steps.

5   Conclusions

A web solution was developed, which originated in the Faculty of Obstetrics and Childcare of the Santa María Catholic University, to modernize and optimize the learning system about emergency obstetric hemorrhage care, which is hosted on a web server free (www.somee.com), which was selected based on certain criteria. The web solution is available 24/7 for the use of students who require it, as well as for the administrator. Complementing with the documentation of the project, in each of the phases annexes were developed, among which are the database, data dictionary, source code (digital) and user manuals of/ administrator.

The information provided by the system is focused on the category of emergency obstetric hemorrhage (red key), this does not mean that the system is static, since it has a process management (obstetric emergencies) that allows keeping the information updated to available to all active users. Tools and feedback were integrated into a web solution to complement the current learning system and the application of knowledge. The GEO Web application improved the performance in the evaluations, the results being better on the platform than the evaluation that had the same parameters demonstrating the efficiency of the system.

The implementation of information technologies in the specialty of education complements the teaching practiced in classrooms today. This implementation has encouraged the improvement of teaching quality through the integration of a new distance self-learning model with the classroom model, achieving a mixed model which favors those involved in the learning process (students and teachers).

References

1. WHO, UNICEF, UNFPA, The World Bank: Trends in maternal mortality: 1990 to 2008. World Health Organization, Geneva (2010)
2. Hogan, M.C., Foreman, C., Naghavi, M., et al.: Maternals mortality for 181 countries 1980–2008: a systematic analysis of progress towards Millenium Development Goal-5. The Lancet 375(9726), 1609–1623 (2010). https://doi.org/10.1016/S0140-6736(10)60518-1
3. OMS: Salud en Sudamérica. Panorama de la situación de salud y de las políticas y sistemas de salud, 2012 Ed. OPS, Washington, DC (2012)
4. World Health Organization, United Nations Population Fund, World Bank, United Nations. Population Division & United Nations Children's Fund (UNICEF): Trends in maternal mortality: 1990 to 2013: estimates by WHO, UNICEF, UNFPA, The World Bank and the United Nations Population Division. World Health Organization, Geneva (2014). http://apps.who.int/iris/handle/10665/112682
5. Alkema, L., et al.: Global, regional, and national levels and trends in maternal mortality between 1990 and 2015, with scenario-based projections to 2030: a systematic analysis by the UN Maternal Mortality Estimation Inter-Agency Group. Published online www.thelancet.com. 12 November 2015. http://doi.org/10.1016/S0140-6736(15)00838-7
6. OMS: Recomendaciones de la OMS para la prevención y tratamiento de la hemorragia postparto, Ginebra (2014)
7. REGION DE SALUD AREQUIPA: Análisis de la situación de salud Región Arequipa (2016)
8. Tavara, L.: Los cuidados obstétricos de emergencia como estrategia para la reducción de la muerte materna. Rev Per Ginecol Obstet., 54, 231–234 (2008)
9. MINSA: Boletín Epidemiológico, Lima (2016)
10. OPS: Guía para la atención de las principales emergencias obstétricas, 2da. Edición. Washington DC (2019). Series Publicación científica CLAP;1616. http://iris.paho.org/xmlui/handle/123456789/51029
11. Fescina, R., De Mucio, B., Ortiz, E.: Guía para la atención de las principales emergencias obstétricas, Montevideo (2012). Publicación científica CLAP 1594.pdf. http://clacadigital.info/handke/123456789/782
12. UCSM: Plan estratégico institucional, Arequipa (2015)
13. JHPIEGO: Programa ACCESS, Mejores prácticas en atención materna y neonatal: Un paquete de recursos de aprendizaje para la atención esencial de emergencias obstétricas y neonatales, Baltimore (2008)
14. MINSA: Guía de práctica clínica para la atención de emergencias obstétricas según nivel de capacidad resolutiva, MINSA, Ed., Lima (2007)

15. MINSA: Evaluación de las funciones obstétricas y neonatales en los establecimientos de salud, MINSA, Ed., Lima (2012)
16. Arenas, E., Cabrera, L.: Diseño, desarrollo e implementación de una solución web para la integración de las guías y evaluación de emergencias obstétricas para la Facultad de Obstetricia y Puericultura Tesis Facultad de Ciencias físicas y formales. UCSM. Arequipa (2016)
17. Ortiz, J., Carpio, G., Cobos, I., Cedillo, P., Prado, T., Robalno, M.: Tecnologías de información y comunicación- TIC-para mejorar la calidad de la atención materna y neonatal en los servicios públicas de la provincia del Azuay. Universidad Politécnica Salesiana, Ecuador, Cuenca (2010). http://dspace.ups.edu.ec/handle/123456789/11193
18. Sanchez, J.: Servidor de aplicaciones Web. Centro Don Bosco Villamuriel de Cerato, Palencia (2012)
19. Peña, A., Arada, A., Herrera, G., Rodríguez, Y., González, E.: Educative software for developing practical-professional skills in the subject Gynecology and Obstetrics. Rev Ciencias Médicas [Internet], **19**(1), 77–88 (2015) [citado 2020 Ene 15]. http://scielo.sld.cu/scielo.php?script=sci_arttext&pid=S1561-31942015000100011&lng=es
20. Arenas-Alarcón, E., Cabrera-Diaz, L., Sulla-Torres, J., Escobedo-Vargas, J.: Effectiveness of the implementation of a web solution in the evaluation of emergency obstetric hemorragy (red key). In: Arenas-Alarcón, E., Cabrera-Díaz, L., Sulla-Torres, J., Escobedo Vargas, J. (eds.) Proceeding of the Congreso Internacional Sobre Educación y Tecnología en Ciencias - CISETC 2019 (Arequipa, Perú, 10–12, December 2019, pp. 245–256). CEUR-WS.org, Aachen
21. Trigas, M.: Metodología SCRUM, TFC gestión de proyectos informáticos (2011). openaces.uoc.edu/webapps/02/bitstream/10609/17889/1/trigasTFC0612memoria.pdf
22. Jacobson, I., Booch, G., Rumbaugh, J.: El proceso unificado de desarrollo de software Addison-Wesley, Otero, A. (eds.) Pearson Educación S.A., Madrid, p. 464 (2000)
23. Presman, R.: Ingeniería de Software: Un Enfoque Práctico, 7ma.Edición, Mac Graw Hill, Madrid (2006)
24. MINSA: Manejo estandarizado de las emergencias obstétricas y neonatales: Módulo 1 (Modelo de intervención para mejorar la disponibilidad, calidad y uso de los establecimientos que cumplen Funciones Obstétricas y Neonatales. MINSA, Ed., Lima (2010)
25. Bordon, D., Carcaga, M., Avendaño, A., Villalobos, E.: Nacer: Desarrollo de un software multimedial para optimizar la docencia en Obstetricia y Puericultura, En: La informática en la práctica docente. Universidad Nacional de Educación a Distancia, vol. 1, pp. 441–444. Madrid.2000.URl//hdl.handle.net/11162/60839
26. Breijo Madera, H., Crespo Fernández, D., Breijo Madera, G.: Aten-pre. Simulador de atención prenatal. Rev Ciencias Médicas [Internet], **11**(2), 40–49 (2007). [citado 2020 Ene 15]. http://scielo.sld.cu/scielo.php?script=sci_arttext&pid=S1561-31942007000200006&lng=es
27. Atria, A., Salinas, H., Naranjo, B.: Software obstétrico para asistente personal digital Revista Cubana de Información en Ciencias de la Salud (ACIMED) 24(2) (2013)
28. JHPIEGO: Helping mothers survive bleeding after birth. Trainig Package, Baltimore (2016)

Written Reconstruction of School Scientific Experiments: The Use of Narratives in Secondary Chemistry Education

Roxana Jara[1] , Cristian Merino[1] , Marcela Arellano[1] , Gisselle Inzunza[1] ,
Miriam Satlov[1] , and Agustín Adúriz-Bravo[2](✉)

[1] Instituto de Química, Facultad de Ciencias, Pontificia Universidad Católica de Valparaíso,
Avenida Universidad 330, Curauma, Valparaíso, Chile
roxana.jara@pucv.cl

[2] CONICET/Universidad de Buenos Aires, Instituto CeFIEC, Facultad de Ciencias Exactas
y Naturales, 2° Piso, Pabellón 2, Ciudad Universitaria, Avenida Intendente Güiraldes 2160,
Ciudad Autónoma de Buenos Aires, Argentina
aadurizbravo@cefiec.fcen.uba.ar

Abstract. In this chapter, we present an implementation of scientific narratives in a chemistry laboratory in secondary school; those narratives were directed to improving students' learning outcomes in the topic of oxidation-reduction reactions. The aims of our study were: characterizing the written narratives that students produced, and categorizing different 'types' of narratives related to the ways in which they approached the reconstruction of the emerging scientific knowledge. As a result, we expected to identify the application of various 'cognitive-linguistic' skills in the narratives. Students conducted a series of school science experiments following the guide of a worksheet of standard protocols. Once the lab activity was completed, students were asked to write an interpretive text that became an integral part of their laboratory reports. Our analysis on the narratives showed that many students approached the written reconstruction of the experiments in a 'descriptive' way, but other modes were also present.

Keywords: Secondary school chemistry · Narratives · Written reconstruction of experiments · Redox reactions · Lab work

1 Introduction

Along the process of teaching chemistry at school, it results essential for teachers to obtain information on what students are learning and on the ways in which they systematize and communicate what they are learning. An important means to get this information is via school scientific experimentation: teachers encourage students to formulate and answer questions on phenomena of the natural world through planning, conducting and analyzing experiments. Experimentation in the school laboratory contributes to the understanding of core scientific concepts and procedures, to the use of key scientific notions and skills in order to develop new understandings, and to the discussion of ideas on the nature of the scientific activity [1, 2].

© Springer Nature Switzerland AG 2020
K. O. Villalba-Condori et al. (Eds.): CISETC 2019, CCIS 1191, pp. 128–140, 2020.
https://doi.org/10.1007/978-3-030-45344-2_11

We believe that it is of the utmost importance to develop and implement school science activities that allow students to *theoretically* rebuild their knowledge on chemical phenomena; such 'rebuilding' can be fostered and at the same time made visible by engaging students in the production of written texts. The activity of reconstructing school scientific experiments through writing involves what can be called 'cognitive-linguistic skills' [3, 4]: procedures based on complex cognitive capacities and conveyed through oral, written or multi-semiotic texts, which foster the development of competences of scientific thought [4]. The process of reconstructing experiments through the use of very elaborate modes of discourse –such as explanation, argumentation, or justification– constitutes a way of gradually incorporating the normative, model-based knowledge of chemistry and of using it to make sense of the world in chemical terms.

Scientific conceptualization of the natural world is based on a set of cultural representations of the objects and interactions under study that are shared at the interior of a specific knowledge community. Although reality exists beyond its representations, theories that explain it are built on the basis of languages with strong syntaxes, invented during the long history of science. Therefore, from an epistemological point of view, reality is to a certain extent 'constructed' through sophisticated talking and writing on phenomena. Theoretical models, as conceived by the American philosopher Ronald Giere [5], can be considered the representational tools that help scientists –and students– understand phenomena, intervene on them, and construct text-based explanations and argumentations [4, 6].

Many studies have been conducted in didactics of science (i.e., science education understood as a scientific discipline) regarding the nature of students' understanding of natural phenomena. These have shown that, before formal learning, students hold their own conceptions of chemical entities and processes, and activate their own explanations on phenomena. When explaining the world, students use everyday language, which differs –in terms and syntax– from the language of scientists, thus establishing structural relations between ideas that are usually very different (and sometimes incompatible) with scientifically accepted relations.

In what has now become a classic text, Osborne and Bell [7] distinguish between what they call 'students' science' and 'scientists' science': the former comprises worldviews, conceptualizations and vocabulary that students have acquired before receiving science instruction, while the latter refers to the theoretical views widely accepted in the scientific community, which become the object of science teaching.

Science learning is a continuous and autonomous process of knowledge-building by each individual, though not in an isolated manner, but rather through rich and extensive interaction with other people and objects (teachers, peers, teaching materials, experimental artifacts, digital information). In science classes, teachers ask students to read, write and talk; in the lab, students make observations and interventions, and communicate their results, usually through 'reports'. This variety of activities constitutes a conglomerate of processes under on-going communication and evaluation, and this is precisely what enables the construction of scientific knowledge among students. Different authors [8–10] state that learning science is done through the progressive appropriation of scientific language, in association with the incorporation of new ways to see, think, talk and act on facts. As we have highlighted, such ways differ from every day, common-sense ways of seeing, thinking, talking and acting. Thus, through scientific language, students can get access to a different culture, the scientific culture, which is a historical conquest.

In this chapter, we discuss the implementation of *narratives* in a chemistry laboratory in secondary school. The 'scientific narratives' that we propose are directed to improving the learning of a specific topic of chemistry: oxidation-reduction (redox). The aims of the study that we report here were: 1. characterizing the written narratives that a group of students produced in order to 'reconstruct' their lab work, and 2. identifying and categorizing different 'types' of narratives, in relation to the ways in which those students approached the reconstruction of the emerging scientific knowledge. As a result, we expected to identify the organized application of a variety of 'cognitive-linguistic' skills in the narratives.

The thirty students participating in our study (aged 16–18) conducted a series of school science experiments on reactions of oxidation-reduction following the guide of a worksheet of standard protocols provided by the teacher. Once this laboratory activity was completed, students were prompted to write an interpretive text, which we called an 'experimental narrative'. Those narratives, which became part of the students' laboratory reports, constitute the corpus for our empirical analysis.

2 Theoretical Framework

2.1 Scientific Narratives

From a theoretical perspective, a narrative serves the purpose of framing and grounding any substantive linguistic exchange: "We can conceive narrative discourse more minimally and more generally as verbal acts consisting of someone telling someone else what happened" [3]. This 'minimal' definition makes reference to a narrator (someone saying), a recipient (someone who receives the narrative, which in this case will be called the 'reader'), events (something that happened), and a timeframe [11, 12]. Linguists also identify other characteristics of any well-constructed narrative: e.g., structure (i.e., correct concatenation of elements), agency (actors performing actions to advance the storyline), and purpose (the aims towards which the agency is directed) [12].

The implementation of our didactical strategy involving narratives in the science laboratory aims to help moving language and thought from the everyday to the scientific. Therefore, the incorporation of narratives into chemistry teaching is valuable to students' learning insofar as it encourages the development of the communication skills of explaining and arguing, which serve an *epistemic* function: they stimulate deeper reflection on the learnt scientific notions and they permit to construct plausible and founded explanations [12, 13].

According to Sanmartí and Jorba [14], narrative is the most common structure appearing in the texts that we usually use in everyday life. Narrative as a textual category often includes all others, as a narrative text can contain dialogues, descriptions, explanations, assumptions, etc. To be considered a narrative, the text as a whole needs to have some additional traits: cohesion, identifiable context, subjectivity (i.e., a viewpoint), and chronological ordering of events.

2.2   Characteristics of the Narrative Structure

Following [14], it can be said that the structure of a narrative is always developed in three distinct phases: introduction of the situation, development, and outcome. A narrative resorts to various linguistic elements that relate the events with time, i.e., temporal connectors and adverbs (Table 1).

Table 1. Elements in a narrative structure.

Types of text	Morphology and syntax	Key textual aspects
Written or oral texts: – Stories, reports, narrations of events, etc – Biographies – Fictions, tales, legends, myths – News, historiography, etc	Perfective verbs: distant past or recent past Elements that provide structural relations to verb tenses: – Time adverbs and locutions – Temporal connectors, conjunctions, etc	– Chronological order of events and 'narrative order' (alterations of the chronology for rhetorical purposes) – Parts of the narrative: introduction, development (with a climax), outcome ('dénouement') – Narrative viewpoints: characters' perspectives, external narrator, etc

Scientific narratives in the form of scientific reports are a discursive genre that can be used by science students to express their ideas on the scope, validity and limitations of a certain scientific position. In a study on the rhetoric of the experiment [15], Azuela states that scientific narratives in general, and experiment reports in particular, are *pieces of rhetoric* (in a conventional definition of the term), as their objective is to persuade or influence an interlocutor or an audience. Scientific discourse is a discourse of power, in which rhetoric should be understood as the use of language with the aim of being effective in all aims of communication; this includes convincing through discourse and suggesting ways of seeing and courses of action.

In our study, we conceptualize a scientific narrative as a discursive sequence that includes a concatenated set of ideas on the natural world that the author wishes to transmit, the facts that justify those ideas with reference to scientific models, the contexts of effective application of such ideas, and the author's own conceptions regarding science and its development [16].

In the context of school science, scientific language is learned by talking, reading and writing, and by thinking about these processes through the different genres employed by science. Unfortunately, too much emphasis is given to the writing and evaluation of very stereotyped texts, such as lab reports [17]. Therefore, the use of scientific narratives can be a distinct contribution, since it implies understanding scientific language, at least in some of its aspects, as genuine literary language [18], as a tool for creating and comprehending the world. In the narration of their own scientific ideas, students need to understand a set of key concepts in order to reasonably describe how they are conceiving phenomena and how they explain them to themselves and others. In the process of textualizing the ideas in an elaborate format, those ideas, and the words students use to shape them, become more and more coherent with the theoretical models that they sustain [11].

Narratives on experiments are an instrument that can have advantages for reporting on laboratory practice [9, 11, 16]. An experimental narrative is a way to reconstruct first-hand experience with a phenomenon in order to give meaning to that experience through technical language. Such reconstruction can be understood as the production of an elaborate 'factuality' combining 'real' facts accessible to experience and very stylized transformations of those facts through linguistic resources [11].

Our decision to use experimental narratives is based on acknowledging that it has been shown that they represent a means of facilitating modeling processes. Narratives are also a strategy for improving the 'memorability' of the activities; they increase interest in learning and expand the comprehension of what has been learnt. In addition, they can be used to reflect the fundamental structure of students' conceptualizations: making public students' private thought [19]. Narratives facilitate the appropriation of diverse cultural knowledge, providing a framework for dialogue between emotions, reason and experience [20]. They can be used as a tool to 'play' with experiences in a two-way reconstruction of ideas: making the incomprehensible comprehensible (i.e., giving meaning, explaining) and making the comprehensible incomprehensible (i.e., problematizing, debunking common sense). Both these epistemic actions contribute to our knowledge of the world and how we interact with it [18].

2.3 Cognitive-Linguistic Skills

Jorba et al. [17] suggests that skills are basic processes through which we deal with information, process data, draw conclusions, etc., based on acquired knowledge. Using those skills, students articulate new knowledge into already established structures formed from a set of representations of behavior and spontaneous ways of reasoning, which are specific to each individual at each stage of their development. Jorba posits that 'cognitive-linguistic' skills are those processes that are activated to produce different text types, and that they are 'transversal' to all areas of curriculum, while at the same time being formed in different ways in each of those areas. As a result, these skills cannot be approached *solely* from the perspective of the school subject Language, they must also be developed in every curriculum area in order to avoid the mistake of producing texts whose structure follows the conventional characteristics demanded by the typology but which are devoid of content. Cognitive-linguistic skills include: describing, defining, summarizing, explaining, justifying, arguing and demonstrating.

Studies [11, 14, 16, 17] suggest that, in general, when talking about skills that must be taught in order to learn science, we normally think of those that are acquired through performing scientific experiments, such as observing, proposing hypotheses, identifying and combining variables, designing experiments, collecting and transforming data, and stating conclusions. In opposition, there are very few examples that consider teaching skills related to expression and communication of ideas: describing phenomena and images related to them, defining, summarizing, explaining, arguing in favor of a thesis, or writing reports, summaries and critical assessments. It should always be considered that, in the construction and evolution of science, experiments have been a key motor, but even more important were the collective discussion of their results and their theoretical interpretation. Historical experiments are just as essential to science as the books and papers that are subsequently written in order to structure and publicize ideas.

In a scientific text, entities that anyone can easily identify transform into entities that not everyone can initially relate to, as they are highly abstract. These give meaning to the text within the framework of theoretical models [21]. This means that, when students create texts using ideas that relate to two different levels –i.e., everyday ideas translated into ideas based on a scientific theory– the way is open for them to meaningfully learn science. The linguistic skills that generally give evidence of scientific understandings are description, definition, explanation, justification and argumentation.

According to Jorba et al. [17], description, explanation, justification and argumentation are sequentially related in order of complexity. In the first place, describing produces statements about the qualities of the objects, facts or phenomena that are being described. If a causal connection is made between the description and other 'reasons', we have an explanation. If the statements and reasons have theoretical validity, showing scientific knowledge, this is justification. Finally, if the acceptability of the reasons for changing the epistemic value of the object of study is examined, we move into argumentation.

Following these ideas [17, 22], we propose that explanation, argumentation and justification are higher-order cognitive-linguistic skills that allow students to gradually appropriate the language of chemistry and give them the ability to build and communicate ideas about the world applying scientific theories.

2.4 Scientific Models and Narratives

In this chapter, we adhere to what is known as a 'semantic' view of scientific models, taken from the philosophy of science of the last quarter of the 20th century [23]. We use such a meta-theoretical portrayal of the nature and function of models in order to engage students in model-based practices when they are learning science. Semantically defined, theoretical models are the 'projections' of a scientific theory onto the world, or their 'potential realizations'. Models (of a theory) are the formal correlates of the pieces of reality that the theory intends to explain. 'Model-phenomena' (i.e., stylized reconstructions of facts by means of theoretical principles) are thus integral parts of all theories, and not their a-posteriori implementations [5, 23].

A shift in focus to a semantic understanding of models would imply paying less attention to the most formalized aspects of theories and more attention to *meaningfulness* in the learning of science [23]. Thus, the semantic conception of models opens the possibility to work with written reconstructions of experiments in school science laboratories. When doing this, models would function as the theoretical representations of phenomena that hold together the architecture of the scientific texts, including narratives.

In [24], one of us has inspected the function of the so-called 'narrative rationality' in science education, under the hypothesis that this mode of thinking can be recognized in historical scientific texts and in the texts used when teaching science. This mode of creating scientific meaning would be substantively linked to the historical development of the disciplines, which configures the famous 'context of discovery'. 'Hybrid' texts, which present scientific explanations in a narrative 'vehicle' or 'container', could prove very fruitful for science education, since they can incorporate ampliative (and especially abductive) reasoning, hypothesis generation, and the consistent use of evidence. Such texts would then require that scientific models play a very specific role: giving structure to evidence and supporting explanations. Students would use the theoretically reconstructed evidence as mediation when 'projecting' the model to the experimental results, and the detailed presentation of this process would become the core of the experimental narrative.

2.5 Students' Identified Difficulties in Redox

The literature has classified the recurrent difficulties faced by students (of different educational levels) when thinking about oxidation and reduction into two types: conceptual and procedural [25]. Conceptual difficulties include the following:

- The notion that oxidation and reduction reactions can occur independently.
- The explanation of electron transfer.
- The meaning and designation of states of oxidation.

Procedural difficulties include the following:

- Identification of reagents as oxidizing or reducing.
- Imprecise terminology and linguistic complexity hindering the identification of the involved substances and their roles.
- Solving equations that are difficult to understand, giving excessive emphasis to the importance of following established procedures (e.g., ion-electron method).

Another difficulty frequently seen is the definition of redox related to 'oxygen transfer': this idea is very appealing to students, as they can argue the participation of oxygen instead of electron transfer. A study [26] shows that when students are asked why a metal changes appearance, most of them explain it from a macroscopic viewpoint, arguing that this change is caused by the exposure of the metal to conditions such as moisture, sun, water, etc. Few students refer to the redox process, though they understand that electrons are involved in a reaction. The same study also shows that there is a conception that oxygen always participates in a redox reaction.

When students give explanations on redox phenomena, they generally have problems with the microscopic explanation and the abstraction of the behavior of atoms and the interaction of particles. They thus illustrate phenomena through facts, such as the coloring of the solution, which help identifying the experimental behavior of the system, but do not account for what has occurred.

3 Methods

The main objective of our study was to identify and characterize the narrative styles among secondary school students when they explain oxidation-reduction reactions through the written reconstruction of experiments.

Our study is based on students' original productions: the written experimental narratives. We categorize and describe 'types' of 'school scientific narratives' using two indicators: how they approach scientific knowledge, and how they use cognitive-linguistic skills.

We analyzed the narratives constructed on an experimental activity performed by students who use a protocol they were given. Once the activity was completed, the students were asked to write a text ('experimental narrative') about the subject in question (oxidation-reduction). The narratives formed part of the students' laboratory reports, and data was collected from them for this investigation. The corpus of data is constituted by the narratives written by a class of 30 high-school students (aged 16–18) who participated in the laboratory activity.

The suggested task was the following: "After completing the lab activity, we would like you to write down your experience. Please write a minimum of one page on the full laboratory experiment you have just done. Do not leave out any details: describe what you did, what you saw, what you analyzed, how you felt, and what you learned. Also try and relate the things you studied in the laboratory with processes that occur in everyday life".

Considering that data for our research is under the form of written texts with thematic unity, our data analysis, in accordance with Bardin's [27] prescriptions, is based on text segmentation into units of analysis, thus allowing identification of different meaning units that make up the narrative text. This requires assigning codes in order to be able to classify the units of register in the document, and classifying the written material for subsequent description and interpretation. This so-called 'open coding' aims to express the data in the form of concepts, corresponding to a first-order analysis. The texts were coded in order to:

- Establish regularities to identify different structural dimensions in the narratives: (a) introduction, (b) development, and (c) conclusion.
- Establish regularities to recognize different cognitive-linguistic skills in the narratives: (a) description, (b) explanation, (c) justification, and (d) argumentation.

These last four categories are understood as follows:

- Description involves producing statements that present the qualities, properties, characteristics, etc., of an object, organism or phenomenon.
- Explanation entails producing reasons or arguments in an orderly manner following cause-effect relationships.
- Justification needs providing reasons or arguments in relation to a corpus of knowledge or theory.
- Argumentation is also producing reasons or arguments, but with the main aim of persuading or convincing.

4 Results and Discussion

For the purpose of categorizing the 30 narratives that we collected, two analyses were performed: one on the structural elements, and one on the cognitive-linguistic skills that are used.

4.1 Analysis of the Structural Elements in the Narratives

Forms of Introducing: Connection to Knowledge. The first structural element is the introduction. Critically assessing allows identifying the different starting points and the ways in which students deal with their own prior knowledge and its confrontation with the phenomena. While some students only describe the instructions received, others begin by proposing ideas on the phenomenon and use their past experience as an element to frame and give meaning to what they have done (Table 2).

Table 2. Introduction

Types	f %	Examples
Summary	40	In this lab I had the experience of doing 5 oxidation-reduction experiments, in which we used 5 minerals and 3 different solutions
Descriptive	20	All the materials were placed on the table. Then the reagents were added to the solutions
Emotive	20	This lab has been a fun experience for me, because I had never done anything like this before
Reflective	10	After doing the oxidation-reduction experiment, I realized that when using different materials and reagents in a precipitation beaker, not all the materials react together
Degree of importance	10	This experiment strengthened my knowledge of oxidation and reduction

Forms of Developing: Connection with Phenomenon. Development is the longest part of the text and mainly includes descriptions of the procedure, ways to approach the phenomenon, and decision-making in the execution of the lab. Students establish a dialogue with the activity, they describe the steps taken for each redox reaction, the reflections, the physical changes observed, the successes and failures, and they even include some anecdotes (Table 3).

Forms of Concluding: Reflections on the Activity. In the conclusions of the texts, we identified more reflections from the students on the implications of the experiment, the expectations they had, their difficulties, and the expected learning (Table 4).

Table 3. Development

Types	f %	Examples
Descriptive	30	We started by identifying the solutions: copper sulphate was blue; iron sulphate was yellow and hydrochloric acid was clear; we put them separately into 5 beakers
Emotive	20	… this change was surprising because I thought it would stay the same, and so I became more interested in the experiment
Reflective	50	It seems that reaction using SO_4^{2-} with Fe generates more changes

Table 4. Conclusion

Types	f %	Examples
Emotive	40	Personally, I didn't feel anything special, maybe because I expected to see the reactions more clearly
Summary	30	From what we could see, they were all redox reactions due to the oxidising-reducing nature of the reagents
Critical judgement	30	These experiments helped me see the subject in a different way, not in the simple way I had seen it before

4.2 Analysis of the Cognitive-Linguistic Skills Present in the Narratives

All 30 narratives were again separately considered for this second analysis. They were coded according to the four main cognitive-linguistic skills that we had selected: describing, explaining, justifying, and arguing. The coding corresponds to the presence of fragments in which one of those skills can be identified.

Our analysis led to coding 138 text paragraphs, classified under the three skills that could be found (Table 5).

Table 5. Cognitive-linguistic skills

Types	n	f %	Examples
Describing	120	87	For $AgNO_3$ + Cu, the Cu plate changes from orange to silver, we also saw lumps, it gave me the impression that it was breaking apart
Explaining	15	11	We found that they were all redox reactions due to the oxidizing-reducing nature of the reagents
Justifying	3	2	We analysed the oxidizing and reducing reagents for each case, which take or give away electrons
Arguing	0	0	–

In general, description is the skill most commonly identified in the narratives of the experiment, with a frequency of 87%. This may be showing that students favor visualization of the phenomenon in terms of observation.

On the other hand, argumentation is not seen in any of the texts, showing the difficulty faced by most students when they intend to elaborate a strongly organized set of ideas in a written format that requires precision, coherence and the use of warrants or backings. This last finding may also be related to the traditional way in which science classes are conducted, beginning by presenting the 'sheer' concepts without any associated phenomena to be modeled. Such classes are neither aligned with current proposals on chemistry teaching based on a constructivist approach, nor consistent with what the philosophy of science tells us on the ways in which scientific knowledge is generated. This could explain the lack of higher-order abilities, such as explanation and justification, in students' narratives.

5   Conclusions

In the light of our preliminary results, which we have presented here, the inclusion of experimental narratives in chemical education is only the first step towards the development of higher-order scientific skills, such as explaining, establishing a theoretical basis, providing evidence, justifying, and finally arguing. Considering that a high proportion of the students are only descriptive in their retelling of the scientific experiment, it is necessary to generate scenarios in which they can be helped to make concrete advancements in the development of more robust texts that include more elaborate skills.

According to the categories employed in this study, experimental narratives favor a space of reflective 'textualization' of the scientific experiences. The narratives created by students show that for them this genre is a useful means to summarize the activity. It is our contention that narrative writing constitutes a task where students can think back on the experiment and express their impressions, and even emotions, regarding it in a more reflective way.

The multiple values of this task that we proposed lead us to conclude that it has a positive influence in students' learning, beyond what is usually achieved in this kind of activities when the traditional experiments are performed, but no written model-based reconstruction is demanded. Specifically, regarding the acquisition or consolidation of theoretical concepts, though many of the 'descriptive narratives' use more colloquial than scientific language, it can be seen that some incorporate more critical and reflective elements to account for the results of the experiments.

Villalba-Condori and his colleagues [28] state that "[t]here is a need for a pedagogical model framework, instructional design, and guides that integrate students and help reach common and desirable learning outcomes [and also a] need to analyse the necessary conditions regarding their validation". In our study, we had as an important objective the clear presentation of all the theoretical foundations, including the pedagogical model from which we designed our intervention and made didactical (i.e., instructional) decisions [29]. As a natural continuation of this first piece of research, we want to design other teaching environments in which the validation conditions of our proposal on experimental narratives can be further evaluated.

Acknowledgments. This scientific product is derived from:
- Research Project Fondecyt 11130445. Comisión Nacional de Investigación Científica y Tecnológica. Government of Chile.
- Research Project PICT-2017-3397. Agencia Nacional de Promoción Científica y Tecnológica. Government of Argentina.

References

1. Lunetta, V.N.: Learning and teaching in the school science laboratory: an analysis of research, theory, and practice. In: Abell, S.K., Lederman, N.G. (eds.) Handbook of Research on Science Education, pp. 393–441. Lawrence Erlbaum Associates, Mahwah (2007)
2. Hodson, D.: Experiments in science and science teaching. Educ. Philos. Theor. **20**(2), 53–66 (1988). https://doi.org/10.1111/j.1469-5812.1988.tb00144.x
3. Norris, S.P., Guilbert, S.M., Smith, M.L., Hakimelahi, S., Phillips, L.M.: A theoretical framework for narrative explanation in science. Sci. Educ. **89**(4), 535–563 (2005). https://doi.org/10.1002/sce.20063
4. Izquierdo Aymerich, M., García Martínez, Á., Quintanilla Gatica, M., Adúriz-Bravo, A.: Historia, Filosofía y Didáctica de las Ciencias: Aportes para la Formación del Profesorado de Ciencias. Universidad Distrital Francisco José de Caldas, Bogotá (2016)
5. Giere, R.N.: Explaining Science: A Cognitive Approach. University of Chicago Press, Chicago (1988)
6. Gilbert, J., Treagust, D.: Multiple Representations in Chemical Education. Springer, New York (2009). https://doi.org/10.1007/978-1-4020-8872-8
7. Osborne, R., Bell, B.: Science teaching and children's views of the world. Eur. J. Sci. Educ. **5**(1), 1–14 (1983). https://doi.org/10.1080/0140528830050101
8. Sanmartí, N.: Didáctica de las Ciencias en la Educación Secundaria Obligatoria. Síntesis, Madrid (2002)
9. Izquierdo, M., Sanmartí, N., Espinet, M.: Fundamentación y Diseño de las Prácticas Escolares de Ciencias Experimentales. Enseñanza de las Ciencias **17**(1), 79–92 (1999)
10. Lemke, J.: Talking Science: Language, Learning, and Values. Ablex Publishing, Norwood (1990)
11. Ramos, L., Espinet, M.: Utilizar las Narrativas en el Trabajo Experimental. In: Merino, C., Gómez, A., Aduriz-Bravo, A. (eds.) Áreas y Estrategias de Investigación en la Didáctica de las Ciencias Experimentales, pp. 197–210. Universitat Autònoma de Barcelona, Barcelona (2008)
12. Adúriz-Bravo, A., Revel Chion, A.: El Pensamiento Narrativo en la Enseñanza de las Ciencias. Inter-Ação **41**(3), 691–704 (2016)
13. Izquierdo, M.: Estructuras Retóricas en los Libros de Ciencias. Tarbiya **36**, 11–34 (2005)
14. Sanmartí, N., Jorba, J.: Strategies promoting self-regulation in science learning. In: Novak, J. (ed.): Proceedings of the Third International Seminar on Misconceptions and Educational Strategies in Science and Mathematics. Cornell University, Ithaca (1993)
15. Azuela, L.F.: Claude Bernard, el Sebo de Vela y la Originalidad Científica (2007). http://www.medigraphic.com/pdfs/bmhfm/hf-2007/hf072k.pdf. Accessed Feb 2020
16. Marzàbal, A.: Anàlisi dels Llibres del Pare Vitoria, Director del l'IQS (1905–1955), com a Exemple de la Incorporació Progressiva de les Innovacions Científiques al Camp Docent. In: IX Trobada d'Història de la Ciència i de la Tècnica. Societat Catalana d'Història de la Ciència i de la Tècnica, Barcelona (2006)
17. Jorba, J., Gómez, I., Prat, A.: Hablar y Escribir para Aprender: Uso de la Lengua en Situación de Enseñanza-Aprendizaje desde las Áreas Curriculares. Síntesis, Barcelona (2000)

18. Ochs, E.: Narrative. In: Van Dijk, T. (ed.) Discourse as Structure and Process. Sage, London (1997)
19. Eisner, E.W.: Cognition and Curriculum Reconsidered. Teachers College Press, New York (1994)
20. Egan, K.: Imagination in Teaching and Learning. University of Chicago Press, Chicago (1992)
21. Sensevy, G., Tiberghien, A., Santini, J., Laubé, S.: An epistemological approach to modeling: case studies and implications for science teaching. Sci. Educ. **92**(3), 424–446 (2008)
22. Erduran, S.: Methodological foundations in the study of argumentation in science classrooms. In: Erduran, S., Jimenez-Aleixandre, M.P. (eds.) Argumentation in Science Education: Perspectives from Classroom-Based Research, pp. 47–70. Springer, Dordrecht (2008). https://doi.org/10.1007/978-1-4020-6670-2
23. Adúriz-Bravo, A.: A semantic view of scientific models for science education. Sci. Educ. **22**(7), 1593–1612 (2013). https://doi.org/10.1007/978-3-030-30255-9_2
24. Adúriz-Bravo, A.: Pensamiento "Basado en Modelos" en la Enseñanza de las Ciencias Naturales. Revista del Instituto de Investigaciones en Educación **6**(6), 20–31 (2015)
25. de Jong, O., Treagust, D.F.: The teaching and learning of electrochemistry. In: Gilbert, J., de Jong, O., Justi, R., Treagust, D.F., van Driel, J. (eds.) Chemical Education: Towards Research-Based Practice, pp. 317–338. Kluwer, Dordrecht (2002)
26. de Jong, O., Acampo, J., Verdonk, A.: Problems in teaching the topic of redox-reactions: actions and conceptions of chemistry teachers. J. Res. Sci. Teach. **32**(10), 1097–1110 (1995). https://doi.org/10.1002/tea.3660321008
27. Bardin, L.: L'Analyse de Contenu. Presses Universitaires de France, Paris (1977)
28. Villalba-Condori, K.O., García-Peñalvo, F.J., Lavonen, J., Zapata-Ros, M.: What kinds of innovations do we need in education? In: Villalba-Condori, K.O, Lavonen, J., Zapata-Ros, M., García Peñalvo, F.J. (eds.) Proceedings of the II Congreso Internacional de Tendencias e Innovación Educativa – CITIE 2018,Arequipa, Perú, 26–30 November 2018, pp. 9–15. CEUR-WS.org, Aachen
29. Jara, R., Merino, C., Arellano, M., Inzunza, G., Satlov, M., Adúriz-Bravo, A.: Written reconstruction of school scientific experiments: the use of narratives in secondary chemistry education. In: Villalba-Condori, K., Adúriz-Bravo, A., García-Peñalvo, F., Lavonen, J. (eds.) Proceeding of the Congreso Internacional Sobre Educación y Tecnología en Ciencias - CISETC 2019, Arequipa, Perú, 10–12 December 2019, pp. 50–59. CEUR-WS.org., Aachen

Design of the Tutor Module for an Intelligent Tutoring System (ITS) Based on Science Teachers' Pedagogical Content Knowledge (PCK)

Adán A. Gómez[✉] [iD], Elvira P. Flórez[iD], and Laura A. Márquez[iD]

Universidad de Córdoba, Montería, Colombia

{aagomez,epatriciaflorez,lauramarquezg}@correo.unicordoba.edu.co

Abstract. Pedagogical content knowledge (PCK) is a construct used to represent teacher's understanding. PCK have used for different purposes, among which are the design of technological tools and curriculum materials. An Intelligent Tutoring Systems (ITS) is a type of Intelligent System, which incorporates AI techniques to know what to teach, who to teach and how to teach individually to each learner. The main module of an ITS is the tutor module. Thus, this study presented the design of the Tutor Module of an ITS using the theoretical assumptions of the METAGOGIC metamodel and the perceptions of the science teachers about their PCK. The research phases developed allowed: collection of the Science Teachers' Perceptions, content Analysis of these Perceptions and finally the design of Model for the Tutor Module of an ITS based-on Science Teachers PCK using METAGOGIC Metamodel.

Keywords: Pedagogical Content Knowledge (PCK) · Intelligent tutoring systems · Tutor module · Metagogic

1 Introduction

Pedagogical content knowledge (PCK) is a construct used to represent teacher's understanding [1] of how to help students learn specific subject matter [2]. Five basic elements structure the PCK: *Orientations to teaching science, Student thinking about science, science-specific strategies, Science curriculum,* and *Assessment of students' science learning* [3, 4]. PCK in science is used to analyze the development over time of the pedagogical and disciplinary science teachers' knowledge. In this way, each one of the PCK components are used by in an integrated way for the lesson planning before, during and after of carrying out an instruction [5]. Researchers have used PCK for different purposes, among which are the design of technological tools and curriculum materials [1, 6]. Thus, the Technological Pedagogical Content Knowledge (TPACK) that was first proposed by Mishra and Koehler [7], describes an integrated connection between content knowledge, pedagogical knowledge, and technological knowledge. Thus, the Technological Pedagogical Content Knowledge (TPACK) that was first proposed by Mishra and

K. O. Villalba-Condori et al. (Eds.): CISETC 2019, CCIS 1191, pp. 141–157, 2020.

https://doi.org/10.1007/978-3-030-45344-2_12

Koehler, describes an integrated connection between content knowledge, pedagogical knowledge, and technological knowledge. this being a framework for teaching of science, which allow: (i) model knowledge structures or learning patterns, (ii) develop more in-depth and integrated understanding of concepts and process, (iii) improve the development of skills scientific, (iv) understand complex and dynamic scientific phenomena, (v) promote collaborative network in the community of learning for the construction of knowledge and sharing of data, among others [8].

Artificial Intelligence (AI) techniques into education has been widely used for improve teaching efficiency and effectiveness, create smart learning environments and provide tools to teachers which facilitate knowledge generation in the teaching services [9]. The use of AI in education allow knowledge generation, dissemination, update, and management [10]. For this reason, IA possibilities the redesign and creation of new learning environments, changing the traditional teacher-student interaction and learning evaluation methods [10]. AI attempts to produce similar behaviors of the natural intelligence. In education, one of the uses of this type of computational techniques is the simulation of the teacher behavior. ITS is a particular type of Intelligent System, which incorporates AI techniques to know what to teach, who to teach and how to teach individually to each learner [11, 12]. The evolution of ITS is the result of the findings multiplicity of researches in the field of education and artificial intelligence in recent years [13].

The intelligence of this type of systems consist in the ability to adapt to the performance of each learner throughout own learning process [14]. as well as to the interaction, interpretation and response of the learner [13]. According to Gómez et al. [11], is necessary to know the needs and behavior of the student in order to infer which pedagogical strategy should be applied at a given moment. Also, Latham et al. [15], affirm should be detected and adapting dynamically to an learner's learning styles.

An ITS is a computer program that uses artificial intelligence techniques to teach a person [4]. In the literature, there is a considerable consensus since the early 1980s, ITS is structured in four basic components [16–18]; Initially [19, 20] described the expert module, student module and tutor module. Later [21–23] identified and added several works in graphical user interface module (GUI).

The primary objective of the ITS is to provide personalized instruction [24, 25]. Therefore, the main module of an ITS is the tutor module [24, 26–28]. The tutor module is also known in the literature as Instructional Planner [28, 29]. In ITS, the pedagogical model contained in the tutor module is responsible for determining the Learning Objectives and selecting the most appropriate pedagogical strategies to guide the learning process for a particular student [28, 30].

According to [25] ITS can be a potential method for overcoming the challenges to international curriculum adoption; as well as, tutoring and assessment effectively, combining questions, hints, and error messages [31]. Thus, an ITS could provide instructional experiences informed by strong curriculum knowledge and PCK directly to students [25].

Some ITS based on PCK have been developed, Heffernan and Koedinger [32] developed a ITS *"Sra. Lindquist"* for carry on a tutorial dialog for algebra teaching. This ITS has a separate tutorial model encoding PCK in the form of different tutorial strategies, which were partially developed by observing an experienced human tutor. Other research developed an ITS *"Genie 2"* based on instructional methods that through coding the behavior of Russian math teachers and their PCK, which has the ability to simulate the educational experiences students would receive [25]. Other researches have been based on the TPACK of teachers to develop computational systems for the teaching of algebra, Sciences fractions [33], among others. Nevertheless, these systems in their structure are not based on the teachers' PCK.

The objective of this research is to design of the Tutor Module of an ITS using the theoretical assumptions of the Metagogic metamodel and the perceptions of the science teachers about their PCK. This paper document is structured as follows: The second chapter defines the Pedagogical Content Knowledge (PCK); in the third chapter, we explain the Metamodel of Personalized adaptation of Pedagogical Strategies in intelligent tutoring systems (Metagogic). The next chapter shows the methodology used. The fifth chapter describes the results and discussions. Finally, the conclusions of study are presented.

2 Pedagogical Content Knowledge

PCK is a construct used to represent teacher's understanding [2]. Thus, the teacher looks for the best way to represent and formulate the content to make it comprehensible to others, as well as knowledge on students' subject-specific conceptions and misconceptions [34]. PCK involves the interpretations and transformations of content linked to teachability, teachers' knowledge about its own teaching process and how this knowledge changes over broad spans of time [2, 35, 36]. PCK distinguishes teachers from other experts specialized in a discipline [37].

In Addition, Shulman and others authors [2, 3, 5, 38, 39], have proposed differences in this model from the domains of teacher's knowledge. Because the knowing of science although is a necessary, is not sufficient condition for teaching processes. Science teachers must also have knowledge about *orientations to teaching science, student thinking about science, instructional strategies in science* and *the assessment of students' science learning.*

The Fig. 1 shows an adaptation of models proposed by PCK model used in this study. This model is based-on theoretical assumptions (Schneider and Plasman [2], Magnusson [3], Abell et al. [5], Grossman [39], Loughran [40], Herrera et al. [38] and Park and Oliver [41]). In this model, components related to how teachers' knowledge is developed across science topics content. These components are structured by categories, which are described below.

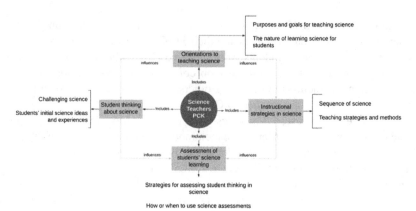

Fig. 1. Model of PCK for Teaching Science based on theoretical assumptions Schneider and Plasman [2], Magnusson [3], Abell et al. [5], Grossman [39], Loughran [40], Herrera et al. [38] and Park and Oliver [41].

Orientations to Teaching Science (OTS)

This component involves teachers' ideas about the purposes and goals for teaching science and the nature of teaching and learning science [36]. OTS is a set of interrelated knowledge or beliefs of a teacher about the purposes and goals, expectations for teaching science and the nature of learning science for students [3, 40, 42]. According to [2] OTS is composed by *purposes and goals for teaching science, the nature of science,* and *the nature of teaching and learning science for students.*

Student Thinking About Science

This component is centered on teachers' ideas about student misconceptions, as well as, the exploration of previous knowledge and the identification of difficulties or limitations in learning [1, 40]. The student thinking about science is centered on the following categories: *Students' initial science ideas and experiences, development of science, how students express science ideas, challenging science ideas for students* and *appropriate level of science understanding* [2, 39, 43].

Instructional Strategies in Science

The improves instructional strategies in science is the key to insuring students' internal interests [44–46]. The Instructional strategies in science is composed by *inquiry strategies, science phenomena strategies, discourse strategies in science* and *general student-centered strategies for science* [2].

Assessment of Students' Science Learning

This component is centered on the includes teachers' knowledge about how and when to use science assessments and strategies for assessing student thinking in science [40, 47]. The *strategies for assessing student thinking in science* and *how or when to use science assessments* are main categories of this component [2].

3   Metamodel of Personalized Adaptation of Pedagogical Strategies in Intelligent Tutoring Systems (Metagogic)

Metagogic is a metamodel that allows generation of models for personalized adaptation of pedagogical strategies in the tutor module of an ITS. According to [48], a metamodel is a set of basic concepts which are related to each other, these can be used to define models, which are instances of the metamodel [49]. A metamodel can build models with key specifications that enable consistently address the complexity of this type of process [50]. Metamodeling is a technique which has the objective of automate the process of model generation in software engineering [51], because without a metamodel, the semantics of domain models can be ambiguous [52]. Thus, METAGOGIC describes the concepts commonly used in modeling a pedagogical module in ITS. The metamodel contains concepts and relationships that are present in the following tasks related to the design of instructional strategies: instructional planning, assessment of instruction and advice on learning activities [11].

Metagogic is organized in five packages: *Metacore, Planner, Advisor, Assessment* and *Users* [11] (Table 1).

Table 1. Functional packages of Metagogic.

Packages	Function	Main elements
Metacore	Is composed by concepts and relationships commonly used in the main functions of the module tutor in an ITS	– *Functional Elements* – *Basic Elements*
Planner	This package is centered on the selection of the most adequate pedagogical strategies for each student	– *Context* – *PedagogicalApproach Class* – *Learning Activity*
Advisor	This package contains the concepts used to configure and generate feedback in ITS	– *Feedback* – *FeedbackTrace*
User	This package contains the necessary components to model user profiles of an ITS	– *TeacherProfile* – *StudentProfile*

4   Methodology

This research is based on a Modeling Methodology proposed by Barchini [53] which belongs to the category of rational methods that, in turn, are also parts of the Research + Development methodologies used in computing science. The author affirms that this type of methodology allows to create abstractions with the purpose of explaining reality. The research phases developed in this project were: (i) Collection of the Science Teachers' Perceptions about their Pedagogical Content Knowledge (PCK); (ii) Content Analysis of these Perceptions and (iii) Design of a Model for the Tutor Module of an Intelligent Tutoring System based on Science Teachers' PCK.

The first research phase consisted in a qualitative analysis which was aimed to describe and interpret the educational reality from within through of a phenomenological study [54]. In this way, this study intends to inquire about the Pedagogical Content Knowledge presented by science teachers of a secondary school based on the meanings that they attribute to their knowledge from a pedagogical and disciplinary view point. The study sample were three Science teachers from a Public School in Colombia, which constituted a twelve percent of total population of the teachers of that school. The research phase was carried out during six weeks, where three in-depth interviews were conducted following the theoretical assumptions of (Herrera, Espinet and Izquierdo [38]; Schneider and Plasman [2]; Loughran et al. [40]). The second research phase consisted in the design of semantic networks based on a content analysis process using the Atlas.ti software. This software-based analysis used line by line codification of each one of in-depth interviews carried out to the Science Teachers. The last research phase is structured by the design of a Tutor Module using both Metagogic Metamodel as well as the selection process PCK main features identified as additional components susceptible to computationally modeling.

5   Discussion and Results

The first research phase was based on the qualitative analysis of content revealing accurate information about perceptions of science teachers on its PCK. In this phase questions were applied to three teachers in the area of science. The results obtained were key to the execution of the following phases. (See on [54]).

The second phase consisted in the design of semantic networks through of a software-based content analysis process. This process allowed to identify two epistemological components of the Science Teachers' PCK: Pedagogical Knowledge and Disciplinary Knowledge. The codes found in this analysis process emerged from each one of the voices

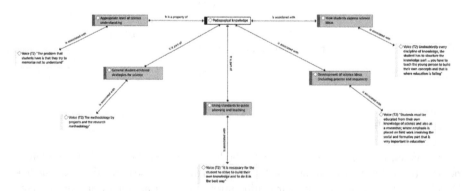

Fig. 2. Semantic network of pedagogical knowledge.

got from interviewed and they are related with the two central categories previously indicated, as can be observed in the following semantic nets:

Figure 2 shows that the science teachers' perception about their Pedagogical Knowledge is structured by five PCK Categories: *Appropriate Level of Science Understanding, General student-centered strategies for Science, using standards to guide planning and teaching, Development of Science ideas* and *How students express science ideas.*

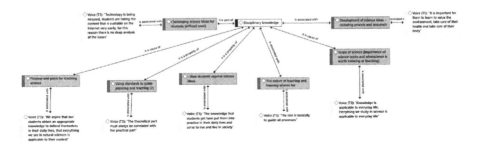

Fig. 3. Semantic network of Disciplinary Knowledge.

Figure 3 shows the Disciplinary Knowledge according to Science Teacher's perceptions is composed by seven PCK categories, which are: *Challenging science ideas for students, Scope of science* (importance of science topics and what science is worth knowing or teaching), *Development of science ideas* (including process and sequence), *How students express science ideas, using standards to guide planning and teaching, Purpose and goals for teaching science* and *the nature of teaching and learning science.*

The following categories are placed in the two types of knowledge expressed by the interviewed teachers: *using standards to guide planning and teaching, Development of Science ideas* and *How students express science ideas.* The reason why teachers perceive that these categories underlie both types of knowledge is consistent with [55] which states that the pedagogical knowledge refers to teacher knowledge about instructional practices, strategies, and methods that allow students' learning. While disciplinary knowledge refers to capacity that have a teacher for synthesizes information from across domains and applicate of knowledge to new contexts in the pursuit of specific end goals.

The third research phase identified the diverse classes which will be added to each one of the packages that will structure the Tutor Module of the ITS. These packages are obtained from Metagogic Metamodel. The additional classes emerged from of the identified categories in the previously phase. The Table 2 presents these classes and the components and categories of the PCK from which they were extracted as well as the voices of the teachers interviewed that were used as a source of this analysis process (See Table 2).

Table 2. Teachers' voices about their PCK and tutor module classes.

Voices	Type of knowledge	PCK component	PCK category	Class of the tutor module
"The problem that students have is that they try to memorize not to understand" (T2)	Pedagogical knowledge	Student thinking	Appropriate level of science understanding	UnderstandingLevel
Undoubtedly every discipline of knowledge, the student has to structure the knowledge part... you have to teach the young person to build their own concepts and that is where education is failing" (T2)			How students express science ideas	Askme
Students must be educated from their own knowledge of science and also as a researcher, where emphasis is placed on field work involving the social and formative part that is very important in education (T2)			Development of science ideas (including process and sequence)	PerfomanceLevel Checklist
"It is necessary for the student to strive to build their own knowledge and to do it in the best way"		Science curriculum	Using standards to guide planning and teaching	Standards

(continued)

Table 2. (*continued*)

Voices	Type of knowledge	PCK component	PCK category	Class of the tutor module
The methodology by projects and the research methodology" One of the strategies could be, application of Natural Sciences, but through "educational games" through workshops" (T2)		Instructional strategies in science	General student-centered strategies for science	LearnerStrategies
"Technology is being misused, students are taking the content that is available on the Internet very easily, for this reason there is no deep analysis of the issues" (T3)	Disciplinary knowledge	Student thinking about science	Challenging science ideas for students (difficult level)	StudentDifficultlevel PreviousKnowledge
"Knowledge is applicable to everyday life. Everything we study in science is applicable to everyday life" (T3)		Science curriculum	Scope of science (importance of science topics and what science is worth knowing or teaching)	LearningScope
"It is important for them to learn to value the environment, take care of their health and take care of their body" (T1)		Student thinking about science	Development of science ideas (including process and sequence)	Sequence

(*continued*)

Table 2. (*continued*)

Voices	Type of knowledge	PCK component	PCK category	Class of the tutor module
"The knowledge that students get here put them into practice in their daily lives and serve to live and live in society" (T1)		Student thinking about science	How students express science ideas	Askme
"The theoretical part must always be correlated with the practical part" (T3)		Science curriculum	Using standards to guide planning and teaching	Standards
"We aspire that our students obtain an appropriate knowledge to defend themselves in their daily lives, that everything we see in natural sciences is applicable to their context" (T3)		Orientations to teaching science	Purpose and goals for teaching science	Expectations
"The role is basically to guide all processes" (T1)		Orientations to teaching science	The nature of teaching and learning science	Assesment trigger

The analysis process of each one of the voices allowed to identify others PCK categories and components which are independently interrelated to the initial classification of the interview questions. For this reason, the PCK Model initially used for the design of the interview and the later design of the Tutor Module was modified using these new categories and components. The new PCK Model used for the Tutor Module design process is shown below. (See Fig. 4):

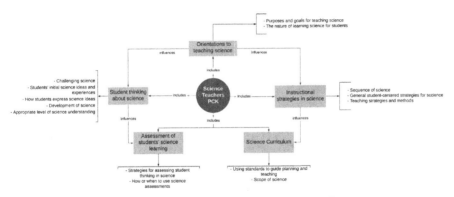

Fig. 4. New PCK model used for the Tutor Module design process.

All of the above allowed the design of the tutor module of an ITS using the Metagogic Metamodel packages and the additional classes that emerged from the analysis process of the science teachers' perceptions about their PCK. Below are each of the five packages of this Tutor Module. Figure 5 shows de Metacore Package. This Package not presented modifications.

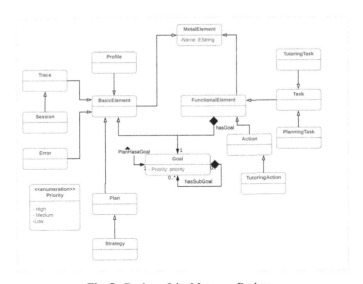

Fig. 5. Design of the Metacore Package.

Figure 6 presents the Planner Package where were added the following classes: *Expectations, Sequence, UnderstandingLevel, Standards, Learning Scope, CheckList,* and *LearnerStrategies.*

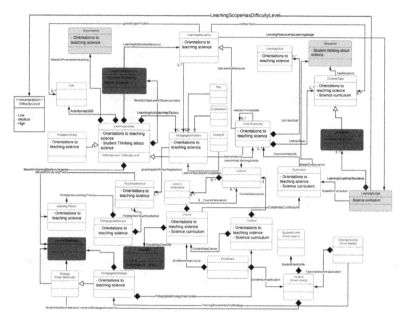

Fig. 6. Design of Planner Package.

The classes *PerformanceLevel* and *Askme* were added to the Advisor Package (See Fig. 7).

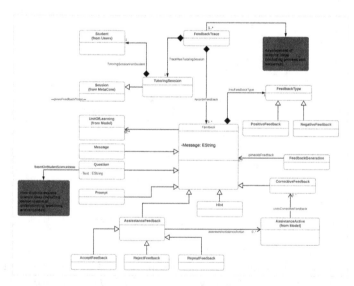

Fig. 7. Design of Advisor Package.

Just one the AssesmentTrigger Class were added to the Assesment Package (See Fig. 8).

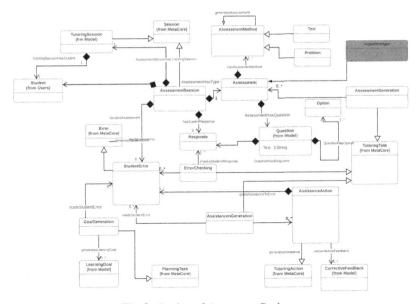

Fig. 8. Design of Assesment Package.

The user package was modified by adding only the classes *PreviousKnowledge* and *Test* (See Fig. 9).

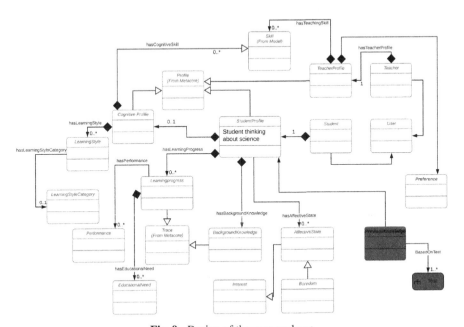

Fig. 9. Design of the user package.

6 Conclusion

This study presented the design of the Tutor Module of an ITS using the theoretical assumptions of the Metagogic metamodel and the perceptions of the science teachers about their PCK. The research phases developed in this research were: (i) Collection of the Science Teachers' Perceptions using an in-depth interview designed from an adaptation of the PCK Frame-work; (ii) Content Analysis of these Perceptions which was carried out both manual and software-based way; and (iii) Design of a Model for the Tutor Module of an Intelligent Tutoring System based on Science Teachers PCK using the classes of the Metagogic Metamodel and the different categories emerged from analysis process of the previous research phase.

The first research phase allowed collected different voices from three science teachers which answered questions classified according to the components and categories of the PCK Model designed for the interview. These voices were used as information source for a manual and software-based content analysis process which allowed to identify two epistemological components of the Science Teachers' PCK: Pedagogical Knowledge and Disciplinary Knowledge. Also, new PCK categories were identified in this process and they were associated to the two epistemological components identified. These new PCK categories allowed to modify the PCK Model designed for the research and to create new classes which were added to each package which structure the Tutor Module of the ITS. Thus, this research describes a computational model which present in detail each class that structure the packages of an Tutor Module of a ITS based on Science Teachers PCK.

This research allowed to conclude that the PCK not only is a fundamental piece for education since it allow to the teacher to be aware of his pedagogical work but also for potential value in the design of intelligent didactic tools which facilitate the mediation process of the scientific knowledge into the classroom.

References

1. Shulman, L.: Knowledge and teaching: foundations of the new reform. Harv. Educ. Rev. **57**, 1–23 (1987). https://doi.org/10.17763/haer.57.1.j463w79r56455411
2. Schneider, R.M., Plasman, K.: Science teacher learning progressions: a review of science teachers' pedagogical content knowledge development. Rev. Educ. Res. **81**, 530–565 (2011). https://doi.org/10.3102/0034654311423382
3. Magnusson, S., Krajcik, J., Borko, H.: Nature, sources, and development of pedagogical content knowledge for science teaching. In: Examining Pedagogical Content Knowledge, pp. 95–132. Kluwer Academic Publishers (2006) https://doi.org/10.1007/0-306-47217-1_4
4. Cooper, R., Loughran, J., Berry, A.: Science teachers' PCK: understanding sophisticated practice. In: Re-examining Pedagogical Content Knowledge in Science Education, pp. 70–84. Routledge (2015) https://doi.org/10.4324/9781315735665
5. Abell, S.K., et al.: Preparing the next generation of science teacher educators: a model for developing PCK for teaching science teachers. J. Sci. Teach. Educ. **20**, 77–93 (2009). https://doi.org/10.1007/s10972-008-9115-6
6. Jang, S.J., Chen, K.C.: From PCK to TPACK: developing a transformative model for pre-service science teachers. J. Sci. Educ. Technol. **19**, 553–564 (2010). https://doi.org/10.1007/s10956-010-9222-y

7. Mishra, P., Koehler, M.J.: Technological pedagogical content knowledge: a framework for teacher knowledge. Teach. Coll. Rec. **108**, 1017–1054 (2006). https://www.learntechlib.org/p/99246/?nl=1

8. Srisawasdi, N.: Developing technological pedagogical content knowledge in using computerized science laboratory environment: an arrangement for science teacher education program. Res. Pract. Technol. Enhanc. Learn. **9**, 123–143 (2014)

9. Good, R.: Artificial Intelligence and Science Education (1987)

10. Liu, M.: The Application and Development Research of Artificial Intelligence Education in Wisdom Education Era

11. Gomez, A., Fernando, M., Piñeres, C.: Meta-Modeling Process of Pedagogical Strategies in Intelligent Tutoring Systems Personalization of pedagogical strategies in Intelligent Tutoring Systems View project (2018). https://doi.org/10.1109/ICCI-CC.2018.8482046

12. Lu, C.H., Wu, S.H., Tu, L.Y., Hsu, W.L.: The design of an intelligent tutoring system based on the ontology of procedural knowledge. In: Proceedings - IEEE International Conference on Advanced Learning Technologies, ICALT 2004, pp. 525–530 (2004). https://doi.org/10.1109/icalt.2004.1357470

13. Alhabbash, M.I., Mahdi, A.O., Abu Naser, S.S., Abu, S.S.: An Intelligent Tutoring System for Teaching Grammar English Tenses (2016). https://philarchive.org/archive/ALHAIT

14. Rodrigues, J.J.P.C., Joao, P.F.N., Vaidya, B.: EduTutor: an intelligent tutor system for a learning management system. Int. J. Distance Educ. Technol. **8**, 66–80 (2010). https://doi.org/10.4018/jdet.2010100105

15. Latham, A., Crockett, K., McLean, D.: An adaptation algorithm for an intelligent natural language tutoring system-computer interface intelligent tutoring systems interactive learning environments teaching/learning strategies. Comput. Educ. **71**, 97–110 (2014). https://doi.org/10.1016/j.compedu.2013.09.014

16. Aguilar, R., Muñoz, V., González, E.J., Noda, M., Bruno, A., Moreno, L.: Fuzzy and multiagent instructional planner for an intelligent tutorial system. Appl. Soft Comput. J. **11**, 2142–2150 (2011). https://doi.org/10.1016/j.asoc.2010.07.013

17. Landowska, A.: Student model representation for pedagogical virtual mentors. In: 2010 2nd International Conference on Information Technology (2010 ICIT), pp. 61–64 (2010)

18. Nwana, H.S.: Intelligent tutoring systems: an overview. Artif. Intell. Rev. **4**, 251–277 (1990). https://doi.org/10.1007/BF00168958

19. Bonnet, A.: Artificial intelligence: promise and performance (1985). https://www.osti.gov/biblio/7011927

20. Barr, A., Feigenbaum, E.A. (eds.): The Handbook of Artificial Intelligence: Vol. 1. Kaufmann, Los Altos (1981). 409 pages, $30.00 (1982)

21. Aleven, V.: Rule-based cognitive modeling for intelligent tutoring systems. In: Nkambou, R., Bourdeau, J., Mizoguchi, R. (eds.) Advances in Intelligent Tutoring Systems, pp. 33–62. Springer, Heidelberg (2010). https://doi.org/10.1007/978-3-642-14363-2_3

22. Burns, H.L., Capps, C.G.: Foundation of Intelligent Tutoring Systems: An Introduction. Found. Intell. Tutoring Syst. 1–19 (2013)

23. Lesgold, A.M., Mandl, H.: Learning Issues for Intelligent Tutoring Systems. Springer, New York (1988). https://doi.org/10.1007/978-1-4684-6350-7

24. Rongmei, Z., Lingling, L.: Research on internet intelligent tutoring system based on MAS and CBR. In: 2009 International Forum on Information Technology and Applications, pp. 681–684 (2009)

25. Khachatryan, G.A., et al.: Reasoning mind genie 2: an intelligent tutoring system as a vehicle for international transfer of instructional methods in mathematics. Int. J. Artif. Intell. Educ. **24**, 333–382 (2014). https://doi.org/10.1007/s40593-014-0019-7

26. Soh, L.-K., Blank, T.: Integrating case-based reasoning and meta-learning for a self-improving intelligent tutoring system. Int. J. Artif. Intell. Educ. **18**, 27–58 (2008)

27. Ting, Y.-L.: Using mobile technologies to create interwoven learning interactions: an intuitive design and its evaluation. Comput. Educ. **60**, 1–13 (2013). https://doi.org/10.1016/j.compedu. 2012.07.004
28. Arias, F., Jiménez, J., Ovalle, D.: Instructional planning model in intelligent tutorials systems. Rev. Av. en Sist. e Informática. **6**, 155–164 (2009)
29. Viccari, R.M., Ovalle, D.A., Jiménez, J.A.: ALLEGRO: teaching/learning multi-agent environment using instructional planning and cases-based reasoning (CBR). CLEI Electron. J. **10**, 1–20 (2007). https://doi.org/10.19153/cleiej.10.1.4
30. Minsky, M.: Steps toward artificial intelligence. Proc. IRE (1961). https://doi.org/10.1109/JRPROC.1961.287775
31. McGuire, P.: Using online error analysis items to support preservice teachers' pedagogical content knowledge in mathematics. Contemp. Issues Technol. Teach. Educ. **13**, 207–218 (2013). https://www.learntechlib.org/p/40389/
32. Heffernan, N.T., Koedinger, K.R.: An Intelligent Tutoring System Incorporating a Model of an Experienced Human Tutor (2002). https://doi.org/10.1007/3-540-47987-2_61
33. Heffernan, N.T., Koedinger, K.R.: An intelligent tutoring system incorporating a model of an experienced human tutor. In: Cerri, S.A., Gouardères, Guy, Paraguaçu, Fàbio (eds.) ITS 2002. LNCS, vol. 2363, pp. 596–608. Springer, Heidelberg (2002). https://doi.org/10.1007/3-540-47987-2_61
34. Krauss, S., Brunner, M., Baumert, J.: Pedagogical content knowledge and content knowledge of secondary mathematics teachers. J. Educ. Psychol. (2008). https://doi.org/10.1037/0022-0663.100.3.716
35. Van Dijk, E.M., Kattmann, U.: A research model for the study of science teachers' PCK and improving teacher education. Teach. Teach. Educ. **23**, 885–897 (2007). https://doi.org/10.1016/j.tate.2006.05.002
36. van Driel, J.H., Verloop, N., de Vos, W.: Developing science teachers' pedagogical content knowledge. J. Res. Sci. Teach. **35**, 673–695 (1998). https://doi.org/10.1002/(SICI)1098-2736(199808)35:6%3c673::AID-TEA5%3e3.0.CO;2-J
37. Shulman, L.S.: Those who understand: Knowledge growth in teaching. Educ. Res. **15**, 4–14 (1986). https://doi.org/10.3102/0013189X015002004
38. Edith, H., Espinet, M., Izquierdo, M.: Teachers' perceptions on the obstacles in the teaching of science through the GOWIN V. PART 13 STRAND 13. 1791 (1709)
39. Grossman, P.L.: Un estudio comparado: Las fuentes del conocimiento didáctico del contenido en la enseñanza del inglés en secuandaria (2011)
40. Loughran, J., Milroy, P., Berry, A., Gunstone, R., Mulhall, P.: Documenting science teachers' pedagogical content knowledge through PaP-eRs. Res. Sci. Educ. **31**, 289–307 (2001). https://doi.org/10.1023/A:1013124409567
41. Park, S., Oliver, J.S.: National Board Certification (NBC) as a catalyst for teachers' learning about teaching: the effects of the NBC process on candidate teachers' PCK development. J. Res. Sci. Teach. **45**, 812–834 (2008). https://doi.org/10.1002/tea.20234
42. Friedrichsen, P., Driel, J.H., Van Abell, S.K.: Taking a closer look at science teaching orientations. Sci. Educ. **95**, 358–376 (2011). https://doi.org/10.1002/sce.20428
43. Carlsen, W.: Domains of teacher knowledge. In: Gess-Newsome, J., Lederman, N.G. (eds.) Examining Pedagogical Content Knowledge, pp. 133–144. Springer, Dordrecht (1999). https://doi.org/10.1007/0-306-47217-1_5
44. Kinyota, M.: Students' Perceptions of Factors Influencing Choice of Science Streams in Tanzania Secondary Schools. Master's Capstone Proj. 166 (2013)
45. Kelly, G.J.: Handbook of Research on Science Education. Google Libros (2007)
46. Treagust, D.F.: General instructional methods and strategies. In: Handb. Res. Sci. Educ, pp. 373–391 (2007)

47. Hashweh, M.Z.: Teacher pedagogical constructions: a reconfiguration of pedagogical content knowledge. Teach. Teach. Theor. Paract. **11**, 273–292 (2005). https://doi.org/10.1080/13450600500105502

48. Atzeni, P., Cappellari, P., Bernstein, P.A.: ModelGen: model independent schema translation. In: 21st International Conference on Data Engineering (ICDE 2005), pp. 1111–1112 (2005). https://doi.org/10.1109/ICDE.2005.90

49. Oei, J.L.H., Van Hemmen, L., Falkenberg, E.D., Brinkkemper, S.: The Meta Model Hierarchy: A Framework for Information Systems Concepts and Techniques (1992)

50. Seidewitz, E.: What models mean. IEEE Comput. Soc. **20**, 26–32 (2003). https://doi.org/10.1109/ms.2003.1231147

51. MOF, O.M.G: OMG Meta Object Facility (MOF) Core Specification. Version 2.4.2, April 2014 (2015)

52. Ali, A., Razak, S.A., Othman, S.H., Mohammed, A.: Towards adapting metamodeling approach for the mobile forensics investigation domain. In: International Conference on Innovation in Science and Technology (lICIST), p. 5 (2015)

53. Barchini, G.E.: Métodos "I+D" de la Informática. https://doi.org/10.1174/021470394321513834

54. Florez Nisperuza, E., Gómez Salgado, A., Marquez García, L.: Science teachers perceptions of their pedagogical content knowledge (PCK). In: Villalba-Condori, K.O., Bravo, A.A., Garcia-Peñalvo, F.J., Lavonen, J. (eds.) Proceedings of the International Congress on Educational and Technology in Sciences 2019, Arequipa, Perú (2019)

55. Kereluik, K., Mishra, P., Fahnoe, C., Terry, L.: What knowledge is of most worth: Teacher knowledge for 21st century learning. J. Digit. Learn. Teach. Educ. **29**, 127–140 (2013)

Why Do Peruvian School Students Choose Science and Technology Careers?

Alvaro Darcourt$^{(\boxtimes)}$ ⓘ, Sadith Ramos ⓘ, Giovanna Moreano ⓘ,
and Wilmer Hernández ⓘ

Ministerio de Educación del Perú, Oficina de Medición de la Calidad de los Aprendizajes,
Lima, Peru
adarcourt@pucp.pe, {sramos,gmoreano,whernandez}@minedu.gob.pe

Abstract. The present study examined the interest of Peruvian school students in careers related to science and technology and the variables that predict such interest. PISA 2015 data was used for this purpose. Students' expectations for pursuing scientific careers were identified by asking the occupation they expect to be working in by the age of 30. The results were interpreted in the light of the expectancy-value theory, a model that emphasizes attitudes towards goals and the self in explaining self-directed behavior. Accordingly, constructs as instrumental motivation, achievement motivation, science self-efficacy, and interest in broad science topics were studied to understand students' interest in scientific occupations. The analysis strategy included descriptive analysis, confirmatory factor analysis, binary logistic regression, and interaction effects. The results confirmed the international trend wherein being a woman is associated with lower possibilities of choosing a scientific career. In the same way, socioeconomic status and scientific capital were positive related to scientific career expectations. Both findings might suggest equity issues affecting students' expectations for scientific and technological occupations. Finally, attitudinal and motivational aspects, especially instrumental motivation, demonstrated to play a role in the intention to study science and technology careers. Recommendations for science teaching in schools and study limitations are addressed.

Keywords: Science · Technology · Career · Expectancy-value theory

1 Introduction

Scientific knowledge provides the most comprehensive and reliable explanations about the material world, a virtue that identifies it as one of the greatest achievements of modern societies [1]. Technologies derived from it directly influence productive activities, health care, recreation, communication and, in general, our understanding of the world [2]. Also, many of the most important global challenges today (e.g., global warming or the prevalence of diseases such as HIV/AIDS) require scientific knowledge for proper conceptualization and the search for effective solutions [2]. Therefore, it is crucial for societies to have citizens who, from an early age, develop interest and willingness for choosing careers related to science and technology.

© Springer Nature Switzerland AG 2020
K. O. Villalba-Condori et al. (Eds.): CISETC 2019, CCIS 1191, pp. 158–173, 2020.
https://doi.org/10.1007/978-3-030-45344-2_13

However, numerous evidences suggest a growing lack of interest in school science among students [2–4]. This trend has increased in recent decades, especially in countries such as England, Norway, Australia and New Zealand [2]. In Peru, according to the II National University Census 2010, of the total undergraduate students enrolled that year, 23% studied a basic sciences, engineering and technology career; while, in graduate school, this proportion decreased to 6% [5]. This panorama shows limitations in the availability of professionals involved in science, technology and innovation.

PISA 2015 addressed this concern and raised, as part of its conceptual framework, that science interest is also part of science literacy. By arguing that science literacy consists of "the ability to engage with science-related issues, and with the ideas of science, as a reflective citizen" [6], PISA highlights that the development of science literacy is not limited to the acquisition of skills and knowledge but it also involves the development of favorable attitudes towards science, expressed in interest in scientific and technological issues [6]. In accordance with this definition, PISA 2015 examined the interest showed by 15-year-old students towards scientific and technological careers. The present study used PISA 2015 data to analyze Peruvian students' expectations to get involved in scientific and technological careers and to identify factors related to those expectations.

1.1 Factors Influencing Scientific and Technological Careers Choice

Career choice results from a complex and dynamic process [7, 12]. Such factors can shed lights on the decision-making process involved in choosing scientific and technological careers and help understand how interest in science is nurtured. In order to better understand the current rates of students involved in science and technology careers, it is necessary to comprehend the contextual and individual aspects that accompany the making of these decisions [8].

Sociocultural and Contextual Aspects

From the social sciences standpoint, career choice is based on sociocultural issues related to the process of the construction of identity, especially in late modern societies. In these contexts, individuals have a greater freedom at articulating in this process interests, goals and personal values [9]. However, it should be emphasized that late modernity implies the *idea* of free choice, something that will not always faithfully reflect the restrictions imposed by structural factors of social life [2].

The importance of family and socioeconomic background in science-related career choice has also been highlighted [10]. Thus, Aschbacher, Li and Roth [11] found that science high-achieving students used to come from high income families, something that can be explained by a greater presence of scientific capital. This construct integrates cultural capital (e.g., having a highly developed scientific literacy), practices or habits (e.g., watching television programs on science topics) and social capital related to science (e.g., having parents with scientific knowledge or careers) [12]. In this line, Archer, DeWitt and Willis [13] argued that the probability that a child expresses and maintains his interest in science will be strongly associated with his family scientific capital. Another relevant aspect is age; evidence suggests that science interest arising from a very early stage might influence science vocational choices [4]. However, such interest might decline by the age of ten [3] and become stable during secondary education [14].

Gender roles also explain the choice of science-related careers. Thus, evidence shows that women are usually more interested in medical, biological and health sciences [15] than in mathematics, engineering and computer science, careers that draw more attention among males [16]. These differences might be explained by the influence of cultural beliefs and patterns related to gender roles on students' career expectations [2]. For example, there is evidence that women are more willing to make professional sacrifices than men to assure their family's wellbeing [17]. In addition, they perceive that scientific careers will not allow them to harmonize between their work and personal life [18]. Similarly, women, unlike men, often prefer careers that allow them to interact and develop altruistic and reciprocal relationships with others [17]. Overall, these findings suggest that choosing certain careers might be influenced by cultural values associated with them, as well as gender-related role expectations.

Regarding school variables, the quality of teaching has shown a significant influence on participation and good performance in science courses [19]. Thus, a study carried out in USA with university students found that one of the most relevant predictors of good performance in these courses was high school education [20]. In contrast, transition from primary to secondary school, low levels of experimental work in class, as well as the lack of references from the scientific field might cause adverse dispositions towards science in school [14, 21].

Individual Aspects: Attitudes Towards Science

Academic motivation and occupational decisions have been studied from socio-cognitive and motivational approaches such as self-efficacy theory, self-determination theory, the development of interest theory, attribution theory and expectancy-value theory. The present study considers the expectancy-value theory as analytical framework because it integrates social, psychological and cultural aspects in the explanation of motivated behavior; dimensions that were explored by PISA 2015.

The expectancy-value theory states that individual differences in decision making, involvement and persistence in certain activities can be explained based on attitudes related to how well one can perform in these activities and the assessment attributed to that task [22]. Such assessment is formed by the value of interest (enjoyment), the value of utility (the instrumental quality of the task for the achievement of personal goals), the value of achievement (the relationship between the task and core personal values) and the cost (what you should give up when making a particular decision) [17]. According to this model, people will be more likely to choose a science-related career as long as they trust in having the necessary skills to have a good performance in this field and as long as they believe that obtaining a scientific degree is, on a personal level, more valuable than get one in another area or discipline [17]. Among the relevant dimensions of the expectancy-value theory are attitudes, motivational orientations and beliefs about the self.

Attitudes can be defined as individuals' feelings and appraisals towards certain objects [4]; to that extent, they precede and guide behavior in various life domains. Attitudes have cognitive, affective and behavioral components, and vary according to their content (e.g. attitudes toward science), direction (positive, negative or neutral) and intensity (e.g. agree/disagree). Regarding attitudes towards science, they are defined as students' affections, beliefs and values towards school science, specific scientific topics and science implications for society and daily life [19]. Among these attitudes, achievement-related emotions can have a positive or negative effect on behavior. For example, science enjoyment mirrors positive emotions of achievement, and reflects the willingness to learn science and to consider such learning as valuable and meaningful. Contrarily, science anxiety reflects a fearful emotional state towards science learning [1].

Motivational orientations, which are closely related to emotions, can be divided into intrinsic and instrumental. Closely related to intrinsic motivation is interest in science, which emerges when people establish a relationship with a specific science object or topic [23]. It has been found that students with high levels of interest (intrinsic motivation) are able to acquire new knowledge, persevere and meet goals, get involved in scientific activities, etc. [23]. In addition, empirical research is consistent in pointing out that science interest is crucial for scientific careers choice especially when it is acquired in early stages of schooling [24]. Instead, instrumental motivation is related to the expected outcomes and consequences of behaviors, rather than the joy of learning itself, and to students' beliefs that science learning will be useful in the future [1]. Longitudinal evidence suggests that this variable is one of the most important predictors in the selection of science-related courses and in the process of vocational choice [1].

Another relevant aspect has to do with self-efficacy, which reflects subjective beliefs about one's ability for performing optimally in specific tasks, and is based on previous mastery experiences ("If I did it before, I can do it again"), vicarious experiences ("If someone else can do it, maybe I'm capable too"), social persuasion ("If my friends think I can do it, I trust that I can do it") and physiological activation [1, 25–28]. According to the social cognitive career theory [28], self-efficacy, outcome expectations and goals inform career expectations. Thus, students might avoid science goals if they have a low sense of self-efficacy or low outcome expectations [26].

1.2   Interest in Science-Related Careers in Peruvian Students

Regarding the Peruvian context, a study published by the National Council of Science, Technology and Technological Innovation identified the following factors as specifically relevant in the process of (not) choosing scientific and technological careers: (a) the poor scientific culture and misinformation about what characterizes a career in science and technology; (b) the limited amount of school experiences related to scientific and technological issues; (c) the absence of "professional models" in the field of science and technology that could show the benefits and positive aspects of this type of careers; (d) the stereotypes surrounding professionals in this field; (e) the ambivalence that exists at the social level about these type of careers (importance vs. little recognition); (f) the inadequate preparation of science school teachers; (g) the lack of programs for visits to schools carried out by Peruvian universities; and (h) the little support and guidance that young people usually receive during their career choice processes [5]. Together, these factors contribute to the formation of an unfavorable context for the development of interest in science-related careers in Peruvian school students.

The present study examined the role of background, expectations, motivational orientations, self-beliefs and attitudes in the interest in choosing scientific and technological careers in Peruvian school students. Specifically, the study poses the following research questions: What are the students' scientific and technological career expectations? Which factors are associated with students' science and technological-related career expectations?

2 Method

2.1 Sample

The Peruvian sample evaluated in PISA 2015 consisted of 6971 students (50.2% male, 49.7% female) from 281 schools, aged between 15 and 16 ($M = 15.66$, $S.D. = 0.47$), selected through a probabilistic, stratified, and two-stage cluster sampling. Ninety-three percent of the participants had Spanish as their native language, while 6% and 1% had an indigenous language and a foreign language, respectively. Seventy-six percent attended upper secondary education (timely enrollment), while 24% attended secondary education (school backwardness).

2.2 Variables

Table 1 shows the variables used in the study and their definitions. Relevant psychometric information can be found in Table 3. The student socioeconomic status (SES) index was constructed by the Office of Learning Quality Measurement of the Ministry of Education of Peru and has proven to be a valid and reliable measure in Peruvian educational contexts [29]. Except for SES, all variables used in this study come from the PISA 2015 student questionnaire [6, 30].

Table 1. Study variables.

Variables	Definition and coding
Gender	0 = Male, 1 = Female
Native language	0 = Spanish, 1 = Indigenous language, 2 = Foreign language
Student socioeconomic status (SES)	Index that represents the student socioeconomic status (SES). To test possible interaction effects, SES was transformed into a categorical variable (SES level): high, medium, low and very low

(*continued*)

Table 1. (*continued*)

Variables	Definition and coding
School SES	Average of student's SES in a school
Timely enrollment	0 = No (students enrolled in lower secondary education) 1 = Yes (students enrolled in upper secondary school)
Science-related parent occupation	0 = No, 1 = Yes Variable coded by PISA 2015 based on an open-ended question about parental occupation
Instrumental motivation	Index that reflects the willingness of students to strive in their science studies because they perceive that this will be useful in the future. This variable was measured with a 4-point agreement scale
Test anxiety	Index that reflects the activation condition that causes physiological, emotional and cognitive changes and prevents the effective use of knowledge while performing an evaluation. This variable was measured with a 4-point agreement scale
Achievement motivation	Index that reflects the aspiration, the effort to excel and the persistence to achieve academic objectives. This variable was measured with a 4-point agreement scale
Science self-efficacy	Index that reflects the subjective beliefs of the students about their own ability to successfully perform specific tasks in science. This variable was measured with a 4-point agreement scale
Science activities	Index that reflects the involvement of students in a series of science-related activities in their spare time, such as watching science TV shows, buying or borrowing science books, etc. This variable was measured with a 4-point frequency scale
Enjoyment of science	Index that reflects the willingness to learn and work in science due to the enjoyment and sense of freedom that this produces. This variable was measured with a 4-point agreement scale

(*continued*)

Table 1. (*continued*)

Variables	Definition and coding
Interest in broad science topics	Index that reflects the degree of interest of the student in general scientific topics, such as "the biosphere", "force and movement", "the history of the universe", "disease prevention". This variable was measured with a 5-point interest scale
Parents emotional support	Index that reflects students' perception about interest showed by their parents in school matters, about parental support received when performing tasks, and about being encouraged to trust themselves. This variable was measured with a 4-point agreement scale
Inquiry-based science teaching	Index that reflects the students' perception of the frequency the teacher seeks to involve them in practical activities and experimentation, in addition to posing challenges and encouraging them to develop a conceptual understanding of scientific ideas. This variable was measured with a 4-point frequency scale
Interest in scientific and technological careers	0 = No, 1 = Yes Variable coded by PISA 2015 based on an open-ended question about the work that students would like to do at the age of 30

2.3 Analytical Strategy

First, national percentages of students interested in science and technology careers according to gender, SES level and scientific performance in PISA 2015 were calculated in order to describe interest in science among Peruvian students. Regarding SES, this variable was transformed into a categorical one in order to classify the sample according to their SES level: high, medium, low and very low [29]. Second, unidimensional factor structures of the different scales showed in Table 1 were tested through confirmatory factor analysis (CFA). Due to the ordinal nature of the data, polychoric correlations matrices and the Weighted Least Squares adjusted by Mean and Variance estimation method were employed. The following fit indices were used to assess the CFA's goodness of fit: Comparative Fit Index (CFI), Tucker-Lewis Index (TLI), Root Mean Square Error of Approximation (RMSEA) and Standardized Root Mean Square Residual (SRMR). Then, factor scores (indexes) derived from the CFAs were estimated. Third, binary logistic regression models were estimated in order to explore the relationship between different variables and the chances that students were interested in science-related careers. These variables were introduced in blocks and sequentially in nested models. In addition, moderation (interaction) effects (according to gender and SES) were also tested. The quality of the final model was assessed through the Bayesian

Information Criterion (BIC) and for its capacity to classify the observed data. These models were evaluated based on the following equation:

$$logit[Y_p = 1|x_1, \ldots, x_k] = \beta_0 + \beta_1 x_1 + \ldots + \beta_k x_k. \tag{1}$$

Where p represents the probability of choosing a scientific or technological career $(Y = 1)$ given the linear combination of a set of predictor variables $(x_1, x_2, \ldots x_k)$; β_0 is the slope or constant term when $x_k = 0$; and $\beta_1, \beta_2, \ldots \beta_k$ are the regression coefficients. All statistical and graphical analysis were carried out using the $R\ 3.6.1$ language [31] and the following packages: $intsvy$ [32], $glmm$ [33] and $ggplot2$ [34].

3 Results

This section reports the results of the descriptive and inferential analyzes performed. First, the interest in scientific and technological careers by Peruvian students evaluated in PISA 2015 is described according to the following strata: gender, SES level and performance in the science test. Next, CFA's goodness of fit indices of the scales used in the measurement of different attitudinal and motivational variables are reported. Finally, the results of the different binary logistic regression models estimated to explain the interest in careers related to science and interaction effects are reported.

Table 2. Distribution of interest in scientific and technology careers by stratum.

		Science and technology careers				Other careers (%)
		Science & engineering (%)	Health professionals (%)	Communication technology professionals (%)	Scientific technicians (%)	
National		21.9	13.4	3.8	0.5	60.5
Gender	Male	29.4	6.9	6.5	0.8	56.4
	Female	14.2	19.9	1.0	0.2	64.7
SES level	Very low	17.7	12.5	1.6	0.4	67.8
	Low	22.2	11.9	3.7	0.8	61.4
	Medium	24.6	14.7	6.4	0.5	53.8
	High	27.9	15.6	4.5	0.2	51.8
Science Performance (PISA 2015)	Below level 2	18.0	12.9	2.4	0.6	66.1
	Level 2	25.9	13.6	5.0	0.3	55.1
	Level 3	30.5	14.3	6.7	0.4	48.0
	Above level 3	26.2	18.0	8.8	0.00	47.1

Source: OECD. PISA 2015 data. Own elaboration.

3.1 Descriptive Analysis

Table 2 shows the percentages of students who aspire to a science or technology career according to student's characteristics. As mentioned, 39.5% of the students reported having the expectation of performing in a science-related career at 30 years old while 60.5% did not report such interest. In general, the engineering career was the one that generated the most interest (21.9%), followed by health careers (13.4%). Technological and technical careers had lower percentages of interested students.

At a disaggregated level, the national trend for the four types of careers is maintained, although some percentages stand out. Male students (as well as those with higher socioeconomic status and higher performance in the PISA science test) showed a greater willingness to opt for engineering careers. On the contrary, women were more interested in health careers.

3.2 Confirmatory Factor Analysis (CFA)

The psychometric evaluation of the scales employed, and the estimation of derived factor scores were carried out using CFAs. For each factor a unidimensional structure was assumed. In all cases, goodness of fit indices showed appropriate values and factorial loads were high enough. It is worth noticing that despite PISA 2015 provides indices or scores (through an Item Response Theory approach) for these variables, CFAs were performed exclusively with national data in order to assure a better fit for Peruvian student population.

Table 3. Goodness of fit indicators for the tested unidimensional models.

Variables	CFI	TLI	RMSEA	SRMR
Instrumental motivation	0.999	0.998	0.073	0.014
Test anxiety	0.973	0.946	0.090	0.042
Achievement motivation	0.989	0.978	0.093	0.051
Science self-efficacy	0.995	0.993	0.053	0.029
Science activities	0.989	0.985	0.123	0.062
Enjoyment of science	0.999	0.999	0.042	0.009
Interest in broad science topics	0.983	0.966	0.151	0.052
Parents emotional support	0.999	0.998	0.003	0.009
Inquiry-based science teaching	0.983	0.977	0.093	0.051

Note. CFI = Comparative Fit Index; TLI = Tucker-Lewis Index; RMSEA = Root Mean Square Error of Approximation; SRMR = Standardized Root Mean Square Residual.

3.3 Binary Logistic Regression Models

Odds Ratios
Table 4 reports the results of the binary logistic regression models. It should be mentioned that exponential coefficients ("odds ratios") associated with the predictors are reported for each model. For the change in a unit in the predictor, an exponential coefficient above 1 reflects greater chances ("odds") that the student is interested in a scientific or technological career, while an exponential coefficient below 1 reflects a decrease in these chances. Specifically, "odds" are defined as the ratio between the probability of an event occurring (e.g., showing interest in studying medicine) and the probability that such event will not occur (e.g., not showing such interest). On the other hand, an "odds ratio" is defined as the ratio between two odds. For example, if one were interested in knowing the relationship between interest (or disinterest) in the medical career and having (or not) a parent who is a doctor, one should calculate:

$$\text{Odds ratio of interest in a medical career } = \frac{\frac{A}{C}}{\frac{B}{D}} \qquad (2)$$

Where each of the following variables expresses the number of students:
A = Interested in medicine and have a parent who is a doctor
B = Interested in medicine and none of their parents is a doctor
C = Not interested in medicine and have a parent who is a doctor
D = Not interested in medicine and none of their parents is a doctor

Base Model
In model 1, women were associated with decreased odds of interest in science-related careers ($OR = 0.664$, $p < .05$), compared to men. Also, having an indigenous ($OR = 0.852$, $p < .05$) or foreign native language ($OR = 0.771$, $p < .05$) were associated with decreased odds of interest in these careers, compared to Spanish native language. Additionally, a higher student ($OR = 1.174$, $p < .05$) and school SES ($OR = 1.051$, $p < .05$), as well as being timely enrolled ($OR = 1.363$, $p < .05$), were associated with increased odds of choosing a science and technology career. Finally, having at least one parent dedicated to a scientific or technological occupation was related with greater odds of interest in these types of occupations ($OR = 1.733$, p $< .05$).

Partial Models
In model 2, after controlling for the base model variables effects, instrumental motivation ($OR = 1.377$, $p < .05$), achievement motivation ($OR = 1.209$, $p < .05$), involvement in scientific activities ($OR = 1.139$, $p < .05$) and interest in science ($OR = 1.271$, $p < .05$) were all positively associated with increased odds of interest in science-related careers. Contrarily, no significant results were found for test anxiety, science self-efficacy, enjoyment of science and emotional support of parents. In model 3, a greater frequency

in the use of pedagogical strategies based on inquiry was associated with decreased odds of showing interest in careers of this type ($OR = 0.878, p < .05$).

Interaction Effects

Interaction effects were modeled in order to verify if previously found relationships differed according to strata (models 4, 5, 6 and 7). Thus, it was found that the relationship between anxiety and scientific aspirations depended on the student's gender (model 6). In this way, at higher anxiety scores, women had a greater chance of remain interested in science-related careers than men ($OR = 1.336, p < .05$). It was also found that the association between instrumental motivation and interest in science-related careers varied according to the student SES level (model 7). Therefore, as instrumental motivation scores increased, students with a higher SES had a greater chance of aspiring to pursue a career in science or technology ($OR = 1.139, p < .05$). Finally, although at first there was no significant interaction effect between socioeconomic status and inquiry-based

Table 4. Summary of models predicting science-related career aspirations (PISA 2015).

Models[a]								
Variables	(1)	(2)	(3)	(4)	(5)	(6)	(7)	(8)
Gender (Female)	0.664*	0.619*	0.619*	0.619*	0.613*	0.619*	0.619*	0.619*
Language (Indigenous)[b]	0.852*	1.116	1.185	1.197	1.185	1.197	1.139	1.150
Language (Foreign)[b]	0.771*	0.787	0.712	0.719	0.726	0.698	0.705	0.712
Student SES	1.174*	1.105*	1.116*	1.116*	1.116 *	1.116	1.105	1.105*
School SES	1.051*	1.185*	1.174	1.174	1.162	1.174	1.185*	1.162
Timely enrollment	1.363*	1.363*	1.336*	1.336*	1.336*	1.336*	1.336*	1.323*
Science-related parent occupation	1.733*	1.716*	1.699*	1.699*	1.699*	1.716*	1.716*	1.733*
Instrumental motivation		1.377*	1.377*	1.377*	1.390*	1.391*	1.336*	1.336*
Test anxiety		0.914	0.896	0.896	0.887	0.771*	0.896	0.771
Achievement motivation		1.209*	1.234*	1.234*	1.234*	1.234*	1.234*	1.234*
Science self-efficacy		0.951	0.951	0.951	0.951	0.951	0.951	0.951
Science activities		1.139*	1.197*	1.197*	1.197*	1.197*	1.197*	1.197*
Enjoyment of science		1.041	1.073	1.073	1.073	1.073	1.062	1.062
Interest in science		1.271*	1.271*	1.271*	1.271*	1.271*	1.259*	1.259*
Parents support		1.030	1.020	1.020	1.020	1.020	1.030	1.030
Inquiry-based science teaching			0.878*	0.827*	0.896	0.878*	0.869*	0.835
Female x Inquiry				1.139				1.174
SES x Inquiry					0.905			0.878*
Female x Anxiety						1.336*		1.350*
SES x Inst. motivation							1.139*	1.162*
Intercept/Constant	0.595*	0.613*	0.619*	0.619*	0.619*	0.619*	0.625*	0.625*
n (Students)	6603	5025	4737	4737	4737	4737	4737	4737

*$p < .05$. [a]For each model, the exponential coefficients (odds ratios) associated with the predictors are reported. For a one-unit change, an odds ratio above 1 reflects a greater odd that the student is interested in a science and technology related career, while an odds ratio below 1 reflects a decrease in this odd. [b]Reference = Spanish language.

science teaching (model 5), this effect became significant in the final model (model 8). All significant interactions included in the final model appear graphically in Fig. 1.

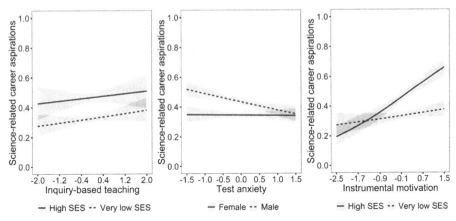

Fig. 1. Interaction effects: inquiry x SES, Anxiety x Sex, instrumental motivation x SES

Final Model

The final model (8) integrates information from previous models. Here, most of the trends observed in partial models remained, except for those described below. Native language (indigenous and foreign), school SES and inquiry-based science teaching ceased to be significant predictors after controlling for the rest of the variable's effects included in the final model. Additionally, the effect of interaction between inquiry and SES (model 5) became significant in the final model. This effect, however, was not consistent with its graphic representation in Fig. 1 and may not be reliable (therefore, it will not be discussed in the final section of the article). Finally, this model showed a better fit to the data (BIC = 6235.7) than a null model without predictive variables (BIC = 9305.4). In addition, it adequately classified 63.4% of the data.

4 Discussion

This research aimed to (1) explore the scientific and technological career expectations shown by Peruvian students; (2) explore the factors associated to interest in this type of careers; and (3) to analyze interaction effects in the relationship between affective and motivational variables with student interest in science-related careers. In general, the results allowed to identify that approximately 40% of students expressed the intention of being involved in scientific careers at 30 years old, with engineering and health careers as the ones that concentrated greater interest. Evidence shows that career expectations are differentiated by gender, which correspond to the international trend: women tend to prefer health careers while men prefer engineering careers [15]. It is important to mention that gender differences in socialization often take place both in educational and family contexts, and this is also the case in Peru. It is likely that parents and teachers are inclined to encourage and reinforce more intensely among male students the active exploration of environments and the manipulation of objects, which are essential features of scientific work. On the contrary, women might place a greater emphasis on activities related to interpersonal care (e.g., health careers). In sum, gender stereotypes might generate different routes in the development of vocational and occupational interests [17]. Given this, it will be crucial for teachers to reflect and become aware of the disparities that affect female students and the conditions that reinforce them in order to address them effectively.

The results also showed the importance of students' background as well as motivational and attitudinal aspects. Among variables related to students' background, a positive relationship was found between science related careers expectations and student's SES, timely enrollment, and having at least one parent working in science. The latter would evidence the importance of the student's scientific capital in the construction of identity related to science and, as Archer, DeWitt and Willis [13] have suggested, would support arguments about the early influence of scientific capital on the expression and development of science interest. Thus, having parents involved in science-related jobs might drive interest in scientific subjects and occupations, consumption of cultural products, participation in out-of-school science activities, interaction with people involved in science, as well as the development of favorable dispositions toward this field [12].

In addition, the present study found that domains highlighted by the expectancy-value theory showed to be important antecedents of interest in scientific and technological careers such as instrumental motivation, achievement motivation, engagement in scientific activities and interest in science topics. These results also coincide with previous evidence according to which the persistence and effort to excel in science courses, the spontaneous participation in science-related activities during free time, as well as the disposition for being informed on science topics show a positive influence on interest in scientific and technological careers [20]. Regarding pedagogical practices, a negative association was found between interest in science-related careers and inquiry-based teaching (a relationship which turned into a non-significant one in the final model). Although these findings are counterintuitive since it would be expected that inquiry nurture interest in science, they are consistent with results from studies reporting that this teaching approach is negatively associated with science performance in standardized tests [35].

On the other hand, instrumental motivation proved to be one of the most relevant factors when predicting interest in science-related careers. Results showed that the study of science in school has, for Peruvian students, an essentially utilitarian value, especially among (a) female students, (b) students who attend public schools, as well as those (c) who have a lower SES. In contrast, enjoyment of science was not a significant predictor of interest in these types of occupations. This would suggest that many Peruvian students approach science primarily because of the revenues it could generate and not because of an enjoyment or internalization of the values associated with it. This makes particularly noticeable the role of school as a provider of meaningful experiences focused on the enjoyment of learning science in the classroom, which is, promoting the development of an intrinsic motivation related to school science.

Regarding interaction effects, instrumental motivation was found to favor science career choice, especially in those students with a higher SES. These students are likely to have a more favorable environment (e.g., greater scientific capital) for the development of vocational paths that reflect their expectations and interests, whether instrumental (as verified in the present study) or intrinsic. Also, it was found that as anxiety increases in evaluation contexts, men are more likely to give up their interest in science and technology careers. This may suggest that women have a greater ability to persist in their academic goals, particularly in unfavorable conditions. It is also likely that, in the presence of difficulties, men will have greater freedom to give up interests or goals and opt for others.

In general terms, the results of this study emphasize the importance of gender roles, socioeconomic status and scientific capital in the formation of interest in studying a scientific or technological career. In addition, attitudinal and motivational factors showed their importance in science career interest as postulated by the expectation-value theory [17]. As the main limitation of the study it is important to point out that, due to its cross-sectional design, it is not possible to make causal inferences or to generate conclusions about the process of development of interest in science and technology careers. Thereupon, the use of longitudinal designs is recommended to track fluctuations of science interest and other associated variables.

References

1. Schiepe-Tiska, A., Roczen, N., Müller, K., Prenzel, M., Osborne, J.: Science-related outcomes: attitudes, motivation, value beliefs, strategies. In: Kuger, S., Klieme, E., Jude, N., Kaplan, D. (eds.) Assessing Contexts of Learning. MEMA, pp. 301–329. Springer, Cham (2016). https://doi.org/10.1007/978-3-319-45357-6_12
2. Henriksen, E.K.: Introduction: participation in science, technology, engineering and mathematics (STEM) education: presenting the challenge and introducing project IRIS. In: Henriksen, E.K., Dillon, J., Ryder, J. (eds.) Understanding Student Participation and Choice in Science and Technology Education, pp. 1–14. Springer, Dordrecht (2015). https://doi.org/10.1007/978-94-007-7793-4_1
3. Bennett, J., Hogarth, S.: Would you want to talk to a scientist at a party? High school students' attitudes to school science and to science. Int. J. Sci. Educ. **31**(14), 1975–1998 (2009)
4. Regan, E., DeWitt, J.: Attitudes, interest and factors influencing STEM enrolment behaviour: an overview of relevant literature. In: Henriksen, E.K., Dillon, J., Ryder, J. (eds.) Understanding Student Participation and Choice in Science and Technology Education, pp. 63–88. Springer, Dordrecht (2015). https://doi.org/10.1007/978-94-007-7793-4_5
5. Corilloclla, P., Granda, A.: Situación de la formación de capital humano e investigación en las universidades peruanas. 2do. Censo Nacional Universitario, 2010 (2014). http://hdl.handle.net/20.500.12390/97
6. OECD: PISA 2015 Results (Volume I): Excellence and Equity in Education, PISA. OECD Publishing, Paris (2016). https://doi.org/10.1787/9789264266490-en
7. Bøe, M.V., Henriksen, E.K.: Expectancy-value perspectives on choice of science and technology education in late-modern societies. In: Henriksen, E.K., Dillon, J., Ryder, J. (eds.) Understanding Student Participation and Choice in Science and Technology Education, pp. 17–29. Springer, Dordrecht (2015). https://doi.org/10.1007/978-94-007-7793-4_2

8. Darcourt, A., Ramos, S., Moreano, G., Hernández, W.: Interest in scientific and technological careers in peruvian school students. In: Villalba-Condori, K.O., Adúriz-Bravo, A., García-Peñalvo, F.J., Lavonen, J. (eds.) Proceeding of the Congreso Internacional Sobre Educación y Tecnología en Ciencias - CISETC 2019, Arequipa, Perú, 10–12 December 2019, pp. 136–145. CEUR-WS.org, Aachen (2019)

9. Giddens, A.: Modernity and Self-identity. Self and Society in the Late Modern Age. Polity Press, Cambridge (1991)

10. Bourdieu, P., Passeron, J.-C.: Reproduction in Education, Society and Culture. Sage Publications, London (1990). (R. Nice, Trans. 2nd edn.)

11. Aschbacher, P.R., Li, E., Roth, E.J.: Is science me? High school students' identities, participation and aspirations in science, engineering, and medicine. J. Res. Sci. Teach. **47**(5), 564–582 (2010). https://doi.org/10.1002/tea.20353

12. Archer, L., Dawson, E., DeWitt, J., Seakins, A., Wong, B.: "Science capital": a conceptual, methodological, and empirical argument for extending bourdieusian notions of capital beyond the arts. J. Res. Sci. Teach. **52**(7), 922–948 (2015). https://doi.org/10.1002/tea.21227

13. Archer, L., DeWitt, J., Willis, B.: Adolescent boys' science aspirations: masculinity, capital, and power. J. Res. Sci. Teach. **51**(1), 1–30 (2014)

14. Barmby, P., Kind, P.M., Jones, K.: Examining changing attitudes in secondary school science. Int. J. Sci. Educ. **30**(8), 1075–1093 (2008)

15. Schoon, I., Eccles, J.S.: Gender Differences in Aspirations and Attainment: A Life Course Perspective. Cambridge University Press, Cambridge (2014)

16. Eurydice: Gender differences in educational outcomes: Study on the measures taken and the current situation in Europe. Eurydice, Brussels (2010)

17. Eccles, J.S., Wang, M.-T.: What motivates females and males to pursue careers in mathematics and science? Int. J. Behav. Dev. **40**(2), 100–106 (2016). https://doi.org/10.1177/0165025415616201

18. Hakim, C.: Women, careers, and work-life preferences. Br. J. Guidance Couns. **34**, 279–294 (2006)

19. Tytler, R., Osborne, J.: Student attitudes and aspirations towards science. In: Fraser, B.J., Tobin, K.G., McRobbie, C.J. (eds.) Second International Handbook of Science Education, pp. 597–625. Springer, Dordrecht (2012). https://doi.org/10.1007/978-1-4020-9041-7_41

20. Tai, R.H., Liu, C.Q., Maltese, A.V., Fan, X.: Planning early for careers in science. Science **312**, 1143–1144 (2006)

21. Sadler, P.M., Sonnert, G., Hazari, Z., Tai, R.: Stability and volatility of STEM career interest in high school: a gender study. Sci. Educ. **96**(3), 411–427 (2012)

22. Wigfield, A., Eccles, J.S.: Expectancy-value theory of achievement motivation. Contemp. Educ. Psychol. **25**(1), 68–81 (2000). https://doi.org/10.1006/ceps.1999.1015

23. Krapp, A., Prenzel, M.: Research on interest in science: theories, methods, and findings. Int. J. Sci. Educ. **33**, 27–50 (2011). https://doi.org/10.1080/09500693.2010.518645

24. Maltese, A.V., Tai, R.H.: Eyeballs in the fridge: sources of early interest in science. Int. J. Sci. Educ. **32**(5), 669–685 (2010)

25. Bandura, A.: Perceived self-efficacy in cognitive development and functioning. Educ. Psychol. **28**, 117–148 (1993). https://doi.org/10.1207/s15326985ep2802_3

26. Falco, L.D., Summers, J.J.: Improving career decision self-efficacy and STEM self-efficacy in high school girls. J. Career Dev., 089484531772165 (2017). https://doi.org/10.1177/0894845317721651

27. Jansen, M., Scherer, R., Schroeders, U.: Students' self-concept and self-efficacy in the sciences: differential relations to antecedents and educational outcomes. Contemp. Educ. Psychol. **41**, 13–24 (2015). https://doi.org/10.1016/j.cedpsych.2014.11.002

28. Lent, R.W., Brown, S.D., Hackett, G.: Toward a unifying social cognitive theory of career and academic interest, choice, and performance. J. Vocat. Behav. **1**, 79–122 (1994)

29. Ministerio de Educación: Desafíos en la medición y el análisis del estatus socioeconómico de los estudiantes peruanos. Oficina de Medición de la Calidad de los Aprendizajes, Lima (2018)

30. OECD: PISA 2015 technical report. OECD Publishing, Paris (2017). http://www.oecd.org/pisa/data/2015-technical-report

31. R Core Team: A language and environment for statistical computing. R Foundation for Statistical Computing, Vienna, Austria (2018). http://www.R-project.org/

32. Caro, D.H., Biecek, P.: intsvy: an R package for analyzing international large-scale assessment data. J. Stat. Softw. **81**(7), 1–44 (2017). https://doi.org/10.18637/jss.v081.i07

33. Knudson, C.: glmm: Generalized Linear Mixed Models via Monte Carlo Likelihood Approximation. R package version 1.3.0 (2018). https://CRAN.R-project.org/package=glmm

34. Wickham, H.: ggplot2: Elegant Graphics for Data Analysis. Springer, New York (2009). https://doi.org/10.1007/978-0-387-98141-3

35. Chi, S., Liu, X., Wang, Z., Won Han, S.: Moderation of the effects of scientific inquiry activities on low SES students' PISA 2015 science achievement by school teacher support and disciplinary climate in science classroom across gender. Int. J. Sci. Educ. **40**(11), 1284–1304 (2018). https://doi.org/10.1080/09500693.2018.1476742

Author Index

Printed in the United States
By Bookmasters